THE ABOLITION
OF LIBERTY

PETER HITCHENS is a well-known and controversial commentator, a columnist for the *Mail on Sunday* and a frequent
broadcaster. His first book, *The Abolition of Britain*, made an
impact on both Left and Right with its argument that Britain had
chosen the wrong future in the 1960s, and that Thatcherism had
not only failed to halt the moral and cultural revolution launched
by the Left, but had in many ways accelerated it.

THE ABOLITION OF LIBERTY

The Decline of Order

and Justice in England

PETER HITCHENS

Atlantic Books

London

Originally published in Great Britain as *A Brief History of Crime* in 2003
by Atlantic Books, an imprint of Grove Atlantic Ltd

This revised and updated paperback edition published in 2004.

The author and publisher wish to thank the following for permission to quote
from copyrighted material: David Higham Associates for *Chronicles of Wasted
Time* by Malcolm Muggeridge (1979); Simon & Schuster for *The Closing of the
American Mind* by Allan Bloom (1987).

1 2 3 4 5 6 7 8 9

A CIP catalogue record for this book is available from the British Library.

ISBN 1 84354 149 1

Printed in Great Britain by Mackays of Chatham

Atlantic Books
An imprint of Grove Atlantic Ltd
Ormond House
26–27 Boswell Street
London WC1N 3JZ

To my parents

Society cannot exist unless a controlling power
upon will and appetite be placed somewhere,
and the less there is within, the more
there must be without.
Edmund Burke

There are more instances of the abridgment
of the freedom of the people by gradual and
silent encroachments of those in power
than by violent and sudden usurpation.
James Madison

Contents

	Preface	xi
	Acknowledgements	xv
	Introduction	1
I	Your papers, please	19
II	The causes of crime	31
III	'Bobbies on the beat'	52
IV	The slow, bureaucratic death of George Dixon	96
V	Making bad people worse	122
VI	Evil drug-dealers	159
VII	Twelve angry persons	180
VIII	Institutional defeatism	208
IX	Justice denied	233
	Postscript	245

Preface

Jonathan Swift said that you could not reason a man out of a position that he had not been reasoned into in the first place. That is why I have, with some sadness, ripped two chapters out of this book, originally published in April 2003 as *A Brief History of Crime*. In truth, I ought to have known better in the first place. As I wrote that book, originally meant to explain what had gone wrong with the English criminal justice system, it became clear to me that I had stumbled on to a much bigger subject. The more I researched, the more it seemed to me that there was a threat to the liberty of the English – and British – people, emanating from their own trusted government. This threat was gathering and increasing, largely unnoticed, and it faced no serious opposition. It was even more important than the issue of unchecked crime and disorder, though linked to it.

I am convinced that the only way to affect politics in this country is to influence the left. As I described in my 1999 book *The Abolition of Britain*, the left now holds power in almost all the important cultural and moral citadels of the country, as well as in government. I do not believe that all its supporters intended many of the bad results which their policies have had. I continue to hope that, if I can persuade them that those results truly are caused by their ideas, they may – change their minds – as I have done. Any political book which does not reach the left might as well not have been written. Influencing the counsels of the Tory Party is about as much use in British politics as gaining the favour of the Habsburgs would be in present-day Continental diplomacy. In any case, the Tory Party is, if anything, even more hostile to my sort of thinking than is the

Labour Party. In its declining years it has become far too ready to reach for the false solutions of pseudo-conservatism, at home and abroad – unrestrained market forces and confrontations with foreign bogeymen. It is afraid to be genuinely conservative, and almost entirely closed to original or unconventional ideas. It is considered brave for Conservatives to adopt the dreariest and most played-out policies of the Fabian mainstream, but it is foolhardy for them to say or think anything genuinely reactionary. The Conservative Party is actually more likely than any other political force to pronounce the cliches 'You can't put the clock back', or 'Change is inevitable'. The arrival of Michael Howard as Tory leader diminishes any chance that it will make a serious effort to defend liberty, since Mr Howard is personally associated with past attempts to undermine jury trial, reduce the rights of the accused person, and to reintroduce identity cards.

So I should have realized that it was foolish to make it so hard for the left to listen to my arguments. This is not to say that I withdraw anything I said in *A Brief History of Crime*. I remain convinced that the moral, logical and practical case for the death penalty is excellent and irrefutable. Likewise, I am sure that arguments for gun control are empty and that it has proved worthless in practice, judged on its own terms. However, opposition to capital punishment and a passion for gun control are articles of faith with the modern left. Facts and logic have no part to play in these opinions. In general, the stronger and better the arguments against these two positions, the angrier the response will be. People do not like to be made to think about their faith, in fact they positively resent attempts to make them do so.

That is why I have removed these chapters from this edition. For on the other issues which I deal with here, the left has not made up its mind with anything like the same determination, nor with the same emotional, irrational conviction. Its more intelligent supporters recognize that crime and disorder fall most painfully on the poor. Some of them may even concede that the current state of our prisons is atrociously cruel, and I agree with them that these places lack any purpose or justification as they stand. The idea that the police are best employed patrolling the streets on foot is gaining in strength and supporters all the time, and I like to think that I have played some part in this important change of mood. Those who know what drugs have done and are doing to the English poor and unemployed must also have doubts about the glib defeatism of the London establishment on this subject. My re-examination of the Scarman and Macpherson reports must at least be of interest to anyone who hopes for racial harmony in this country, an objective shared by all civilized people.

But when we come to the attack on jury trial and the other protections of liberty, the danger is so great that even the most unlikely allies must join together to fight it. And now that the British government is stealthily preparing the introduction of identity cards, it is essential that all those who oppose this slippery, dishonestly-presented and fundamentally nasty project link arms to stop it. It was successfully beaten in Australia, where it was initially as popular as it is now in Britain. It can be defeated here as well, and perhaps such a defeat will bring about a rebirth of the old English mistrust of authority and instinctive love of liberty and private life. This is why I have added a chapter devoted to this topic, which explains its historical origins and sets out the many reasons why its alleged benefits are illusory, while its implicit threat to freedom is undeniable. If you have done nothing wrong and have nothing to hide, even so you have much to fear from this damned card.

This country is free partly because for four centuries neither of its two great political factions has been able to destroy or finally overcome the other. Royalist and Roundhead, Whig and Tory, Socialist and Conservative have all eventually come to terms with the existence of the opposing movement. It is in the differences between them that, in a way, we all live. From time to time, critically in 1688 and most recently in 1940, both sides have forgotten their differences for the sake of England and later of Britain. I believe there is now a genuine threat to the liberty of this country, a threat that comes from its own governing class (as has happened before), as good an excuse as any for offering the hand of alliance across the gulf.

Oxford,
November 2003

Acknowledgements

My thanks to David Miller, Toby Mundy and Clara Farmer, for helping to turn an idea into a book; to Peter Wright, Editor of the *Mail on Sunday*, for encouraging and helping me to pursue this most important subject, and likewise to Eric Bailey; to Fred Broughton and Tony Judge (whose book *The Force of Persuasion* was invaluable to me) for indispensable advice on how to find what I was looking for; to Louise Stemp of the Home Office Library, who helped me far beyond the call of duty both with a superb bibliography and access to unique documents, and to her colleagues Lorna Brook and Marilyn Saklatvala; also to Wendy Sainsbury and Ian Harris of the Prison Service Headquarters library and Paul Levay, Assistant Librarian of the National Police Training Library at Bramshill; to Brian Butler, head of information at the Home Office, to many diligent press officers at the Home Office and the Lord Chancellor's Department who responded so willingly to my requests for arcane information; to the librarians of the London Library, the British Library and the Westminster Reference Library for always finding what I needed, however ancient and obscure; to the librarians at Associated Newspapers, superb keepers of one of the best archives in Britain; to Norman Dennis, for his dissection of the Macpherson report; to Colin Greenwood, a real expert; to Stephen Moore, for allowing me into prison at Wormwood Scrubs, and letting me out again even though he knew how sceptical I was about the modern prison service; to Neil Clark, for pointing out the Labour Party's changing view of the death penalty; to the many readers of the *Mail on Sunday* who have written to me about their experiences as police and prison officers, or as victims of the scourge of crime and disorder; above all, and as always, to my wife Eve for companionship, support and comfort – and to Ribs, Daniel and Jonathan for the encouragement that only they could give. All these should share in any credit. I take all the blame.

P.H.,
Oxford,
December 2002

THE ABOLITION OF LIBERTY

Introduction

Necessity is the plea for every infringement of
human freedom. It is the argument of tyrants;
it is the creed of slaves.
William Pitt

Let us at least agree that there is something wrong.

Once it was modish to argue that we were suffering from an
ailment called 'moral panic' and to make light of worries that crime
and disorder were at perilous levels. Then the liberal left began
reluctantly to admit that perhaps the problem might exist even
though conservatives said it did. From that came the seemingly
simple slogan 'Tough on crime – tough on the causes of crime'
which the Labour Party used before 1997 to suggest that it had
grown out of its anti-police phase.

That slogan hides an awkward truth, which its apparent ferocity
is designed to conceal. The left is still convinced that crime is a social
and economic disease, produced by poverty, bad housing, poor
schools and all the other ills that socialism claims to be able to cure.
This is understandable. If this belief were false the left would lose
most of the justification for its existence. Why have all that high taxation, those regiments of social workers and that maze of targeted
benefits, not to mention the bureaucracies needed to organize
them, if they do not actually make people more content and better
behaved? Being 'tough on the causes of crime' means continuing to
accept that public officials and public money can cajole and bribe
the people into being good, when they would otherwise be bad.

Being 'tough on crime', on the other hand, means that Labour can from now on ignore what is left of its liberty-loving wing and cheerfully enact laws that increase the power of the state and the police to search, listen, file, survey, arrest, hold suspects and seize property, while weakening jury trial and the other safeguards that our wiser ancestors devised to protect us if evil times should come again.

Behind this recipe for repression lies another problem – too large for this book to deal with in full but bound to grow in importance in the coming decades – the accelerating growth of a European legal system, police force and prosecution service. These are bound to conflict with existing English institutions because they draw their power from different courts and documents. They know nothing of the common law, Magna Carta, the English Bill of Rights (a document that seems genuinely to be unknown to many human rights campaigners who noisily demand a British Bill of Rights as if this were an entirely new idea), habeas corpus, the English law's great safeguard against unlimited detention without trial, or the right to trial by jury.

Consciously or unconsciously, the English legal authorities appear at the start of the twenty-first century to be adapting the English system to fit the very different pattern of Continental law. This unpleasant change has been hastened by the ugly collection of repressive and irrelevant measures gathered into one bill by David Blunkett, the Home Secretary, ostensibly in response to the terrorist massacres in the United States on 11 September 2001.

These include the right to detain certain suspects without trial, a breach of the principle of habeas corpus that is not only bad in itself but also shows a willingness to plead necessity as an excuse for destroying liberty, an attitude that threatens many other freedoms if it is not checked. Mr Blunkett dismissed opposition to this bill as 'airy-fairy', a view shared by the Prime Minister, who was and is quite unmoved by the traditions of English liberty or by the left's own strain of libertarianism.

Mr Blair has often spoken with contempt of civil liberty and those who defend it, notably after his government had suggested that everyone who is arrested should be forcibly tested for traces of illegal drugs, even before being convicted. Mr Blair told the Labour Party conference on 28 September 1999:

> It is time to move beyond the social indifference of right and left, libertarian nonsense masquerading as freedom. This generation wants a society free from prejudice but not from rules. I can announce that we will provide the extra resources for a database where every known offender will have their DNA recorded, and evidence from any scene of crime will be matched with it. And I saw that what we said on drugs and new powers was attacked by civil liberties groups. I believe in civil liberties too: civil liberty to me means just that: the liberty to live in a civil society founded on rights and responsibilities, and in dealing with the drugs menace, that is the society we can help to build.

Incoherent as this is, like most of Mr Blair's speeches, it betrays a powerful man's scorn for the irritating rules that get in the way of his grand and benevolent plans. His impatience with those who have doubts about such measures is a common failing in messianic political leaders. They believe themselves to be exempt from the normal laws of life because of their special goodness.

The September 2001 massacre was also used as a pretext for the introduction of a European Arrest Warrant which will permit prosecuting authorities in any EU country to order the arrest of citizens of other EU nations for a number of vague offences. Several of the offences listed are not actually crimes under English law. They include 'xenophobia', which is not an offence, as such, anywhere in Britain. There is also no safeguard against a Continental magistrate obtaining a warrant for one of the listed offences and then charging the arrested person with a wholly different crime once he is in custody. This measure effectively demolishes the boundaries between the criminal justice systems of EU member states. Since the overwhelming majority of EU countries lack habeas corpus, the presumption of innocence or jury trial it indirectly, but gravely, undermines all of them.

Corpus juris is a plan to give the EU a common legal space, which entails a common jurisdiction, a European prosecutor and a European police force. Ultimately, it will not be able to function unless a common code is in being throughout the EU. Since only England, Wales and Ireland – and to a lesser extent Scotland – differ significantly from the systems used on the Continent, it is more likely that Britain and Ireland will eventually be brought under this civil code system than that the other states will adopt common law, habeas corpus and jury trial. Much of this new system is already in existence or in preparation, justified by supposed campaigns against fraud, and probably in future by similar campaigns against illegal immigration and drug trafficking or any other form of lawbreaking that crosses frontiers and can be portrayed as a public menace so serious that freedom must be abridged in order to deal with it. It is likely to increase its powers much as the FBI has done in the USA, allowing federal intervention in national affairs. The difference, from an English point of view, is that the EU's federal system will lack English protections, whereas the FBI is still restrained by habeas corpus, the Bill of Rights and a universal right to trial by jury. The recent experience of British plane-spotters arrested for spying in Greece has alerted many people to the possible drawbacks of the Continental system. However, it has done little or nothing to halt the changes. Europol, for instance, already has the legal right to operate in the UK and its officers have immunity from prosecution for any action that they may take here.

Other parallel developments, especially the incorporation of the 1950 European Convention on Human Rights into English law, have weakened the specifically English tradition of unconditional liberty – everything is legal unless officially banned. They have replaced it with the codified and conditional Continental system, under which all rights are granted by the authorities and everything is illegal unless specifically allowed. The rights contained in the ECHR are often devices for altering the moral and cultural balance rather than actually for protecting liberty. The Convention contains grandiose provisions such as the right to life and liberty, and the right to respect for private and family life. But it does not offer the effective provisions found in the US Bill of Rights which prevent the state from acting in such a way that these rights would be infringed, by debarring it from making certain laws. 'Congress shall make no law abridging the freedom of speech' is much more use in a court of law (and in a crisis) than a right to free speech which is balanced by a right to privacy and perhaps cancelled by the right of the state to act in self-defence.

This is only the beginning. There is a likelihood that in the long term a European constitution will be created and enforced by the European Court of Justice, a wholly different body from the Strasbourg-based European Court of Human Rights. The EU has already drafted its own Charter of Rights and Freedoms, a rival to the ECHR which gives significantly more rights to the state and fewer to the individual. Many of the rights enshrined in these documents are political or group rights, given to people supposedly discriminated against under the existing system. They are not rights as the English Whigs of 1689 or the American revolutionaries of 1776 would have understood them – freedom from autocratic power, arbitrary arrest, indiscriminate searches or indefinite detention without charge. On the contrary, modern human rights charters tend to be very weak and vague on such issues. They have generally been written by idealists from free countries with little experience of the methods and mechanisms of oppression.

This book cannot deal in detail with Scotland, although much of what has gone wrong in England has been replicated north of the border. Scotland's legal and criminal justice systems have never been fully merged with England's, and now never will be – except perhaps as part of a final all-European code which will submit the whole of the British Isles to the Code Napoléon and corpus juris. Scottish juries are significantly different from English ones; England has no procurators fiscal (a kind of examining magistrate who can decide on prosecutions); and the office of constable is far newer and less significant in Scotland than in England. Northern Ireland's problems are so different and special that they form a whole separate subject, although it is interesting that one of the greatest battles over the political future of the province has involved the nature of its police force. This is why all the facts and figures in this book refer only to England and Wales. Even so, many of its themes affect all parts of what is still officially a United Kingdom. The recent collapse of the rule of law in Northern Ireland has had many subtle and demoralizing effects on law enforcement and trust in the rule of law in the rest of the country.

My purpose is to show that much of the public debate on crime and punishment in modern England is based on mistaken beliefs, misunderstood figures and cheap slogans – especially on imprisonment, drugs and policing. None of the major parties appears to have given any serious thought to the issue for many years. As a result, the actions taken by government in the name of fighting crime are often quite worthless for that purpose. They have, however, gravely damaged the liberty of the law-abiding citizen, which government ministers dismiss as the concern of tiresome eccentrics.

If the new armoury of police and state powers had had the slightest effect on levels of crime and disorder, the government's arguments might have some force. However, these measures have proved useless, as well as menacing to liberty in general. The wicked, the selfish, the loud, the oafish, the inconsiderate and the bully are all freer to behave as they wish than at any time for a hundred and fifty years. Their actions often go unrecorded or are dismissed as petty by the authorities. Yet their effects on people's lives are deep and painful. Even the well-massaged crime figures and the new emphasis on the British Crime Survey (a household survey using random sampling, now generally believed to be more accurate than the centralized crime figures amassed by the police and courts) instead of on classical statistics cannot obscure the truth. England is rapidly becoming a place where the good are afraid of the bad and the bad are not afraid of anything.

The real paradox in the argument is one that the genuinely liberal left needs to grasp swiftly if it is to act in time. The left has now captured the machinery of government and the great bulk of the media and the education system. It alone has the opportunity to put matters right. If it refuses to do so, it is likely that the slide into disorder will soon become unstoppable as the last vestiges of authority and obedience disappear from the streets and the unpoliced countryside. Even at this late stage, there is little sign that the left is prepared to look at the issue as anything other than a propaganda problem. One of the Prime Minister's closest advisers, Peter Mandelson, wrote in *The Times* on 10 June 2002 that the left is failing to cope with 'tough issues that are "cultural" rather than ideological'. Among these he included crime. But he clearly saw this as a question of fighting against the right for a propaganda victory rather than of re-examining principles:

> Fundamentally, we must connect with issues that are disturbing voters and not vacate space to be occupied by the Right. This does not mean pandering to prejudice or headline grabbing; it means advancing workable policies that reflect the essentially tolerant values of the majority. At the heart of the Centre Left's strategy should be building security through strong community action; vigorously promoting economic opportunity, ensuring that everyone gets a proper share of economic success; advancing fairness as a responsibility issue (rewards for

those who work and do the right thing as well as lifting
the poor and disadvantaged out of need); and investing
heavily in education as the key to social mobility.

What this actually means is open to interpretation. None of the
leading thinkers of New Labour writes in clear English – either
because they do not really know what they intend to say or because
they are nervous about saying it. But the warning against 'pandering
to prejudice' is a prohibition against conservative common sense,
always dismissed as prejudice by the left. The 'essentially tolerant
values of the majority' are the essential social liberalism of the intolerant elite. 'Security through strong community action', on the
other hand, is authoritarianism justified by the general will. The
adherence to 'economic opportunity' and 'proper share[s] of economic success' is a reassertion of economic and social
egalitarianism, the very policy that has done so much to promote
crime and disorder in the first place. The fact that this sort of thing
passes for advanced thinking in Downing Street is profoundly
dispiriting. It is a warning that the official left views public concern
about crime as a threat to its popularity rather than as a threat to
society, and that it would much rather undermine liberty than re-
examine its principles in the light of experience. These are people
who would rather infringe the freedom of others than change their
minds. We must hope that there are others on the left with more
open minds, for the left is so entrenched in power that it alone will
carry the responsibility if the law crumbles and the country then
turns to authoritarian government to impose a crude sort of order.
The paradox is this: the more harshly we treat wrongdoers and
the greater the power of the state to punish and pursue them, the
more we preserve liberty for the enormous majority who keep to
the laws. A society that clearly and decisively punishes wicked
actions will have no need to document, restrict or spy on the many
millions who do not do such actions.
Conversely, the more generously and considerately we create

safeguards for transgressors, the fewer freedoms will remain for those who behave themselves. The more we treat crime as the symptom of a social and economic disease, requiring treatment rather than penalties, the more the state will need to become an apparatus of repression. The more the police are required to treat individual offenders with care and consideration, the more the law-abiding population will have to be restrained by the authorities from taking actions in their own defence. The less free ordinary citizens are to use their initiative in dealing with wrongdoers, the more they will yearn to do so. The more bureaucratic and formal the criminal justice system becomes, the less use it will be against the disorderly and disobedient. Such people treat a prison record as a career risk, do not pay fines (huge amounts are uncollected, although the middle class still tend to pay), fail to turn up at court or do not stay long at the same address. It is then simpler and more convenient for the police to pursue the settled and orderly members of society. They are easy to find, can have their regular earnings raided to pay fines and still fear the stigma of a criminal record.

A society where crime is an endemic disease to be contained and placated needs to treat all its citizens as potential suspects all the time. This approach will only reduce crime when the state becomes all-powerful. Even then, it may fail to do so; its failure so far is so blatant that any rational society would long ago have abandoned it. The end of this process, of repression followed by failure followed by yet more repression, will be wretched. If it is not soon halted, it will create a social and legal system so stifling and intrusive as to be uncomfortably close to dictatorship.

When I first sat down to write this book, those words would have seemed overheated. However, since the publication of the Anti-Terrorism Bill in the autumn of 2001 and the contempt of the government for the bill's responsible critics, such alarm is completely justified. Enlightened and thoughtful members of the liberal left ought to remember that they were originally moved to action by a desire for both justice and liberty. In their own interests, they should think again about this tremendous issue. What follows should at least give them some material to consider. I hope it may even create a few doubts in their minds.

Returning to Labour's dishonest and misleading slogan about being 'Tough on crime – tough on the causes of crime', I hope to show why these words are both false and dangerous. I also intend to show why and how the current government and its Conservative forerunners have failed to stop the growth of disorder – and how they have unintentionally encouraged it. I would like to demonstrate that we can do better than this. However, our political leaders, of all parties, cannot make progress until they understand the real nature of a problem that they seem barely to have thought about at all.

The sheer concrete-headed stupidity of most political statements about crime defies belief. Anyone who calls for 'more bobbies on the beat' simply reveals that he – or, in many cases, she – knows nothing about what has happened to the police, especially that there is no longer any 'beat' for 'bobbies' to go on and that the word 'bobby' simply cannot be applied to the paramilitary social workers, jangling with clubs, handcuffs, radios and gas sprays, who have replaced the traditional English constable.

As for those who demand 'tougher' sentences, 'fast-track' prosecutions, juvenile curfews and similar measures, they are announcing that they have not recently visited their own country, let alone taken any interest in it. One of the most astonishing recruits to the 'tough sentences' campaign is the Lord Chief Justice, Lord Woolf, who in February 2002 suddenly urged long prison terms for thieves who stole mobile telephones. Lord Woolf had until then been seen as a member of the liberal wing of the judiciary. His 1991 report on the Strangeways prison riot had been sharply critical of the usefulness of prisons as a whole. His intervention is a worrying sign that the liberal elite, far from recognizing that their whole approach is mistaken, is suffering from the moral panic of which it normally accuses others. Lord Woolf's plan could only work if there were a constant police presence on the streets. Had he been paying attention to real life, he and his fellow campaigners for 'tough' measures would have observed that proper police patrols to catch thieves or enforce curfews are a rarity in most parts of the country, and that most patrolling that does take place takes the form of random appearances by officers in cars. They might also have noticed that even 'long' prison sentences are, in effect, automatically halved as they are passed. They would know that prisons themselves are only terrifying to the innocent or the harmless because they are run by the bad and the strong. They would realize that prosecutions could never keep pace with the quantity of offences now committed unless the rules of justice and evidence were entirely abandoned.

As for the crime figures, in whatever form they are served up, they are not to be trusted fully or taken literally. Like all politically important statistics they have suffered what ought to be called the 'bikini effect' – the things concealed are more interesting than those revealed. This is not to say that they are meaningless: they cannot conceal the grave increase in dishonesty and disorder. However, it is well to bear in mind that police forces campaigning for extra funds or increased manpower may be diligent in recording crime, while forces under pressure to produce results for their political masters may be far less diligent and might even be tempted to 'combine' several offences into one or to reclassify a theft as lost property. In an era when central government assumes responsibility for so many aspects of life, such figures are always susceptible to gentle (and sometimes quite rough) massage. British inflation figures, absurdly, exclude the price of houses. Unemployment figures exclude the 'long-term sick', who may not be sick at all. Anyone with the slightest knowledge of schools knows that league table pressure sometimes prevents weak candidates from taking exams when their performance might drag down the average. It would be sensible to assume that similar rules apply to the collection of crime figures. Certainly, the repeated claims of the current government that crime is falling are risible.

In judging them, we should always ask ourselves what story they are trying to tell and make allowances for it. So, before showing that something enormous and damaging has happened to English society since the Second World War, it is worth quoting an astonishing footnote from Jose Harris's social history of Britain before the First World War, *Private Lives, Public Spirit: Britain 1870–1914*. Dealing with pre-1914 crime figures, she states:

> A very high proportion of Edwardian convicts were in
> prison for offences that would have been much more
> lightly treated or wholly disregarded by law enforcers in
> the late twentieth century. In 1912–13, for example, one
> quarter of males aged 16 to 21 who were imprisoned in the
> metropolitan area of London were serving seven-day
> sentences for offences which included drunkenness,
> 'playing games in the street', riding a bicycle without
> lights, gaming, obscene language and sleeping rough.
> If late twentieth-century standards of policing and
> sentencing had been applied in Edwardian Britain,
> the prisons would have been virtually empty; conversely,
> if Edwardian standards were applied in the 1990s then
> most of the youth of Britain would be in gaol.

As it happens, 1913 was a fairly bad year by the standards of the time, with 98,000 serious offences recorded. This level would not be surpassed again until 1920 when the total rose to 101,000 after a wartime truce during which annual crime tallies sank to as low as 78,000 in 1915. Even convicts were reported to be showing patriotic zeal as they broke their rocks. Measure this against the figure of 2,521,000 recorded in 1980 and, even when you grant that the population had risen from 36 million to 49 million, the figures could be from different planets as well as from different eras.

Set beside A. J. P. Taylor's famous statement that the Edwardian Englishman hardly came into contact with the state at all, except to see a policeman walking past or a postman coming up his front path, these figures raise an interesting point. The numbers of recorded crimes in England and Wales had remained fairly stable for sixty years before the outbreak of war. Occasionally falling to as low as 79,000 (1886) or rising as high as 105,000 (1908 and 1909), the annual figure generally remained between 85,000 and 95,000. Murder, the worst of all crimes, seldom rose above 170 and often fell below 130 in a year (these numbers include deaths from backstreet abortions and infanticides). Courts at that time were far less likely to accept pleas of manslaughter, and primitive medical treatment meant that almost any serious wounding could result in death whereas nowadays thousands of such injuries are successfully treated by the National Health Service.

These totals are striking for a society far poorer than most of us can imagine, in which millions lived in disgusting and miserable slums or survived on wages that would be barely enough to feed a twenty-first-century pet cat. There were no laws restricting the ownership of guns or knives. Transportation and the hulks had been abolished, as had public execution. Even hanging itself had become more humane, a swift breaking of the neck instead of a slow strangulation. There were no social services and very few benefits, targeted or otherwise, offered by the state or local authorities, apart from the workhouse. Nobody had a National Insurance number and hardly anyone had a tax code. Trade union membership was small, council housing non-existent and state pensions for the elderly unknown until the very end of the period. Even if recent suggestions that the crime figures of this era were manipulated are true – and, given that most English police forces were locally controlled and that crime was not a major political issue, one has to wonder why anyone should have manipulated them – the difference between then and now still cannot be explained by worsening social conditions.

What makes the figures for the late Victorian and Edwardian age still more telling is that they cover a period when the population of

Year	Population (England and Wales)	Recorded crime (England and Wales)
1921	37,886,689	103,000
1931	39,948,000	159,000
1941	41,748,000	359,000
1951	43,745,000	525,000
1961	46,166,000	807,000
1971	48,604,000	1,666,000
1981	49,011,000	2,963,000 *
1991	49,890,000	5,276,200
2001	53,137,000	5,200,000 **

*Changes in the law mean that post-1980 figures are not strictly comparable with pre-1980 totals, but no other statistics are available and there appears to be some continuity.
**These figures have been disputed, with suggestions that there is some undercounting – for example, because of failures by the uninsured to report thefts and because police have recorded multiple thefts in one block or street as if they were a single offence. Few who lived through the period believe that crime did not rise between 1991 and 2001. The alternative British Crime Survey gives a different picture but is itself criticized for under-reporting crimes affecting the young. By this time, crime figures had become politically significant and therefore subject to massage and adjustment.

England and Wales increased more rapidly than ever, and when multitudes exchanged the ordered and ancient ways of the country-side for the fetid chaos of the new cities. In 1861, when the annual crime figure was 88,000, the population stood at 20,066,224. In 1911, when the crime figure was 97,000, the population had risen to 36,075,269. This was, in fact, a significant drop in the crime rate and one that was to continue, less sharply but just as convincingly, until the 1930s.

The table above shows the growth of population and of crime in the twentieth century. The idea that poverty or social conditions are causes of crime melts away in the hot blast of these truths. The increase in wrongdoing of all kinds is so huge that supposedly reassuring factors, such as temporary su[...] young men or a greater temptation to steal [...] of so much portable property, are simply too [...] colossal rise. The evidence, which shows that [...] crime in memory have occurred at a time of un[...] health, social welfare provision, good housing an[...] ment, also destroys the idea that increased w[...] to a reduction in crime. On the contrary, it raises the possibility that well-meaning state intervention to improve the lot of the poor can actually lead to increased crime.

Gertrude Himmelfarb argued in *The Demoralisation of Society* that the Victorian achievement of peaceful order owed far more to Sunday Schools and moral values than to any other factor. Exactly the same argument, but in reverse, should be applied to Britain's descent from lawful peace to lawless chaos since the early 1930s. It is the decay and destruction of moral values and self-restraint, accelerated by two terrible wars, that have led to the misery of the modern poor – poor in spirit rather than in goods.

In the companion to this book, *The Abolition of Britain*, I sought to show that there had been a cultural revolution in this country as thoroughgoing as the Chinese upheaval under Mao. The subject of crime, order and justice was too big to be considered properly in that book. It deserves separate treatment – yet, like the rest of the cultural revolution, it has involved changes that were often minute, seldom understood or even noticed at the time they were made, and which, in this case, would be surprisingly easy to reverse. The still better news is that, by correcting these mistakes, an enlightened government could help to revive ideas of responsibility, good and bad, guilt and innocence. This would greatly strengthen the position of the large number of citizens who still believe in self-discipline based on a common morality. It would help in the remoralization of our country. It would be pointless to try to deal with the rise in disorder solely through changes in the law and in police methods. A moral counter-revolution is also needed. Practical reforms,

would help such a counter-revolution to begin and hasten
it had started, provided they were not attempted in isolation.

The balance of power in England, between the criminal and
lawless on one hand and the civilized and law-abiding on the other,
has been disturbed by a number of measures and changes which
could quite easily be repealed or amended. The revolution in the
police force could be reversed by a determined Home Secretary
with the support of Parliament and people. The Police and
Criminal Evidence Act 1984 (PACE), with its many pages of absurd
codes for detention and identification, its guaranteed lawyers and
tape recordings, seems to have been devised by left-wing lawyers
for left-wing lawyers. It is astonishing that it was passed without
serious protest by a Conservative government at the height of its
strength. Based on a complete mistrust of the police, it assumed
that a small number of real miscarriages of justice were typical of
police behaviour. It destroyed what remained of police independence of action. It ensured that constables could no longer do what
the people wanted them to do.

Let us not deceive ourselves about this. The police in former
times repressed crime and criminals without much gentleness or
finesse. We knew, if we were honest, that we were guarded by men
who kept the rough world away from us with rough methods. Now
the police are all but powerless because of regulations imposed by
unrealistic utopians who do not have to live with the consequences
of their reforms. Millions of others do, and long for help. Can
anyone now say that what has followed is better than what went
before, for anybody except the wicked? Now it is the criminals who
rule many parts of Britain with boot and fist. Intimidation of witnesses and juries makes a mockery of hundreds of trials each year
while ensuring that many crimes are never prosecuted at all. A few
innocent people went to prison under the old rules. Too few guilty
people go there now. From the moment it came into effect, PACE –
with the Police Complaints Authority standing behind it to punish
those officers who broke its codes – spelt the end of order for honest

poor people. However, it made wealthy liberals feel good about themselves, and made many liberal lawyers wealthy enough to live in places where they could avoid its consequences. Its repeal would be a symbolic break with the folly of the past which would give hope to all now suffering at the hands of criminals.

Even the prisons, those hopeless warehouses of failure and lassitude largely controlled by their inmates, could at last be given a purpose once again. Their inmates could be forced to work to pay for their keep and provide restitution to those they had wronged. They could be deprived of all but the most austere necessities of life. They might then discover that wrongdoing has severe and unpleasant consequences, and so learn to avoid it.

But before we can begin, all those concerned about this great problem must understand what has gone wrong. Then they must grasp the central and worrying truth, which ought to unite principled men and women of the left as well as the right, that without a serious attempt to restrain crime our liberty will soon be in danger. What are generally dismissed as harsh and illiberal attitudes are actually essential for the preservation of individual freedom and the protection of the kind and gentle. Put simply, if the wicked are not disciplined and afraid, then the good and the bad alike will have to live in a prison state, subject to unending surveillance, surrendering freedom to a powerful armed police force, accepting lower standards of proof in the courts and permitting government interference in the legal system. Quite likely we shall also have to accept censorship of printed and electronic media. Revulsion at the licence of the pornography business is likely to grow. So is the demand for controls on broadcasters who know that violence increases ratings and refuse to accept that there are any limits on their behaviour apart from commercial ones.

The book that follows describes in detail the way in which the best police force in the world has been reduced to bureaucratic uselessness. It shows how egalitarian socialism and limp, unrealistic conservatism withdrew the law's protection from the poor and left the English people defenceless in their own homes.

It explains how and why the prison system has lost all sense of purpose and is a place where the wicked flourish, while the innocent and the harmless are punished.

It argues against the fashionable surrender to the drug culture by amoral liberals and supposedly libertarian conservatives. It states unequivocally that the spread of stupefying narcotics creates demoralization and crime. It suggests that decriminalization or legalization will lead to an increase in human misery.

It examines and dismisses the claims that the police are 'institutionally racist'. It argues that the Brixton riots and the murder of Stephen Lawrence were employed by social liberals to destroy the old conservative ethos of the police and to subject them to a politically-correct inquisition which left them unable to function as a crime-fighting body. It also maintains that this was a serious betrayal of the great majority of black and other minority peoples in England, who badly need the law to be enforced on their behalf.

It shows that juries are not in principle weak and foolish, but that rash egalitarian reforms and liberal tampering have made them so.

Finally, it warns that if these things are not dealt with swiftly, then all but the very rich face a future of increasing danger and insecurity. This will become so severe that ignorant and unscrupulous calls for the abandonment of valuable liberties will grow in strength. Political forces may be unleashed that will lead to the extinction of liberty itself. We may, even now, be living in the British equivalent of the Weimar Republic. Fortunately, we have time for amendment and reconsideration before night falls.

I

Your papers, please

The hanging judge, that evil old man in
scarlet robes and horsehair wig, whom
nothing short of dynamite will ever teach
what century he is living in, but who will at
any rate interpret the law according to the
books and will in no circumstances take a
money bribe, is one of the symbolic figures
of England. He is a symbol of the strange
mixture of reality and illusion, democracy
and privilege, humbug and decency, the
subtle network of compromises, by which
the nation keeps itself in its familiar shape.
George Orwell, The Lion and the Unicorn, *1941*

Orwell might actually have been thinking of Lord Goddard when
he wrote this beguiling description of one of the great English
paradoxes. That paradox is that virtues much valued by liberal
reformers are often enforced and defended by conservative figures, whom they prefer to despise. Goddard was believed by his
foes to relish donning the black cap and ordering death sentences. He was embarrassingly coarse and crude in his private
conversation, at least according to one of his critics, Ludovic
Kennedy, who was shocked at the sort of stories the judge told in
the presence of ladies. He became a target of general hatred and
contempt in his final years on the bench, for his stiff refusal to
modify his belief in an older penal system and his general aura of

personal, merciless nastiness. Yet the same Lord Goddard was an uncompromising and courageous champion of English liberty, whose actions forced an elected Conservative government to abolish identity cards, very much against its will.

Now, as a Labour government stealthily and dishonestly prepares to reintroduce these nasty badges of serfdom, it is worth remembering how and why Lord Goddard, of all people, put an end to them before.

This is in fact the third time that the British people have been faced with government demands that they carry identity documents. The first occasion was towards the end of the First World War. Since the introduction of military conscription in 1916, adult males had been issued with National Certificates of Registration, to prove that they had signed up for war service – useful for fending off white feathers and taunts of cowardice. But in the very last months of the conflict, with rationing at its most severe and a genuine fear of defeat during the last great German offensives, Parliament made it compulsory to produce these documents on demand to any police officer. The requirement was abandoned as soon as the war was over, since there was no longer any excuse for it.

The second attempt to register the population was far more interesting, unexpected and controversial. Given that we are now told that identity cards are a response to national peril, unrestricted immigration and crime, we tend to assume that the documents issued during World War Two were justified by similar things. After all, there was a widespread fear of fifth columnists, the country lived for some years under a genuine threat of invasion by sea or by air, far more pressing and actual than the nebulous and generalized threat of terrorism, and the war is now acknowledged to have led to a great deal of crime, especially connected with the black market.

However, none of these arguments was ever used for the issue of identity cards in the period immediately before the Second

World War. The first people to call for them were – and this is no surprise – Tory MPs, who believed they would be useful to ensure that citizens did not evade military duty when conscription was introduced in early 1939. However, the loyal and patriotic British people immediately proved them wrong, by registering promptly and in their millions for National Service, so that by the long-predicted outbreak of war in September 1939 this country still had no system of registering identity, nor any need for one.

It also comes as some surprise to learn that when the government eventually did legislate for identity cards, the minister involved was not the Home Secretary, but the Minister of Health, the forgotten Walter Elliott. During a brief and heavily-whipped debate immediately after the declaration of war, Mr Elliott argued prosaically that the cards would make it easier to organise food rationing and to direct key workers into war industries. He did not mention security, black markets, German parachutists dressed as nuns, or fifth columnists at all.

The scheme was much mocked by independent-minded MPs. Mr Elliott asserted that a national identity register would be useful because 'In time of war, up-to-date statistics as to manpower and the general population both as to the producing and consuming side of the nation's activities are absolutely essential.' To this, Sir Herbert Williams, a Tory from Croydon, retorted sarcastically: 'On a great many occasions I have tried to discover what would be the purpose of such a register, but I have never yet discovered it.'

Sir Herbert pointed out that the government could find out how many people lived in an area by asking local councils, and obtain workers for industry by advertising vacancies. He predicted there would be 'thousands of girls punching innumerable holes in small cards so that it will be possible to find out how many ladies have size eight feet and pink eyes'.

Another critic, the Gateshead MP Thomas Magnay, scoffed: 'The next suggestion will be fingerprints. Logically, why not?

You might as well tattoo people.' The sceptics did manage to reduce the planned heavy penalties for failing to carry the card, and limit the number of people entitled to demand it. But the costly scheme went ahead. If it was any use at all to anybody, this has not been recorded. The cards were crude cardboard folders, without even a photograph of the holder, easily forged and stolen. They contained a mysterious page on which were printed the words: 'Do nothing with this part until you are told.' On 22 May 1940, as an invasion seemed imminent, everyone was ordered to fill in this page with his address and signature, and to carry the card at all times or face a fine of £50, a huge sum then. It also became an offence to fail to report a change of address.

I have studied the newspaper archives of the period, and have failed to find any cases of spies or saboteurs being caught because they failed to produce identity cards. They do, however, reveal that there was a large black-market trade in stolen blank cards. A man was tried at the Old Bailey for receiving stolen cards in November 1941. Half a million people, unsurprisingly, managed to lose theirs in the first two years of the war. But the documents became a growing excuse for officiousness and interference in people's lives.

In 1942 the authorities refused to issue new ration books to those who could not produce cards. In 1944, police threatened to prosecute those in 'sensitive' coastal areas who collected ration books for neighbours. This miserable inflexibility does not seem to have any practical purpose. A spy trying to uncover details of D-Day preparations would hardly risk detection by asking a citizen to collect his ration book for him. It is in fact typical of the sort of thing that officials do, once they have the power to do it, for no other reason than that they can and it pleases them to do so. One chief constable even warned, grandly: 'No one in the prohibited areas may be without his or her identity card for a moment.' All this ostentatious vigilance might just have been excused by grave national peril, if there were any evidence that it had even once led to the detection of a fifth columnist, spy or infiltrator.

But on the other side, it is worth pointing out that if we had lost the war, German authorities would have found the national register extremely useful (as they found the meticulous registers of other occupied countries so useful) for their plan to deport British males of working age for slave labour on the Continent. They would have found the compulsory recording of addresses even more helpful in rounding up victims for political and racial purges. This danger certainly seems to have occurred to at least one British subject at the time. For in May 1950, a Jewish furrier, Myer Rubinstein, was prosecuted because he had never registered, presumably because he feared in 1939 that his name alone, discovered on national records by a Gestapo officer, might one day cause his death.

Who can blame Mr Rubinstein for his caution? But his case has another interesting lesson for us. Despite having never registered, he had successfully managed to live and work without a card, undetected amidst the regimentation of wartime, for more than ten years. The idea that the oppressiveness of such measures is justified by the increased efficiency they give to the organs of security just does not stand up to scrutiny.

When war ended in 1945 the authorities did not, as they had in 1918, give us back our former freedom. Though the official reason for their existence was over and done with, government found it convenient to hang on to its new powers on the grounds that they might come in handy at some time. This suggests that the real reason for the introduction of cards had always been the state's natural instinct to increase its power over the people at every opportunity, and also to gather knowledge about them in case it might one day be useful. The post-war period was a period of increasing crime and disorder, mainly brought about by the dislocation and demoralization which always follows war. Identity cards do not seem to have been of any great use – if any

this. Yet the uselessness of the cards to the innocent
often demonstrated. The droning mantra 'If you have
hide and have done nothing wrong, you have nothing
to fear' was constantly disproved in practice. In 1945, the
Seamen's Union leader Charles Jarman was held by police for
hours on the ludicrous suspicion of being a smash-and-grab
raider, even though he produced his identity card which ought to
have proved that this was, to put it mildly, highly unlikely. There
were many similar cases involving less prominent people, who
found that, while cards gave the police the power to poke their
noses into their private affairs, they did not provide any protection from the frequent mistakes of insolent and arrogant officials.

By 1951, the public were sick of being pestered for documents
which were of no benefit to them at all. That year Joyce Mew, of
Tunbridge Wells, won a court case after she refused to show her
card to a pettifogging rationing officer who knew perfectly well
who she was. Even the Home Secretary, Chuter Ede, was ready
to admit that that the cards were 'alien to the British mode of life'
but his view was then overruled by the Cabinet when he sought
to abolish them.

Finally, Lord Justice Goddard destroyed the system, while ruling on the case of a motorist who was stopped and asked for his
identity card even though he had committed no offence.
Goddard decided that the letter of the law entitled the police to
behave like this, but added – devastatingly – that it should not be
so. The duty to produce a card, he said, 'tends to make people
resentful of the acts of the police and inclines them to obstruct
the police instead of to assist them.' Those who now claim that
such cards would aid the fight against crime should bear this in
mind, but never do.

The newly-elected Tory government, which had somehow not
got round to dispensing with the cards despite having given the
impression that they would do so, were now forced to act by
Goddard's trenchant judgement. The cards were abolished

within days of the case, on 22 February 1952, and the *Daily Mail* recorded that day: 'Many people did what they have been longing to do ever since the cards were issued – they tore them up.'

Once again the English tradition of common law being superior to political power, and the English love of privacy which this reflects, separated us from most of our Continental neighbours. We had been prepared to submit to this foreign idea during the war, but the war had only served to prove that it was useless in any case, and that unless ordered to abolish it by a powerful senior judge, the authorities would have clung to it for ever. Most European countries have had identity documents for so long that nobody can say exactly when or why they were introduced. Those that do not have compulsory cards instead issue 'voluntary' ones, which are demanded on so many occasions that they are effectively essential to daily life. Many have compulsory registration of home addresses, some demand thumbprints, some have penalties for those who do not carry cards, most expect a new Europe-wide ID card to be introduced before long, which is no doubt part of the impulse behind moves to introduce a British version. They are all used to it, just as they are used to living without juries or habeas corpus. In the old Soviet Union, the thing was known by a name which gives a much better idea of its real purpose. It was called an internal passport, and resembled a passport in every way but one: while the holder was required to show it to register his residency, send his child to school or buy a railway ticket to the next city down the line, he could not use it to leave the country.

When I asked them, spokesmen at most Continental embassies in London could not recall any time when they had not carried such cards, although none could explain how they came into being. The truth is probably that most Continental countries have had systems of registration at least since the days of Bonaparte, have found it convenient to retain them and have no common law through which they could be challenged.

Ireland, Sweden and Norway, all for various reasons outside the European legal and political mainstream, do not have identity cards. Denmark, that ambiguous country whose closeness to Germany has often forced her to act against her own wishes, does not issue cards, but has a system of identity numbers which has the same effect in practice.

There is no evidence that any of these countries has less crime and disorder because of these cards. If there are differences in crime rates, they are easily explained by other reasons. And the claim that the cards are a safeguard against illegal immigrants is also rather feeble. Illegal immigrants gain access to Britain because the United Kingdom's external borders are so slackly patrolled and because the claim of asylum is too readily accepted as giving a right of entry that then cannot be revoked – often because those involved have destroyed their original passports and their home countries will not accept them back. Illegal immigrants are able to work in Britain despite the fact that – officially – documents are required for them to do so. Some obtain forged British National Insurance cards. Others get documents from the ever-growing number of countries in the European Union. Others work without any documents at all, in poorly-regulated industries. It is not the absence of identity documents that allows this to take place, but the inability of the authorities to keep track of so many lawbreakers, and the complicity of many employers who know that illicit labour is cheap and pliable, and who have no interest in checking backgrounds too thoroughly. And it is worth pointing out here that, were British identity cards to become compulsory, the only people in this country who would not be required to carry them would of course be foreign nationals, whose biometric details would not be on any British database and who could pass by any checks with a wave of a forged foreign document. A British national identity card would merely make life more difficult for those who were legally here already.

The argument that identity cards would aid the fight against crime and social security fraud is equally weak. The ineffectiveness of the police, as shown elsewhere in this book, is not because they cannot identify culprits. In many cases, they know them only too well, but cannot or will not restrain or prosecute them because of ludicrous codes of practice or because the overcrowded prisons mean that no serious penalty would follow all their effort. In many more, the police are so absent from most of the places where crime and disorder happen that a wicked person could go from the cradle to the grave without ever meeting a police officer face to face, and would be far more likely to see him on the television, or rushing by in a car, or flying overhead in a helicopter. It is hard to see how identity cards would help the enforcement of law at all. As for benefit fraud, it is seldom the identities that are fraudulent. The real problem is that the claims made – of housing need, destitution or unemployment – are false, and that the officials who should be checking these things are not very active. Many of them are themselves former claimants, whose sympathy lies with the recipients of benefits rather than with the taxpayers who fund them. Meanwhile, a ruthless audit of benefits would make the government very unpopular with the sort of tender-hearted liberal persons who dominate the media, the higher ranks of the civil service and much of Parliament.

As for terrorists and their confederates, the one thing that we can absolutely rely on is that they will always have the most perfect and impressive identity documents in any group of passengers arriving in the country. Since they are often aided by rogue governments, they have access to the best technology. Almost all of the 11 September hijackers, for instance, had perfectly valid US visas and would have passed without problems through any routine document check. Terrorist organizations are careful to use individuals whose records are entirely clean for their operations.

And then there is the great number of *specific* identity proofs we already carry. Some people see this as an argument for a unified, simplified card. But on examination, this idea is not logical. New driving licences carry photographs, though oddly enough these plastic cards are not valid unless accompanied by the old-style paper document. National Insurance numbers now unite our tax and benefit records. Most employers require workers to use electronic photo-passes to enter offices and factories. Banks demand old gas bills before they will open accounts, and debit, credit and cheque cards are increasingly elaborate. Addresses can be checked in moments against the computerized electoral register. These are regrettable features of a mobile, depersonalized and mistrustful society, and enable us to identify ourselves quite satisfactorily to those who need to know that we are who we say we are. But the most important thing about these cards is that each is limited to one purpose. The bank, the taxman, the driving licence office, the employer, know what they need to know about us but no more – and quite right too. The temptation to use information improperly is great, and is best limited by making sure that those who hold it know as little as possible.

Each of the cards we carry has a specific purpose, reasonable and limited, even if annoying. If you do not drive, you do not need to carry a licence. If you do not go abroad, you do not need to carry a passport, and if you do you are only required to show it when you cross into other countries or return to this one. If you deal in cash, you will not need bank cards. If you do use bank cards, then you benefit from the security they provide. And while many might prefer tax records to be separate from benefit records, it is not a gross intrusion into privacy that they are connected. Your employer may wish to be able to record the time at which you enter the office, and have your photograph on file to keep impostors and criminals out of the building. But that information should go no further.

As we well know, modern government is given to using information for illegitimate purposes. The reporter Andrew

Gilligan, who gave the government much trouble over the I war, was surprised to be approached by a government-supporti g newspaper which had mysteriously learned that his confidential tax affairs were in a mess. The family of Rose Addis, who complained about her NHS treatment to the leader of the Tory Party, were shocked when supposedly confidential information about Mrs Addis leaked into the public domain. In these nasty instances, we saw premonitory flashes of the powers a totalitarian – or would-be totalitarian – government might have over us if it had centralized access to all the vast and disparate files which its many different departments hold about us. In my view it already knows far too much about us, compared to what we know about it. If we have to wait thirty years to learn about Cabinet meetings, then the government ought to wait just as long, or longer, before it can get its hands on our medical records.

And this is the point at the heart of this argument: the old question correctly posed by Vladimir Ilyich Lenin, 'Who whom?' Must the state justify its existence to us, or must we justify our existence to it? In the English common law tradition, quite distinct from those of our Continental neighbours, it is the state that is answerable to us. We are presumed innocent in the widest sense of the word. We can walk down any street without being challenged to prove who we are or explain what we are doing. We are, in short, sovereigns over ourselves, left alone to live our private lives as we wish provided we obey a law we have made ourselves. Or rather, this is what we were until our elite state began its great reforms fifty years ago.

If we now submit to a law compelling us first to have our eyeballs scanned and our records assembled, then to have and then to carry and then to show on demand the slave badges proposed by Mr David Blunkett, then we will have become a different sort of country and a different sort of people. It will certainly not be a country where if you have done nothing you believe to be wrong, you will have nothing to fear. That is because what you believe to be wrong, and what the elite state believes to be wrong, will be two quite distinct things. Nor will it be a country where, if you have nothing to hide, you have nothing to fear. For all of us have private things we wish to hide, simply because they are nobody's business but our own. George Orwell rightly pointed out that the greatest distinction between the English people and others was their desire to live privately, to pursue private activities undisturbed, a declaration of freedom more powerful than any street march, peaceful, silent, vast and benevolent. And we know already that our rulers are prepared to drag these private things into the open, to tame us if we are troublesome.

This book seeks to explain elsewhere how a broad and complex assault on liberty has been under way in this country, often excused by crime, disorder and terrorism, for some years. Our present rulers, who openly declare that they are the political arm of the British people as a whole, are accelerating this process. And anyone who doubts that there is a danger should ponder the implications of the introduction of internal passports in the very island where liberty was invented. It is not to be thought of that the British people should be compelled to carry these squalid rectangles of plastic and be required to show them on demand to frowning officers of the state.

II

The causes of crime

He shall keep the simple folk by their right:
defend the children of the poor, and punish
the wrong-doer.
Psalm 72

The single most serious mistake made by modern democracies is to
imagine that criminality can be contained or discouraged by being
more considerate or kinder to criminals. By doing so, they make it
plain that they think that crime is caused, and thus excused, by bad
conditions. They imply that they do not believe crime to be
absolutely wrong in itself. The next step in this logic, which its supporters tend to hide from themselves, is that everybody is a potential
criminal whose good behaviour depends only on his good fortune. In
that case, those who are prosperous are good only because they *are*
prosperous, rather than prosperous because they are good.

This belief demolishes the whole idea of a middle class, open to
all who are diligent and self-disciplined, who will then be rewarded
by a more abundant life. It helps to explain the modern left-
winger's contempt for middle-class values, such as respectability
and conventional moral and social behaviour. It also explains our
cultural elite's withering scorn for the lower middle class, the most
aspirant group of all, the most respectable and conventional of all
because they are so close to the frontier. It may even solve the
mystery of that elite's destructive hatred for the grammar schools
where the poor learned the virtues of the middle class and were
enabled to join it. The comprehensive system, with its equally

passionate loathing for selection by ability, is actively designed to ensure that the process of individual self-improvement is halted. Its main effect is to trap its pupils in whatever social, economic, racial and cultural place they happen to be at the age of eleven. What else could explain the governing party's refusal to adopt for the national education system a principle – selection by ability – that governs every other field of life from science to football?

The socialist state-worshipper thinks that virtue consists of him confiscating other people's money and power for the higher good. He wants all that virtue for himself. Those who believe in this religion of government must design society, as we have, on the assumption that goodness is imposed from above by the wise generosity of the elite state. They will be guided by the belief that, without such wisdom and generosity, people will naturally behave badly. Implicit in this creed – a sort of socialist version of original sin – is the belief that everyone who *can* do bad deeds *will* do bad deeds unless he has the correct housing, income and health care. Usually, however, these correct levels are slightly out of reach, thus forever justifying further intervention by the state – somehow the task is never finished. To help people overcome their sinful state, they need subsidies, handouts, counselling, intervention from social workers, help and treatment. They have no vice or virtue of their own and cannot be expected to behave well unless they are looked after. The elite state has taken all virtue upon itself. Deterrence and punishment are therefore not merely cruel but wrong.

The old, pre-1960s law, based on unchanging moral codes, assumes that conscience is individual rather than social, that man can improve himself by work and free will. It assumes that he can refrain from committing crime through self-control and, if that fails, can be deterred from repeating it by exemplary punishment. If these things are true, then man does not need to rely on his rulers for a better life. This is why a belief in self-reliance, self-control and conscience is now the great heresy.

By sucking all personal responsibility out of the population, government actually does the opposite of what socialism claims and hopes to do. It creates a society of endemic crime which must be unceasingly placated by welfare. If an ungrateful people persist in their violence and dishonesty despite the elite's goodness towards them, it has nothing left with which to control them (and assert its goodness) except external force and fear. This requires the weapons of the strong state, an armed and obedient gendarmerie separate from the people and owing its allegiance directly to the state, with great powers of arrest, search, interrogation, investigation and detention. Communist countries, despite being allegedly based on the popular will, all eventually created harsh legal systems based on naked force, restrained by nothing.

Although social democracy has failed to abolish or even reduce crime and wrongdoing, despite decades of trying to do so, it cannot accept that its ideas are wrong and have failed. The suggestion that socialist reforms might actually have increased crime by undermining morality is impossible for the left to accept. Instead, it insists that it has failed because it has not yet gone far enough, and so demands yet more taxation, yet more spending, yet more social workers, yet more treatment. Forced to admit that crime, disorder and bad behaviour have *still* not responded to this treatment, it reaches increasingly for the crude bludgeons of authoritarian rule, curfews, surveillance, confiscations, limitations on the liberties of all to control the licence of a criminal few. Taken much further than it has already been, this idea will lead to the destruction of personal freedom for all but a very few powerful or rich people.

Lord Woolf's conversion to 'tough' sentencing is the first sign of a general collapse into crude authoritarianism. In the early months of 2002, it was followed by two other interesting straws in the wind. On 8 March, the radical left-wing Labour MP, Tony Banks, made a speech in the Commons bemoaning the decay of order and calling for the arming of the police and the stationing of armed paramilitaries at London railway termini. Mr Banks had recently been the victim of a street robbery. In May 2002 the prominent left-wing intellectual Jonathan Miller complained of graffiti in his wealthy north London street – and not just graffiti. He told the *Evening Standard*:

> 'More and more you notice these gangs of local youths lurking ever closer. They leave their telltale signs in the street – empty KFC boxes and cans of Fosters....
>
> Drug dealing is rife in the high street and around the Tube station and you really have to watch out for yourself.'
>
> Dr Miller said: 'Because of London street crime people here will now avoid going out at night unless they really have to.
>
> It's not worth popping along to the off-licence for a couple of bottles.'
>
> Dr Miller – who has twice had his bank card snatched while attempting to draw cash in Camden High Street – added: 'Call it middle class timidity, but if I travel by bus or Tube at night I always find these gangs – and they are black and white mixed – wearing their hoods and you really do need to avoid making eye contact with them.'

This retreat from liberal complacency – usually via a sudden epiphany when the new barbarism bursts into a previously sheltered life – has been summed up in the phrase 'A conservative is a liberal who has just been mugged'. Yet it is not an open or even a deliberate and conscious process, and the new enthusiasts for armed police forces or 'tough' prison sentences usually fail to see that what they used to advocate may have helped to bring about the disorder which they now protest against. If they would only recognize this connection, they might seek to preserve and defend the old system of liberty under the law before it is too late. Those who support liberal authoritarianism do not really mean to produce the results they obtain. It happens subtly, like many of the most damaging changes of the recent past. These changes soak slowly into the law and the state, thanks to the general acceptance of a series of dangerous but attractive ideas.

Those who believe that crime is committed in response to social conditions must begin to believe a number of other risky things. First, they must think that the job of the law is no longer to punish the wrongdoer but instead to mediate between the 'offender' (that carefully neutral word) and the 'victim'. One astonishing example of this, taken to its outer limits, occurred in Somerset in February 1999 when a woman complained to the police that her car had been vandalized. The constabulary wrote her a letter saying that the culprits 'could be considered to be victims themselves'. For those who find this incredible, here is the full account from the *Daily Mail*:

> When Rebecca Trebble found that her car had been vandalised, she expected the police to treat her as a victim of crime. Even when they told her they would not be sending an officer to investigate what they regarded as a minor matter, she thought they would at least care about her plight.
>
> But when she wrote to them complaining about her treatment, the local police chief in Taunton, Somerset, replied that whoever had damaged her car was a victim deserving of sympathy, too.
>
> Superintendent John Snell wrote back: 'Whilst I have every sympathy with you being the victim of crime, the position regarding victims is not limited to those who suffer as you have done.
>
> 'Many of those who are responsible for the commission of such minor crimes could be considered to be victims themselves.

'To my knowledge some of our prolific offenders are heroin addicts who live in the very worst of housing conditions in our area in relative poverty. It is also true many of them are from broken homes and really have miserable family backgrounds.

'I know this is no excuse and it is difficult to sympathise with such individuals when they commit crime; however, I do think sometimes we should give a thought to those less fortunate than ourselves.' Miss Trebble, a 21-year-old financial assistant, said yesterday: 'I was shocked. I felt I was being patronised and that he was lecturing me. To suggest the criminal was as much the victim was amazing. That's just not what you expect from the police.'

There is another unpleasant side to this excuse-making approach. While helping the 'victim' to cope with his victimhood, you must work on the assumption that his misfortune may well be partly his own fault. Although he must not risk the use of force in guarding his life and property, he may be to blame if he fails to protect his possessions strongly enough with the passive methods that are still permitted, such as alarms, lights, fences and locks. He may own more than he ought to, or be too obvious about his wealth. He may be weak, old or ill and therefore vulnerable, and well-advised to stay indoors as much as possible.

In short, wealth greater than the average is itself immoral, probably obtained at the expense of others. Those who draw attention to their wealth, or fail to protect it, or are too feeble to do so, can reasonably expect to be relieved of it by others. They have no absolute right to it. A frightening sign of how deeply this view has penetrated our society is the way in which criminals, like the muggers who recently attacked the Prime Minister's eldest son in north London, will often describe the ownership of expensive clothes and cars as 'greed' and their robberies of those better off than themselves as 'taxing'. They speak more truly than they know. They did, after all, learn something in their long years at comprehensive school: the dim falsehood that the rich and the middle classes are wealthy at the expense of the poor. This is an argument both for expropriation and for its little brother, theft.

Rather than seeking to frighten, punish and deter those who would prey on the 'victim', the socialist state seeks to educate the 'victim' in how he must fortify his house or alarm his car, how he must not walk in certain areas or leave valuables where a criminal might observe them. Millions are spent on advertising campaigns telling us not to leave our property where a thief might see it. The inability to resist the temptation to steal is seen as an unavoidable fact of life. Theft is treated as an uncontrollable force of nature, like the wind and the rain, against which we must shelter ourselves. Policemen who once patrolled the streets to deter thieves now visit homeowners, calling themselves Crime Prevention Officers and advising on fences, lighting and alarm systems. These are designed to deal with a world in which it is assumed that housebreakers will take any opportunity they can, and will almost always escape detection or capture.

If householders fail in their duty of protecting the dishonest from themselves, then they may lose their insurance against theft. When householders are injured or killed during robberies, police spokesmen are often quoted as saying such things as 'this was a burglary that went wrong'. This implies that, in their minds, there is such a thing as 'a burglary that went right' – presumably one in which nobody is hurt. Neighbourhoods are plastered with posters warning that 'pickpockets operate in this area' or 'thieves operate in this locality, do not leave valuables in your car'.

Even if it does catch him, the system will seek to understand the 'offender' so thoroughly that he will probably not be dealt with in any way that will upset or inconvenience him. At the same time, the 'victim' must be placated, because he cannot be offered the reassurance that his attacker will be punished. He is offered counselling, told the outcome of the case and sometimes asked if he wishes to meet the person who has attacked or robbed him, in a process known as 'restorative justice'. Despite its name, this does not restore the things he most wants – his lost property and his lost peace of mind. Instead he may get an apology.

This managerial, morally empty approach was sharply exposed in an article in the *Daily Telegraph* in May 2000 by its home affairs expert Philip Johnston, dealing with the new type of chief constable now emerging. Johnston, an acute observer of the modernised system, wrote:

> The present generation of senior officers is far removed in social and educational background from most of their predecessors. Almost to a man, they grew up in the Sixties, an era of permissiveness which some say led to the development of the current liberal orthodoxy. Thirty of the 43 chief constables in England and Wales are 55 or under. All but seven have degrees. Thirteen have degrees in social sciences, psychology or business studies; a further 13 graduated in law or criminology. The remaining 10 read a variety of subjects.
>
> A decade ago, only a quarter of chief constables had a degree and none was a graduate when he entered the service. The characteristics of chief officers have also changed. Before the last major police reorganisation in the mid-Sixties, many would have been retired Army officers or civil servants. It was not necessary to have been a policeman. Nowadays, every chief constable has come through the police service and few have ever worked outside it. They have all been on specialist courses at the Bramshill police college in Hampshire. They are far more adept than their predecessors in the law, in criminal theory and in detective techniques. The new generation of police chiefs has been much

influenced by the adoption of management techniques in the public services. It would be wrong to see the 43 chief officers as a homogeneous group but they increasingly speak as one through the Association of Chief Police Officers.

Johnston quoted Robert Reiner, professor of law at the LSE, as saying that many of the new chiefs saw themselves as business executives:

> 'That is what they are groomed for. Basically, they are running very large organisations, with the Home Office as their main client,' he said. The type of degrees some chief constables possess may make them more inclined to a 'society causes crime – don't blame us' approach. During the recent debate about policing, that view was prevalent.
>
> Richard Childs, chief constable of Lincolnshire, said: 'The quick and populist way today is to blame the police for getting it wrong. While sometimes we do, we are, I believe, the messengers of a broader problem of change and unrealistic and insatiable expectations.' The Police Federation, with which chief officers have an uncomfortable relationship, once called them 'clones and butterflies', career officers who possessed a similar outlook and flitted from force to force looking for promotion.

As Johnston pointed out, critics of the existing system believe it rewards caution and conformity and reinforces the culture that has already taken root. Most senior officers are reluctant to offend the Home Office or stray from current orthodoxies because this could threaten their promotion. Some of them also feel entitled to join in the political debate. On 26 April 2000 William Hague, then the

Conservative leader, championed what were subsequently denounced as 'populist' views on law and order. In a speech in Alcester, Warwickshire, he said :

> The Tony Martin case lit a touch paper that has led to
> an explosion of anger and resentment among millions of
> law-abiding British people who no longer feel the state is
> on their side.

He said that the foremost responsibility of the state was to protect its law-abiding citizens. One of those who did not seem to agree was Mr Crispian Strachan, Chief Constable of Northumbria, who accused the Conservative leader of promoting American-style gun law that could 'seriously increase' levels of violent crime and murder.

Kenneth Williams, 56, the Chief Constable of Norfolk, scene of the Tony Martin episode, said it was not the job of his officers, 'to make value judgments about the crimes we investigate'. He said he had been shocked at the ferocity of public reaction to Martin's life sentence, expressed in a flood of abusive phone calls to the police.

Johnston's account explains why chief constables seem so immune to public pressure and why they seem so keen on technological solutions – the favourite resort of the modern managerial reformer. It also gives a clue as to why they are so resistant to returning to the tried methods of the past.

The results of this on the street are far from happy. Instead of the reassuring presence of police constables walking the beat, there is the disturbing electric shrieking of sirens as the police rush to the scenes of crimes that have already been committed, all too frequently killing or injuring innocent pedestrians (and sometimes killing themselves as well) as they hurtle at excessive speeds down shopping streets and suburban roads. In 1999–2000, twenty-five people were killed in high-speed police chases, three times the figure of three years before. Six more died when police cars answering 999 calls crashed. Roughly two thousand people are injured each year in accidents involving police cars chasing suspects or answering 999 calls, according to the Police Complaints Authority and the Home Office.

This miserable wailing racket, together with the fear and danger it betokens, only spreads the idea that crime is abroad and chaos is near. This is exactly the opposite of what a police force should be doing. Its cost in lives and injuries is greater than that of some recent wars. It is worth asking whether the outcomes of most of these calls justify such a level of risk. It is hard to see what the point of it is, except to emulate what police chiefs have seen on American TV shows, where the strobe lights and howling may conceivably be justified by the conditions of the south Bronx or north Philadelphia but certainly are not in the suburbs of Wolverhampton.

This is not the only demoralizing and dispiriting result of modern absentee policing. Many city areas, especially in London, are punctuated with bright yellow 'murder boards' detailing horrific crimes that have taken place nearby, about which the police are seeking information. First used in the mid-1980s to seek witnesses to murders, when one or two might be displayed each month, they are now part of the London landscape, with about two hundred now being deployed each month, describing crimes such as street robbery, serious assault, serious sexual assault, murder and racial crime. They may be effective in finding witnesses, but they are even more effective at spreading the idea that evil is abroad and unrestrained. It is much easier to find such boards than to find a police officer on patrol, as one London borough wittily pointed out when it displayed similar boards asking if anyone had seen a police officer in the area recently.

This sort of reactive, fire-brigade policing is doubly useless. Many of the incidents to which the cars are hurrying with their sirens of doom and their spaceship strobe-lights are not worth the fuss. Some, such as pub fights, would sort themselves out quietly if left alone and simply do not merit the level of attention they receive. Others, such as burglaries, are over and done with before the officers can get there. It is a harsh and unwelcome fact that, unless trained in first aid, a police officer is almost entirely useless *after* most crimes have been committed. All he can do is take notes, offer sympathy and launch a legal process that will probably end in failure. Even Sherlock Holmes reincarnated would be unlikely to be able to track down most culprits. Even then, the Crown Prosecution Service may well decide that it is not worthwhile to proceed. If the CPS does go ahead, the case may collapse at the last minute for bureaucratic reasons. If it is taken to its conclusion, the criminal will probably be punished so lightly (if at all) that he will in future be even less afraid of the law.

Yet this is not the worst of it. There are grim and totalitarian implications in the social-work approach to crime which will not be widely obvious until they are far advanced. We should think about them now. The new system refuses to believe that there are people who are so morally unrestrained that they are prepared to do wicked acts. It cannot accept that they must be punished for those acts and deterred from repeating them by hard and memorable retribution. Instead, it bases all its actions on the view that crime results from inequality, mental disturbance or unpleasant experiences such as child abuse. Authority must then assume that everyone is a potential wrongdoer. The law, the police and the authorities must treat everyone as a suspect.

We are supposed to accept that it is necessary for the police to retain DNA details of as many citizens as possible. Pressure to compel us all to be photographed and fingerprinted is great and growing. Terrorism is only the latest pretext for the Home Office to bring out – once more – its long-prepared plans for identity cards. If these cards are successfully introduced, they will contain great quantities of encoded information as well as fingerprints and photographs. They will be of little use to the police unless citizens are compelled to carry them at all times – a measure that would completely change the relationship between the citizen and the state.

Many of our movements in public and semi-private places, from shopping centres to churches and offices, are monitored without our knowledge or permission by closed-circuit TV cameras. Sadly, as in the case of the abducted child James Bulger, this surveillance is of no use in preventing crime unless someone happens to be watching at the very moment it is committed. If only the cameras that tracked the abduction of James Bulger had been able to cry out a warning or call out a question. They merely recorded the disaster, so that experts could stare at the miserable footage too late to save James Bulger from death or his killers from their crime.

Our most personal details are shared with increasing willingness among government departments. Our recorded telephone calls and e-mails are to be stored. The Regulation of Investigatory Powers Act, now likely to be combined with European legislation and Europol powers, is the basis for this enormous intrusion into places that would once have been considered absolutely private.

While still formally presumed to be innocent until proven guilty, we may have our assets seized without any such proof. The Drug Trafficking Offences Act 1986 gave a court powers to order the seizure of property connected with narcotics offences. Later, through the Criminal Justice Act 1988, this power was extended to the profits from all crimes. These Acts were conviction-based, so that there could be no confiscation of assets without the defendant first having been convicted. However, the Proceeds of Crime Act 2002 gives the police powers to confiscate assets *without a conviction* from persons whom they suspect of drug dealing or other crimes. Drug-dealers, for reasons explained elsewhere in this book, are convenient hate-figures against whom such measures might be popular at present. But this does not alter the fact that an important legal principle, of no punishment before conviction, has quietly but definitely been breached.

We may be detained for long periods if we are accused of 'terrorism'. This is a crime the government pretends to treat with special horror but with which it is in truth happy to negotiate when it suits it. So, if the horror is false, we have the right to suspect that 'terrorism' is no more than an excuse for the taking of powers that the state wants anyway. If we engage in certain kinds of demonstration or political movement, the police have extraordinary new powers, almost always granted with the public's willing support, to detain and obstruct us as if we were threats to the state. The Criminal Justice and Public Order Act 1994, originally passed to deal with unpopular 'rave' parties, is the main basis of these new powers. Our passports can be taken from us if we are believed to be football hooligans. How long before this totalitarian power is extended to cover other people?

Police officers, when we do encounter them, are ostentatiously equipped with devices to restrain, gas and club us, when once they managed with no more than a tactfully concealed truncheon. The new equipment makes it plain that the public are not to be trusted and may at any time need to be pursued, gassed or manacled. The modern police officer is not a public servant except in name. Like his Continental counterparts, he is a powerful representative of the state with whom it is unwise to argue. The old police deference to the middle class was not just the consequence of simple snobbery. It was an expression of the old truth that the law was our servant, not our master. The new type of officer, who defers to nobody but his chiefs, does not care who you are, if you support the law or loathe it. It is all the same to him, although stardom and celebrity, the classless society's aristocracy, may gain his deference. He is the state and you are not. That is why he now has far greater licence to enter our homes and search them than ever before, to listen to our telephone conversations and read our mail. Our right to have our guilt assessed by a jury of people like ourselves has also been seriously undermined and may, in effect, soon disappear for ever for most accused people.

This is a physical expression of a new type of thought. The liberal state has redefined crime in such a way that many actions that used

to be seen as common sense are now dangerous breaches of t̶
Teachers who smack or even restrain children, householder̶
catch vandals smashing their fences and frogmarch them to their
parents for punishment, citizens who put up barbed wire to defend
their homes against thieves, shopkeepers who try to fight off violent
robbers with force, all find that the police are likely to view them as
offenders. The new law believes that the family is itself a seething
nest of abuse from which battered wives and molested children
may at any time need to be rescued. By means of the Children Act
1989 it openly undermines adult authority, zealously pursuing allegations against teachers accused of 'abuse'.

This enthusiasm for pursuing allegations against authority figures
widens the gulf between the police and citizens who once saw
themselves as being on the side of the law. Actions that would at
one time have been seen as helpful to the police are now prosecuted and punished. Faced with such actions – defence of homes,
citizens' arrests of street robbers and so forth – police chiefs complain about citizens 'taking the law into their own hands'. This is an
interesting use of language. The law, as it has existed for centuries,
is in the hands of the English people and is shared by them with a
police force who are supposed to be citizens in uniform.

However, there is now such deep disagreement between the
public view of right and wrong and that held by the state that this is
no longer so. In the one area where the two do apparently agree –
dislike of disorder and disapproval of certain spectacular and
unpopular crimes – there are interesting clashes between appearance and reality. The disapproval that used to be aimed at sexual
deviation of all kinds has now been focused on paedophilia, the one
sexual perversion of which liberals disapprove as much as the rest of
the population. Red light districts and blatant prostitution now
flourish on the verge of legalization. The laws against under-age
intercourse are rarely enforced. In a recent case, police refused to
prosecute a man in his twenties for alleged sexual relations with a
thirteen-year-old girl because the girl herself had not complained

and would not complain, despite the powerful evidence that an offence had been committed and the grief and distress of the girl's parents. What would once have been called 'public indecency', heterosexual or homosexual, is quite unchecked. Sexual and violent abuse of children is made vastly more likely by the breakdown of the stable family. All our fears and worries about sexual exploitation, licence and the victimization of the young must now be assuaged by one of the few remaining laws that acknowledges (quite rightly) that some sexual behaviour is wrong and that children need protection from adult evil.

Perhaps this is why this offence, quite bad enough to start with, has become the focus for angry street demonstrations and for special police and court procedures not applied to any other crime. People accused of this offence – and it is important to remember that they *are* accused until convicted – are subject to trials that are often breathtakingly unfair. Police are allowed to trawl for witnesses, childish denunciations are given the same weight as adult statements, under-age witnesses are protected from the normal rigours of cross-examination and guilt is effectively presumed from the start. Dawn swoops, computer searches and similar tactics, often well publicized by press leaks, seem designed to show the police are doing at least one thing that is popular. Celebrities, although usually rather faded ones, are accused surprisingly often of this offence, again as if to show that the law's old impartiality between great and small still exists, since celebrities are the only privileged aristocracy permitted to exist in our egalitarian times.

One effect of this development is that perfectly reasonable doubts about such prosecutions are liable to be viewed as sympathy for child-molesters, by even well-educated and intelligent people who are unaware of the manipulation being practised upon them. Some readers may even find themselves thinking that this passage is some sort of attempt to excuse or minimize paedophilia. No such sentiment is expressed or intended by the author, who views sexual assaults on children as serious offences deserving harsh punishment and who loathes pornography of all descriptions. It is a sign that something is wrong with our laws and our society when such a disclaimer is necessary. This atmosphere makes it harder for reasonable doubts to be expressed, for fear of the mob cry of 'you must be one too'. Concern for justice and due process is dismissed as tenderness for perverts or killers. The modern show-trial of an alleged paedophile is therefore unfair even before it begins. Even where the charges are obviously true, such trials leave a nasty taste. The same end could have been achieved without breaking the basic rules of English justice.

Rape is also now viewed as a crime against feminism rather than merely an offence against decency, kindness and trust. Thanks to its new ideological importance this offence is treated with politicized horror and subject to special rules, notably the anonymity of the victim and restrictions on the right of the accused to defend himself. The presumption of innocence is damaged beyond repair by the treatment of defendants and accusers in such cases. Most such cases involve 'date-rape' where both parties know each other and the alleged assailant claims that consent was given. The name of the accused is made public, in a case where it is generally one person's word against another's and there are no independent witnesses. Even if acquitted, he is subject to the exposure of his private life and behaviour which can never be expunged or forgotten. The accuser, however, retains her anonymity even if the charge is dismissed. This appallingly one-sided procedure cannot fail to impress jurors with the idea that the Crown's mind is already half made up before the trial has begun. It also often fails in its objective. A large number of rape cases end in acquittals, very probably because the law makes little distinction between 'date-rape' and violent assaults by strangers, and juries are reluctant to convict on the basis of an uncorroborated accusation. In November 2002 the government proposed to make it harder for a man accused of rape to claim he believed the woman had consented. This will have the effect of compelling male defendants to prove their innocence of such charges. It is political-law-making.

Another strange development raises suspicions that the justice system has become more politicized than it would care to admit. Conservative politicians such as Jonathan Aitken or Jeffrey Archer seem especially liable to accusations of perjury, a crime that is breathtakingly common (the witnesses in many contested trials could in theory face such charges if their side lost) and remarkably rarely prosecuted among the non-political classes, especially in civil cases. Again, the point is not that anyone should feel sympathy for either of these two. The author has no such sympathy and views both men as an embarrassment to the causes they espouse. They are proven liars who deserved to be punished. Nobody should object to such prosecutions if they were intended to discourage lying on oath, a terrible crime which poisons the wells of justice. However, was that their true purpose? Would their prosecutions have taken place at all, or would their sentences have been so long, if they were not prominent members of the dethroned Conservative elite? Were they imprisoned for being perjurers, or for being *Conservative* perjurers? The apparently selective nature of these cases raises questions about their real justification. Susan Edwards of Buckingham Law School found that Archer's four-year sentence was unprecedented in such a case. Between 1981 and 2000 only nine perjurers were imprisoned for three years or more. They had told lies in serious criminal trials involving murder or large-scale corruption. Archer's perjury was in a civil trial.

The ludicrous affair of the sexual allegations against the former Tory MP Neil Hamilton and his wife Christine, attended with phalanxes of police cars and seizure of computer equipment, all taking place in conditions of total publicity, gave yet more force to fears that the police have become far too sensitive to political fashion and media stardom. The Hamiltons have made public fools of themselves and deserve little sympathy, but the willingness of the police to take seriously these laughable allegations against them is disturbing. For whose benefit was this charade intended?

Murder, a shockingly common crime treated with increasing leniency by the courts, is a different matter when the victim is a child or a celebrity. Police forces cannot catch as many killers as they once did and prosecutors often reduce murder charges to manslaughter in order to achieve a swift conviction. However, they will concentrate enormous resources on prominent murder cases. Something akin to a show-trial often results. It is reasonable to wonder whether these spectacular tribunals are designed to prove, at almost any cost, that the law is actually effective after all. In some recent cases, notably those of the Russell murders in Kent and the killing of the TV presenter Jill Dando, there are serious doubts about the quality of the evidence used to convict the suspects.

The law of the new elite, based on utopian social engineering, is displacing the older law, based on common sense and Christian morals, because that elite controls the courts and the modernized police. One of the most important duties of the modern police force is to ensure its total monopoly of violence and enforcement. The common law has been taken from the common people, and their attempts to enforce it themselves are punished more harshly than crime itself. This is why citizens who unintentionally kill suspects during attempted crimes, such as the farmer Tony Martin, are prosecuted and imprisoned while police officers who do the same thing are generally exonerated. It is not the action itself that is wrong – or police officers who have mistakenly shot suspects would have languished alongside Mr Martin. It is the fact that a private individual rather than a representative of the elite state has done the shooting.

The police are now a special body of armed men with special powers far beyond those of the ordinary citizen. Such harsh and determined prosecutions are designed to educate the public into realizing that the law no longer belongs to them, that the police are not citizens in uniform any more. They are servants of the elite state, which owns the law and uses it for its own supposedly wise purposes. The same reasoning lies behind the rapid and determined disarming of the English people, who were once obliged by law to bear arms in support of the civil power and who, a century ago, were as free to bear arms as any American is today.

This division, between what people think the law should be and what it actually is, leads to a permanent suspicion and near-hostility between police and citizens. The police are operating a law that they know to be unpopular. This shatters the old sympathy between police and respectable law-abiding people. The police themselves must in many cases be neutral referees between offender and victim. Their new rules tell them that the offender may have good social and economic reasons for his behaviour. They also tell them that the victim may have brought his trouble upon himself by behaving foolishly, for instance by failing to conceal his unfair wealth or status, failing to bar and bolt and alarm his house and car, or just assuming that the streets of an English city are safe at night.

The new police will often be harsher with the victim than with the offender, especially if he has used violence to defend himself or his property. The point must be made that the old idea, that the police are there to defend life and property against those who attack it, has been repealed. It has been replaced by a new 'civilized' or 'social' law. This calls on the police to seek to understand criminals and help them to return to normal life. It has turned them into the uniformed front line of the equality-loving state. This unspoken rule lies behind the zealous prosecution of those who 'take the law into their own hands'. Once, such people would have been more or less the allies of the police. Now they are trying to enforce an obsolete and abolished law and challenging the state's monopoly over law enforcement. It is not merely insensitivity to public opinion when these things happen, or the result of bureaucrats sticking too closely to the rules. It is a cold and deliberate policy aimed at destroying old assumptions about a citizen's right to protect himself and his property. Once we had the Queen's peace, which was ours. Now we have the people's police, who belong to the elite state.

III

'Bobbies on the beat'

The purpose of a trial is to find out the truth.
But we no longer have trials about who did it –
the trial is always about whether somebody
broke the rules in trying to find out who did it.
Sir David Phillips, Chief Constable of Kent

For years British politicians of all parties have been calling for 'more bobbies on the beat' and audiences have been applauding them for doing it. Most citizens, in town and countryside, keenly support the idea that there should be more police officers walking the streets or bicycling down country lanes to reassure the good and frighten the wicked.

One of the most noticeable facts about modern England is that there are hardly any police officers to be seen. Large regiments of them appear during football matches or at demonstrations, kitted out in glowing yellow jerkins whose main purpose seems to be to emphasize that they are there at all. Sometimes, irregularly and unreliably, they are to be found on the busier streets of major cities or sitting, waiting for something to happen, in vans parked round corners. From time to time there are announcements that plain-clothes officers 'may be required to go back on the beat'.

There are even schemes for the police to do their main task, which is tacitly admitted to be paperwork, in public places such as shops and cafés, so that they can at least be seen to exist. They may be observed soaring overhead in helicopters or hunkered down on rooftops, in baseball caps and bullet-proof jackets, during state visits or outside the trials of alleged terrorists. They were active in suppressing perfectly peaceful and legitimate demonstrations against the visit of the Chinese tyrant Jiang Zemin to Britain in October 1999. They can often be seen hurrying by in cars, usually in pairs absorbed in each other's conversation. Even London's Royal Parks Police, a force whose territory is almost entirely made up of lawns, woodlands and narrow footpaths, tends to patrol (when it does so at all) in cars.

If we call on them in distress or emergency they will eventually arrive, complaining of an impossible backlog of unsolved cases, to give us a crime number, offer us counselling for our grief or loss and advise us to buy new locks, bolts, lights and alarms, while going through the motions of an investigation that will rarely yield any result. Even this form of activity is now in decline, since the number of robberies, burglaries and car thefts is so great that it is often unwise for them to raise hopes of justice or recompense that are bound to be dashed. They can be found milling around the criminal courts, all too often on wasted journeys for trials that are mysteriously cancelled or postponed.

Those trials, once a contest between prosecution and defence attempting to establish guilt or innocence, are now an elaborate game to see if the enormous safeguards and protections given to defendants by law have been fully exercised. The Police and Criminal Evidence Act 1984 was a response to a series of police scandals and wrongful convictions. Rather than seeing these as errors that might be corrected by punishing those responsible, the elite state chose to blame the entire police force. They enacted a great Domesday Book of mistrust and regulation which assumes that every police officer is a latent evidence planter, quote inventor, liar and brute. Every action must be tape-recorded or logged. Every suspect must be provided with a lawyer at the earliest possible moment. The streets must be trawled for people to take part in identity parades, a regulation that has created a minor cottage industry in many cities, where a useful tax-free income is available to those with time on their hands and a vaguely criminal appearance

ın take part in the endless parades. Other measures and judi-
.... ecisions have also forced prosecutors to disclose almost
everything they are doing to the defence. And any long delay –
perhaps caused by the need to assemble mountains of files, stacks
of tapes and battalions of busy witnesses – is likely to lead to the
cancellation of the trial.

One slip and the case collapses. Sir David Phillips, Chief
Constable of Kent, complained in April 2001 that the court system
was quite simply too soft on criminals, following the revelation that
one offender was so undeterred by the majesty of the law that he
had been arrested 186 times before he was seventeen. Sir David
pithily described the new justice system in words that ought to be
written up outside the country's courthouses: 'The purpose of a trial
is to find out the truth. But we no longer have trials about who did it
– the trial is always about whether somebody broke the rules in
trying to find out who did it.' He reflected a general feeling that
there are now too many laws and regulations that give privileges to
defendants. Worse, even when they are tried and found guilty the
courts are reluctant to do anything to them. For instance, during
1999, thirty-seven thousand people admitted or were convicted of
burglary, a serious attack on the peace of mind of many thousands of
people. However, seven thousand of those were let off with a
caution, the authorities' way of saying they could not be bothered to
do anything about it.

Home Office focus groups found in the same year that respect for
the law had seriously declined. Most people now believe that criminals run little risk of being caught. Those that are caught will be
given short sentences by an elite of out-of-touch judges. This is
slightly unfair to judges, who come under unending pressure to
keep the prisons from overflowing and so are reluctant to hand out
prison sentences unless they absolutely have to.

In an amoral society with feeble courts today's police officer has a
difficult task. Even so, the missing police cannot escape blame for
being absent from their proper place of duty. Many of them can be

seen in the columns of the newspapers, suing their forces for sexual or racial discrimination. Others, who have yet to understand that the job has changed beyond recognition, are hauled before disciplinary tribunals, and sometimes the courts, for chastising wayward youths, having wrongly imagined that this was what they were paid to do. Large numbers have joined the force – now more usually known as a 'service' – since its transformation into a motorized bureaucracy. They simply do not know what traditional policing involves and are surprised that anyone should expect it of them.

Some officers even speak about the health problems that arise in what is now semi-officially a sedentary occupation. In April 2000, the *Daily Mail* interviewed a young policewoman, Gill Moriaty, then aged thirty-three. She explained: 'When you join the police you acquire a really good level of fitness because you train regularly for the first 20 weeks. After that there is no mandatory fitness regime and you are left to your own devices. I spend a lot of the time cruising around in a patrol car.' She said there was 'a certain amount of walking around'. A fitness expert, Doug Robertson, concluded that, while she was quite fit, 'it's true to say that Gill's job is not very active and any exercise outside working hours – even chasing her toddler around – will not go amiss.' A waitress and a gardener both had higher fitness scores.

If we try to seek them out in police stations, we will find that these places have often been closed, both in country districts and in city areas. Where they still exist, they are often sited away from town centres and are open during office hours only. When they are open, their counters are frequently not staffed by police officers. In many cases, especially in small country towns, they are deserted for much of the time and equipped with special telephones. The frightened or angry citizen can use these to reach a control room many miles away. Those who answer the phone, often not police officers, may never have heard of the street where the victim lives. They will frequently explain that lack of manpower means that no swift response can be expected.

same is true of the 999 service, hugely overloaded because it is only guaranteed route through which most people can make contact with the police at all. By early 2002, BT was dealing with six hundred and twenty-five thousand 999 calls each week; its competitor, Cable and Wireless, handled a further one hundred and twenty-five thousand (these figures are for the whole of the UK; separate statistics for England and Wales are not available). Genuine emergencies have to fight their way past citizens making daft requests for information, needlessly worried old ladies and cranks – exactly the sort of people who would once have accosted a constable on the beat or queued up for a word with the station sergeant.

The history of the 999 service neatly illustrates the changes that have overtaken British society and policing. It was set up in London following a fatal fire in Wimpole Street in 1936 in which five women died. A neighbour complained that, by the time she reached the operator, the fire engines were already at the scene. The Post Office, which then controlled the telephone system, began the 999 service in London in July 1937 so that emergencies could jump the queue. The system was eventually copied throughout the world, but before the Second World War it was confined to London and Glasgow. In its first month, thirteen thousand Londoners used it. The small number of telephones, public and private, limited its use even when it was expanded to most of the UK in the 1950s. At that time there were fewer than half a million 999 calls each year, 65 per cent of them to the police. By the early 1960s this figure had risen to two and a half million per year, rising to four million in 1970, nine million in 1978, nineteen million in 1988, and over twenty-three million in 1998. By 2001 the explosive increase in the number of mobile phones meant that there were more than thirty-one million calls each year, many of them false or accidental. About 80 per cent of mobile emergency calls are to the police rather than the other emergency services, compared with about 56 per cent of calls from fixed lines. How the police can be expected to respond to this number of calls, or sort them into a reasonable priority, is a mystery. In reality, they cannot be expected to and they do not.

Senior police officers and the Police Federation respond in chorus when complaints are raised about this and the other problems that result from the absence of foot patrols. They cling to the belief of all inefficient nationalized industries, that their problems are caused by a 'lack of resources' rather than by their own actions or failures. They say that more manpower is needed. Opposition politicians sing the same silly song. Governments have several different answers. One is to pass laws – the only thing they can actually do – even if those laws already exist in another form and are not being enforced. Another is to increase police numbers, a hard task at a time when many experienced officers are leaving early and it is all the force can do to maintain its strength. When they cannot afford to provide these resources, they massage the crime statistics and claim that everything is getting better. The Home Secretary, David Blunkett, ludicrously claimed in January 2002 that people were safer from crime than they had been for twenty years. In a speech in Sheffield he said that crime was not as bad as people thought it was. Despite a recent spate of street robberies and a huge increase in mobile phone thefts, he said that the chances of becoming a victim were at their lowest for twenty years. 'Anyone reading recent reports would think that crime and violent crime in particular is now spiralling out of control,' he said. 'The reality is very different. There is a growing problem with street robbery and mobile phones in particular. But overall crime is now falling and has been for some time.'

Politicians also use the public's justified discontent to seek closer and tighter central control of the nation's police – something they have always wanted – on the grounds of increasing efficiency. The Conservative Home Secretary, Kenneth Clarke, did this through the Sheehy Report, much hated within the police force itself. Mr Blunkett, in late 2001, likewise promised an attack on poor working practices and excessive sickness claims, while quietly seeking unprecedented powers to dismiss chief constables, the real point of his measures. Both governments failed to realize that cumbersome organization, unwarranted sickness claims and early retirement, not to mention the endless industrial tribunal and other court cases affecting the police, are the result of their own past reforms. In the end, they both accepted the lazy fiction that the problems of the police can be solved simply by increasing the numbers of officers doing the wrong thing in the wrong place, combined with giving them powers that they are unable to use.

The constant allegation that police operations are hampered by a manpower crisis is the first and most amazing Big Lie of the law and order debate. It is astonishing that it goes unquestioned, although it is so often used and so easily exploded. Examine the figures in the table below for population and police strength in England and Wales throughout the twentieth century.

The changes that have taken place over this period are boundless: in health and strength, wealth and housing, education, morality, religion, diet, means of transport, general social welfare, migration, the role of women. One of those changes is shown by the startling increase in the number of female officers (insignificant before the Second World War) which began nearly thirty years ago. What is more, these women officers, who were once given separate duties, are now treated exactly as if they were men, an interesting change in an organization whose effectiveness once depended heavily on the size and strength of its members. The far greater use of women, who simply cannot be as strong and imposing as male colleagues, is a symptom of the change in the role of the police officer. The modern police is an increasingly bureaucratic service rather than a preventive force whose impact used to depend on the implied ability to intervene and on sheer force of personality.

Now-discarded height regulations and rules against the wearing of glasses did not discriminate specifically against women (or myopic bookworms) but against all, male or female, who would be unlikely to overawe a drunken troublemaker on the midnight streets. Plainly, there are women who can produce such an effect and women who are happy to take part in physically demanding operations. Such atypical individuals do this despite the fact that female upper-body strength is seldom more than 60 per cent of that of men. There is no doubt that many women have the necessary courage or personality. But no amount of such qualities can make up for raw strength and size. Attitudes towards women among the educated middle class have been transformed over the past forty years. However, the educated middle class do not need the police to keep them in order. Attitudes remain largely unchanged among the sort of people the police are supposed to control. Few football hooligans, drunks or wife-beaters are *Guardian* readers and it is no use women officers – or small, bespectacled male officers, come to that – appealing to their progressive instincts when the punches start to fly. Thanks to the censorship of any dissent as 'sexism', few in the

Year	Population (England and Wales)	Police strength (England and Wales)	men	women
1901	32,527,843	42,484		
1911	36,075, 269	51,203		
1921	37,886,689	56,914		
1931	39,948,000	58,656		
1941	41,748,000 (estimated)	56,193	55,868	325
1951	43,745,000	63,116	61,610	1506
1961	46,166,000	75,161	72,829	2332
1971	48,604,000	95,759	91,937	3822
1981	49,011,000	118,081	107,379	10,702
1991	49,890,000	125,294	110,396	14,898
1995	n/a	124,710	107,022	17,688
1999	n/a	123,051	103,084	19,967
2001	53,137,000 (estimated)			

THE ABOLITION OF LIBERTY

police now dare to express such doubts. Those who are still free to debate in public have a duty to ask whether this change is good for the police, the public or the individual women involved.

Many of the recent changes in our world might be thought likely to make for a more law-abiding society rather than a more lawless one. For much of the twentieth century they did have exactly that effect. Perhaps the most peaceful single year was 1951, with a low level of crime, especially violent crime, following a brief increase in bad behaviour following the war. The average daily prison population for that year was 21,370. Forty years later, in 1991, we were recognizably in modern times. The average daily prison population stood at 44,809, and crimes of all kinds were rising sharply and were far more common than forty years earlier. Over the same period the number of police officers increased from roughly 1.4 per thousand in 1951 to roughly 2.5 per thousand in 1991. It is true that the number of officers has fallen slightly since the late 1990s while the population has risen but it is still the case that there are now far more police officers per head than in any other era.

This increase has coincided with an increase in crimes of all kinds. It is important to add that the police have been joined in their large new office buildings by tens of thousands of back-room staff whose job is to do the tedious paperwork that is supposed to be tying down so many officers. They have also been relieved of many duties – enforcing car-parking rules, checking shops and factories by night, organizing prosecutions. These are done, respectively, by local authorities, private security firms and the Crown Prosecution Service. So the true increase in manpower is even greater than appears from the figures.

Excuses about overstretched resources and poor manning are also undermined by a great number of other developments which might be thought to make the job of the police easier rather than harder. In roughly the same four decades, the management experts have been set loose on every police force in the land. They have been merged into larger units, supposedly to cut down on bureaucracy and increase efficiency. They have been given huge fleets of cars and vans, computerized central records, personal radios and greatly increased powers of search, surveillance and arrest. They clatter as they move, their belts hung with costly equipment supposedly designed to make them more effective. They even have a small air force of helicopters and the active help of broadcasters, through programmes such as *Crimewatch*, allowing them to hurry details of suspects to millions rather than the few hundred who might have seen a poorly printed 'Wanted' poster in the old days. Enormous networks of closed-circuit TV cameras survey hundreds of town centres, railway stations and shopping malls, supposedly doing the work of dozens of constables.

A deliberate policy of graduate recruitment has raised educational levels to previously unknown heights. Senior officers are more likely to have a university degree than ever before. This may actually be a disadvantage. A university degree in modern Britain is not necessarily a sign of great attainment or intelligence. However, it is almost always a sign that its holder has been indoctrinated in the modern ideology of social welfare, egalitarianism and moral relativism that has dominated the campuses of this country for thirty years. Perhaps, while developing an interest in anarchism like the Oxford-educated Metropolitan Police Deputy Assistant Commissioner, Brian Paddick, they have forgotten what they are employed to do. This may help to explain why they seem so absent and so inefficient, why they no longer patrol the streets and why they respond with indifference or excuses to calls for help from the public.

Like so many of the problems of modern England, this one has its origins in the 1960s and in the mind of Roy Jenkins. To begin with at least, it seems to have been mainly a matter of fashionable innovation, coping with shortages of recruits and cost-cutting, without any co-ordinated political motive at all. Only later did it turn into an opportunity to amend the country's constitution. Economic crisis, like war, is the reformer's ideal opportunity to ram through long-desired change.

From the first patrols of Sir Robert Peel's Metropolitan Police in 1829, the purpose of the force was to prevent crime from happening in the first place, to reassure the lawful and discourage the wrong-doer. Peel deliberately excluded middle-class and officer types from his force because he wanted men who could deal easily with the man in the street. The uniform, originally intended to be scarlet and blue finery, was in the end kept deliberately dull and understated so as not to overawe or stand out too much. The constable's oath was not a declaration of loyalty to the state but to the law, which in England is the property of the whole people. This distinction is deeply significant, which is why there was alarm when during 2002 there were proposals to give it a more politically-correct form. A typical version (each force has its own) runs:

> I do declare that I will well and truly serve Our Sovereign
> Lady the Queen in the office of constable without favour
> or affection, malice or ill-will; and that I will to the best of
> my power cause the peace to be kept and preserved, and
> prevent all offences against the persons and properties of
> Her Majesty's subjects; and that while I continue to hold
> the said office I will to the best of my skill and knowledge
> discharge all the duties thereof faithfully according to
> law. So help me God.

Legally, this gives the individual policeman great powers of initiative and independence so long as he remains within the law. It does not separate him from his fellow citizens or raise him above them.

From the beginning, the English police force was not intended to be a separate gendarmerie. As the 1929 Royal Commission on Police Powers emphasized, the office of constable is very ancient in England, with its powers rooted in the common law. The Commission stated: 'The police of this country have never been recognized, either in law or by tradition, as a force distinct from the general body of citizens.' And the Commission reiterated to the

Home Secretary that there was

> an instinctive feeling that, as a matter of principle, they
> should have as few powers as possible which are not
> possessed by the ordinary citizen, and that their authority
> should rest on the broad basis of the consent and active
> co-operation of all law-abiding people... the utmost
> discretion must be exercised by them to avoid
> overstepping the limited powers which they do possess.
> A proper and mutual understanding between the police
> and the public is essential for the maintenance of law
> and order.

From the start of English policing the chosen method of activity was designed to embody the special relationship between constable and public: that of allies on the same side in support of a law that belongs to all. Plenty of other models were available. This one was chosen because it was the only one that was not likely to threaten liberty.

The standing instructions then given to officers were consciously based on the idea of the constable as a uniformed citizen who kept the peace by persuasion, example and tact, whose influence depended on close contact with the public:

> The primary object of an efficient Police is prevention
> of crime, the next that of detection and punishment of
> offenders if crime is committed. To those ends all the
> efforts of Police must be directed. The protection of life
> and property, the preservation of public tranquillity, and
> the absence of crime, will alone prove whether those
> efforts have been successful.
>
> In attaining these objects, much depends on the
> approval and co-operation of the public, and these have
> always been determined by the degree of the esteem and

respect in which the Police are held. Therefore every member of the force must remember that it is his duty to protect and help members of the public, no less than to bring offenders to justice. Consequently, while prompt to prevent crime and arrest criminals, he must look on himself as the servant and guardian of the general public and treat all law-abiding citizens, irrespective of their race, colour, creed or social position, with unfailing patience and courtesy.

By the use of tact and good humour the public can normally be induced to comply with directions and thus the necessity for using force, with its possible public disapproval, is avoided. He who in this way secures the object he has in view is a more useful police officer than his comrade who, relying too much on the assertion of his authority, runs the risk of seeing that authority challenged and possibly, for the time being, overborne.

The chosen method was regular, intensive patrolling so that everyone knew that an officer was never far away. Sir Richard Mayne, first Commissioner of the Metropolitan Police, said he intended to achieve his objectives by having constables in uniform walking the streets observing and being observed by members of the public. The constable was to be alert and to see every part of his beat once every ten or fifteen minutes so that a citizen in need of assistance had only to remain in one place until the law arrived.

A century after the founding of the Metropolitan Police, the introduction to the 1929 Royal Commission on Police Powers still stated that the first duty of the police was the 'Prevention of crimes and offences, rightly regarded by the police themselves as their most important duty'. Investigation was said to come second, followed by 'other duties which have been imposed on the police', by which they meant mainly the control of traffic, already becoming a serious diversion and preoccupation.

There had been no change in this attitude when another Royal Commission reported more than three decades later, in 1962. Nothing had happened to persuade them that the preventive beat was outmoded or useless. On the contrary, they were convinced of the importance of having 'a sufficient quantity of constables on beat duty in close touch with the public'. They believed that this view was shared by both police and public. It is interesting that it had clearly survived not just two world wars but the transformation, already well under way, of the English cityscape into widespread suburbs linked by busy roads in which the car was fast becoming the main method of travel. It is also interesting that forces were beginning to worry about the decline of beat policing, even though they recognized that it was superior to any known alternative and had proved itself thoroughly in practice. The then Metropolitan Police Commissioner, Sir Joseph Simpson, said: 'The policeman in a car, on a motorcycle or absent from his beat becomes a cypher... the greatest safeguard of public relations, as well as the greatest preventive measure against crime, lies in making good deficiencies on the beats.'

These expressions of confidence and continuity seem prehistoric now. This is not because there was any sudden revolution in the science of policing. There was not and never has been. It was because the next few years were to see a series of revolutions in police organization and methods, and also in law and justice, which have changed policing out of all recognition and for the worse. These new methods have also wiped out the memory of the far more effective system that went before. The old system, which existed continuously from the days of Peel and Mayne to the 1960s, is nowadays often ignorantly mocked by the defenders of the disastrous status quo. Any sort of comparison between current levels of crime and disorder and those of the early 1960s must make any unbiased person wonder if the changes were for the better.

So what happened to abolish the long and successful career of the constable on the beat? It may seem unbelievable now, when a far larger police force is equipped with cars and motorcycles, computers and helicopters, and supplied with multitudes of clerical staff, but it seems that by the late 1960s the Home Office felt that it could not afford to continue policing at existing levels. It was also worried by the problem of patrolling the large new council housing estates that had sprung up all over the country, as both major parties pledged to solve the post-war housing crisis. The Chief Constable of Lancashire, one of the few graduates in the police force of those days, was Eric St Johnston, an innovator much liked by civil servants and by 'progressive' politicians. He was a rare survivor of the controversial, pre-1939, Trenchard proposal to recruit an 'officer class' of graduates, which had been swiftly killed off by resistance from the ranks. He seems never to have served as an ordinary constable on the beat. He would later become Chief Inspector of Constabulary (and Sir Eric) and his influence over police methods in the past forty years has been profound.

In the early 1960s, police officers were still almost entirely independent as they made their rounds. They had no personal radios and would contact headquarters through police boxes of the type immortalized by the Tardis in BBC TV's *Doctor Who*. They might also summon help from neighbouring beats with whistles or by hammering their truncheons on the pavement, still a realistic way of attracting attention in those days of light traffic at night. Car patrols were rare and mainly aimed at controlling what traffic there was. This state of affairs did not appeal to Eric St Johnston, who saw himself as the first of a new generation of visionary police chiefs. He was much admired by the Labour Prime Minister and Merseyside MP, Harold Wilson, as well as by Roy Jenkins. Wilson, the great enthusiast for creating a 'New Britain', plainly saw in St Johnston the pattern of the sort of police force he wanted. He wrote an effusive preface to St Johnston's memoirs, *One Policeman's Story*, in which he pictured St Johnston as a sort of modernizing Hercules, cleansing stables of outmoded practices. He described how, when St Johnston took over the Lancashire force, 'appalling problems faced him, the territory of the county authority was honeycombed with independent police authority enclaves, large and small, over which the County Constabulary had no jurisdiction. Equally he had a police authority which knew it all, resisted reform and the modernising ideas of one of the most progressive Chiefs in police history.' Wilson leaves no doubt that his government viewed St Johnston as an ally in its sweeping reforms of the country, against a supposedly bone-headed establishment.

> Not all the civil servants of the Home Office viewed his revolutionary ideas with enthusiasm, or would be happy to see him as either Metropolitan Police Commissioner (which he never became) or Her Majesty's Chief Inspector of Constabulary, a post which the [1962 Royal] Commission [on the Police] recommended should be created. It was Roy Jenkins as Home Secretary, despite some Home Office resistance, who appointed him Britain's first HM Chief Inspector.

St Johnston's breezy autobiography reveals that Wilson and Jenkins had chosen wisely, if their intention was to appoint a radical. He was a keen innovator and modernizer of the sort who would nowadays appeal greatly to Anthony Blair. He loved technology and publicity and was personally involved in an event that for ever changed the image of the police in England. In the early 1960s, when there were only two TV channels and a single programme could have a far greater effect than today, the weekly drama *Dixon of Dock Green* kept alive the image of the honest British copper treading the beat in size twelve shoes, an image that still lingers many years after it flickered off the screen. The radical BBC of Sir Hugh Greene (Director-General 1960–69) viewed *Dixon*, which it saw as 'middle class' (and therefore bad) and cosy, with some scorn. Jack Warner, the reassuring actor who practically became Dixon, was a national icon much loved by the unfashionable middle-aged and lower middle class, which Sir Hugh's new wave wanted to shock and unsettle. Greene's BBC, whose heyday of innovation and radicalism coincided with the fall of Harold Macmillan and with most of the 1964–70 Labour government, also felt it needed to win back viewers who had deserted to ITV's pioneer soap opera *Coronation Street*. The BBC approached various forces, including Lancashire, saying that *Dixon* was now too paternalistic and asking for ideas that were more modern. They also wanted to move away from portraying a man on the beat to men in cars, probably influenced by American police series such as *Highway Patrol*, then being shown for the first time in Britain. St Johnston recalled being told specifically that they were worried by the success of *Coronation Street* and its northern appeal. 'They wanted to compete by launching a new programme based on working-class life in the north of England.'

St Johnston was aghast at the slovenly, undisciplined image of the police provided by the first episode of *Z Cars*. He expected to be in serious trouble with his colleagues and political masters as a result. He forgot about his objections when the series immediately turned out to be a surging success. Its main characters continued to appear in *Z Cars* and its successors *Softly Softly* and *Task Force* for years to come. Its personalities, 'Fancy' Smith, Sergeant Lynch and Inspector Barlow, and its theme music completely supplanted those of *Dixon* in the public mind. Given the way that realistic TV drama first reflects real life and then influences it, St Johnston's decision to help and advise the BBC may well have had as much effect on English policing as all his other actions put together. To be fair to Sir Eric, this is saying a good deal.

Lancashire Constabulary was one of the biggest forces outside London and covered one of the largest areas in the days when most local forces were quite small. It had always been open to new ideas. It introduced VHF radio in 1936 to maintain contact between headquarters and patrol cars, then rare in English policing. By 1939 it was operating 140 radio-controlled road patrols, known as 'wireless cars'. It also took part in a now-forgotten pre-war scheme to improve

relations between police and motorist which could have cl
the whole history of policing, the so-called Courtesy Cops sy
This created a separate corps of traffic policemen whose main task
was to improve driving standards by offering advice and warnings,
rather than prosecuting motorists. An idea of the innovating genius
Leslie Hore-Belisha, it had a highly successful start but was abandoned on the outbreak of war in 1939. The failure of the police to
find a way of overcoming the growing friction with middle-class car-
owners has so seriously damaged their standing with those whose
support they most need that it is a great pity that this scheme has
been entirely forgotten.

In the 1950s and 1960s, the Lancashire force still wanted to be first
with new ideas, although of a rather different kind. It introduced
radar speed traps in 1957, consciously copying an American idea, as it
was to do several times. Much like modern speed cameras, the traps
had a great effect to start with but that faded once drivers realized
that there were so few of them. However, the impulse to try new
methods did not fade. St Johnston recalled: 'Of all the innovations
that we introduced into Lancashire during the time that I was there,
undoubtedly the one which has had the most lasting effect on
police technology was the introduction of personal radio.' However,
even he did not see this as substitute for traditional beat policing.
On the contrary, he wrote in his autobiography:

> I am a great believer in the traditional methods of
> policing in this country. If one could only have a
> policeman on his feet in every street in every town,
> the amount of crime and public disorder would be
> minimal. Of course this is not practicable but the fact
> remains that once policemen are taken off their feet
> and put into motor cars, they do lose touch with the
> public. However well-marked the police car may be,
> they are not seen by pedestrians in the same way and
> therefore not available for the passing of information

from the public at large to the policeman.

For this reason I came to the conclusion that we must
attach the wireless to the man rather than to the vehicle,
so that even when away from his car he was still in
contact with his station.

This huge change in the role of the police officer began in the
Lancashire town of Chorley in 1961. Superintendent Frank Gee can
claim to be the man who made personal radios truly portable by
reducing the weight of the equipment from just under three
pounds to less than sixteen ounces. Thanks to his work, the
Lancashire force became the first in the world in which individual
policemen could be constantly in touch with their stations. If modernization had stopped there, it would have been radical enough. A
constable who *can* be in permanent touch with headquarters *will* be
in permanent touch with headquarters. He will come to rely on its
advice, to expect its guidance and to seek it when once he would
have used independent judgement. Without meaning to, Eric
St Johnston had severely weakened the idea that the constable
embodies the common law and the will of the people. The constable was now, more than ever before, the servant of his superior
officers, a man able to call on plenty of support but without initiative
or independence, half his mind always tuned to a radio frequency.
This was a mixed blessing and a mixed curse.

It is possible to argue that the radio brought more benefits than it
took away. We cannot know, because this change was so quickly
followed by another even more radical one. Had constables stayed
on foot patrol, they would still have been influenced by their
regular contact with normal citizens. They would have been able
to observe the streets in a way that is simply impossible from a
passing car.

St Johnston's next step was to introduce what were at first called
Panda Cars. He chose this method because he could not find
enough policemen to give proper cover to the fast-growing town of

Kirkby, on the outskirts of Liverpool. The area, in Harold Wilson's parliamentary constituency, was famous in its early years for being so rough that it was known locally as 'Mob Town'. It was thinly disguised as Newtown in *Z Cars*. The original police sent to live there had very bad relations with the public, although after a short while these improved, along with standards of behaviour. Thanks to the unimaginative building policies of the local authority – matched in scores of similar estates elsewhere – the area was utterly bleak when the first residents moved in, with no shops, pubs, cinemas or even playing fields. St Johnston recalled: 'We were unable to find enough policemen to send to Kirkby and we had at the most only six uniformed men patrolling the town at any one time, and this in a community which had risen to 60,000 by 1963.' This was a serious lack. No old-established town of the same size would have put up with such a miserably small police presence and urgent action was obviously necessary. The pity is that St Johnston and his colleagues chose the solution they did. It was the pivotal moment in the history of policing and crime prevention in modern Britain. While it offered a short-term answer to a special problem, it would come to affect the whole country in an astonishingly short time:

> We decided the foot patrol beat must go, and in May 1965, the eleven foot patrol beats were re-organised into five mobile beats patrolled throughout the 24 hours by a policeman in a car, only the pedestrian shopping precinct being covered on foot. More important, each man carried in his pocket a personal radio which enabled him at all times, whether in the car or out of it, to keep in touch with his station.

Note the use of the words: 'We decided the foot patrol beat must go'. Someone else was shortly to take a similar decision affecting every corner of England and Wales. Parliament never debated it, there was no White Paper, no Royal Commission, no real awareness of what was going on. It was revolution by secret decree, like so many of the changes under governments of both parties that have revolutionized the English justice system in recent years. The introduction of the police in the first place occupied Parliament for nearly forty years and plunged the ruling class into controversy, and it spread across the country entirely because it was so successful and there was a popular demand for it. The new style of policing crept into existence virtually undebated. It spread partly because it appeared to be cheaper and partly because Whitehall bullied forces into adopting it. It was also apparently successful, although this may be because it was pursued so keenly and given all the resources it needed to make it work. Its defenders would certainly say that its later failure was caused by its being starved of men and time. There is little doubt that the Kirkby pilot, like the Accrington one which would follow soon after, was pursued with great enthusiasm and plentiful resources. It has all the signs of an experiment designed in advance to succeed and given ideal conditions in which to do so. St Johnston wrote an article for *The Times* in 1966 in which he said that in the last eight months of 1965 Kirkby experienced a decrease of 31 per cent in reported crimes, while detection rates rose from 29 to 37 per cent. Damage cases fell by 53 per cent, with detection rising from 9 to 21 per cent. Even the number of street accidents was reduced by 16 per cent, a miracle of modern times.

St Johnston also copied American police forces by making the patrol cars stand out from their surroundings, an innovation that now seems commonplace but that symbolized a social revolution. In the grey, brown and dark blue England of those times, the new style was startling. The cars were painted in Cambridge blue with white doors and boldly marked with the words 'Lancashire Constabulary'. Until then, police cars had been deliberately sober and discreet, painted navy blue or funereal black. When the first of the new cars appeared in the garage one mechanic remarked, 'Have you heard the latest mad idea of the Chief? He wants the Kirkby cars to look like bloody pandas.' Hence the name.

The rapidity of the revolution that then followed is typical of the reforms that were unleashed on Britain during this period. Two essential conditions were present: an existing system with no articulate or organized defenders and a determined group of reformers with official backing from the centre. The abolition of the bobby on the beat was never discussed or voted on at an election. To this day, most people believe that, in some way, the old system of policing continues to exist and only lacks enough men and women to restore it to its former splendour. The change was not just a matter of technology and money, but was part of a much wider process of political and social reform. It took hold only after Labour's decisive victory at the polls in March 1966, which transformed Harold Wilson's tentative government into the first full-powered Labour administration since 1950, with a majority of ninety-seven. Those in the Home Office who sought change now had an ally at their side in Roy Jenkins, who had taken over from the more cautious Sir Frank Soskice. While Kirkby was important, it was a special case where special methods were justified. The new type of policing had to be tried on a traditional community if it were to be applied everywhere. So it was.

On Monday, 19 September 1966, the ancient city of Carlisle began its own experiment in what was already being called 'unit beat' policing. The trial was 'at the request of the Home Office'. Frank Williamson, Chief Constable of Cumberland, Westmorland and Carlisle, paid the usual empty compliment to tradition before the scheme got under way: 'There has always been a powerful argument for retaining the foot patrol on the beat to keep contact with the public. In recent years there has been equally forceful argument for increasing mobility at the expense of losing some of this contact. The unit beat policing scheme is an attempt to answer both these arguments.'

The Times reported that the plan aimed 'to increase police efficiency and cultivate a better understanding with members of the public by closer contact with men on the beat and swifter response to calls for assistance.' In a pattern to become very familiar, the city was divided into five areas, each given twenty-four-hour cover by a constable in a car. All the cars would be 'prominently signed' and given a distinctive colour. Each car area would be divided into two beats and on each beat there would be a resident constable. On 7 December *The Times* carried a highly significant report of a supposedly successful experiment in the new methods – yet again in Eric St Johnston's Lancashire. It dealt with what came to be seen as the model for unit beat policing, the town of Accrington. Under the prophetic headline 'Policeman on beat may disappear – Accrington "neighbourhood officer" success', it provided an enthusiastic and uncritical survey of what had happened. The report must have rejoiced the hearts of officials in Whitehall. Civil servants had apparently been yearning to replace the constable on the beat since a system of district policing, mixing radio cars and foot patrolmen, had been introduced in Aberdeen in 1949 and in parts of London in 1953.

Once again, this was no Kirkby New Town in need of special treatment but a traditional place set in its ways and unaware that it desired or needed change. Its only police problem was a shortage of men which (as we have seen) would not last much longer. Previously, Accrington and the surrounding area had been divided into twelve regular beats effectively unchanged since Victorian times. In theory, men worked three shifts per day to keep the beats patrolled for all twenty-four hours. In practice, there were not enough men to go round. In June 1966, obviously influenced by the Kirkby experience, the system was changed. Instead of regularly patrolled beats, eight policemen were given areas to look after. They were supposed to live in these areas and became, in effect, neighbourhood policemen. Times of duty were left to the men, but four other officers in distinctive blue-and-white cars were used to supplement them. A publicity campaign was run in the local newspaper to introduce the policemen to their areas and, said *The Times*, 'according to all reports, the public have responded well. Local information from each area goes back to the main station and the crime figures have so far showed a fall.' A PC Ted Dean was quoted as saying happily: 'This has increased the status of the ordinary policeman… Now the policeman is recognised as a specialist.' Another, John Pilkington, explained that it increased his job satisfaction: 'If I get a complaint here I follow it up myself.' An officer driving a car on duty for the first time said: 'An emergency before depended on your being near a telephone. Now you have a radio and car and you can get there quickly.'

These experiments in Carlisle and Accrington had been under way for a few short months when Whitehall's campaign to abolish the Robert Peel system intensified, with the first trial of the new method in a major city centre. On 10 October 1966, once again 'at the suggestion of the Home Office', the so-called 'neighbourhood' system began trials in the heart of Birmingham. Eight constables would each be responsible for a beat. They would decide their own times of duty. Instead of calling at the station in the morning, they would use personal radios to say they were on duty and telephone reports to a tape-recorder. Typing would be done in the station. Every two beats would also be 'overseen' by a turquoise-and-white patrol car. There was some interest in the fact that the project would cover Balsall Heath, described in the coy language of the time as an 'area with a vice problem'. (Many years later it was to be the scene of a famous confrontation between a prostitution racket and the Muslim community.)

It now became clear that what had begun as a local initiative had become a national campaign. On 18 November 1966 no fewer than three Home Office working parties reported on radical police reform. Their reports were considered and largely accepted by a body called the Police Advisory Board, chaired by none other than the Home Secretary, Roy Jenkins. This meeting of the Police Advisory Board, on 7 December 1966, must count as being one of the most revolutionary gatherings in post-war British politics. Among the ideas discussed was the extension of the responsibilities of traffic s, turning them into underpowered traffic policemen, a regularly revived and abandoned and most recently dusted on ... August 2001. Much more significant was a general 'reshaping of the beat system'. Chief constables were to be told to re-examine their systems of patrolling and to continue with the traditional beat system only in special circumstances. Police should patrol city centres in much the same way as before, but in other parts of the country more use should be made of the Accrington system.

The language of the working party reports, which were published by HMSO in January 1967, shows the force and fierceness of the Home Office's desire for change. It makes it clear that it was driven from the centre, not from below. On the beat system, the working party asserted: 'there is no doubt that the system of policing large areas of the country – which still follows the principles of the beat system started over 100 years ago – should be reviewed as a matter of urgency.' Already, the snobbery of the plain-clothes specialist towards the beat was emerging. The working party felt that there was 'a tendency for beat patrol duties, which account for over half the manpower of the service, to be regarded as inferior to duties in specialist departments'. This, it believed, hindered co-operation within the force and led to the 'lessening of the sense of personal responsibility of the man on the beat'. It also believed that the introduction of lightweight personal radios 'opened up the prospect of new techniques in policing'. At the end came what may have been the most pressing reason for change, the recruitment and retention problems of running a disciplined, semi-military service in an increasingly undisciplined, relaxed and prosperous society. Veterans of the Second World War were ageing. The abolition of National Service in 1958 had left most young people unfamiliar with discipline, uniform or unquestioning obedience to the apparently pointless orders of superiors.

As had become usual with such documents, the working party gave a powerful defence of the Peel system even as it recommended its abolition:

When it is properly worked (that is, when enough men are available to work it), it is possible to arrange for every street in an urban area to be visited by a uniformed policeman at least once in every 24 hours, and in many cases more frequently. By his mere presence the uniformed policeman undoubtedly prevents some crime and affords a degree of protection to life and property. He contributes to the maintenance of order and is available to control traffic, prevent accidents and establish close relations with the people living in his area. By these means mutual confidence and respect can be fostered. And *the concept of a policeman as a citizen in uniform gains reality* [my italics]. Moreover, the 'beat' policeman is able to feed information to his colleagues in the specialist branches of the force, since he knows the movements of people in the locality and is in a position to report irregularities in the routine of day-to-day living. Thus he knows when people are on holiday and houses are shut up, has a keen eye for open windows and gates, and knows in advance the man who is likely to make trouble at closing time on Saturday nights – or rather he would know these things where the same beat is worked regularly.

Its main argument for abandoning the Peel system was that it was no longer practicable with the current manpower shortage: 'There is clearly much of value in this concept of the beat system but we think it also embodies an idealisation from the past which, in the conditions of modern society and, given the chronic shortage of police manpower, is unfortunately no longer attainable.' It spoke of an incompatibility between the original system and the society it was meant to serve. It also noted that many chief constables had already moved away from a rigid beat system. There was also the problem of getting post-war recruits to submit to the sort of discipline needed:

There are probably many young policemen who find it
difficult to derive much interest or satisfaction from
working their beats in the traditional manner in urban
areas... many intelligent young men, fresh from a police
training centre, are unlikely to be convinced that their
mere presence on a street deters potential wrong-doers;
and they are therefore liable, particularly on beats where
little occurs, to suffer from boredom or frustration.

In other words, many policemen did not enjoy the work for which
they were being paid. This was, of course, a problem. However, it
was not by itself an argument for getting rid of a system that was still
working well. Other solutions must have been possible. The order
of the working party's conclusions, in typical nationalized industry
style, placed the welfare of the employees above the needs of their
customers, the tax-paying public.

The working party also shifted delicately from the issue of
recruitment, a matter of fact, to the efficiency of the beat, a matter of
opinion:

Our first ground for criticising the system in its traditional
form is the discouraging effect it undoubtedly has on
many policemen. Our second ground is the doubt we
entertain about its efficiency as a method of policing
many areas in modern conditions.

The question must now be asked whether there is
any longer good reason to retain a system which had its
heyday in totally different conditions from those which
obtain today, when populations tended to be static, crime
was adequately contained, traffic problems barely
existed, and the police lacked the modern resources
of mobility and electronic equipment.

The working party admitted:

> no comprehensive operational research has been
> undertaken in this country into the comparative
> efficiency of different systems of policing until the
> creation, three years ago, of the Home Office Research
> and Planning Branch made systematic research possible.
> Even so, some time must elapse before we shall be able
> to establish conclusively that one form of policing a
> particular area (taking account of its physical nature, the
> character of its population and the hazards) is more
> efficient than another.

In the manner of hundreds of other 1960s reformers, it was not
going to let such doubts stand in its way. Asking whether, in this
'interim period, while we are waiting for the fruits of research, the
police forces of England and Wales should continue to rely primarily on the beat system in its traditional form, or whether a definite
move should now be made towards the introduction of the more
flexible systems of policing made possible by the availability of scientific and technological aids', the working party gave itself the
answer it wanted:

> We have no doubt what the answer to this question
> should be. Together, the two broad criticisms of the beat
> system which we have advanced – its lack of appeal to
> the young man of today and the inefficient use of
> manpower which it involves – constitute a formidable
> indictment of the system as a universal means of
> policing; and when to these criticisms is added the fact
> that the system fails to exploit to the full the advantages
> of modern equipment, we think that the case for a very
> early change to more flexible systems of policing in many
> areas of the country becomes unanswerable.

THE ABOLITION OF LIBERTY

Even in the light of the suspiciously encouraging results of the experiments thus far, this might be described as a rush to judgement. The working party could with justice be said to have made up its mind in advance. There was now pressure on every force to change as rapidly as possible. Those that hung back were to be swept aside by the compulsory mergers that would come two years later. When these took place, traditionalist chiefs and senior officers could more easily be ignored or removed. The new men could step into the leadership of amalgamated super-forces which, for the first time, owed more of their authority to central government than to the locality they served. Any rearguard action to save the beat system would have been crushed by central authority and local ambition.

The working party advised that in future the traditional system should be operated by chief constables only when they believed it had positive advantages over other systems. The traditional method had a 'discouraging effect' on many policemen (that is to say, they found it hard work and rather boring) and there were doubts about 'its efficiency as a method of policing many areas in modern conditions'. More flexible systems should be introduced. It stated that unit beat policing had been introduced not by the local forces that first introduced it but by the Home Office Research and Planning Branch. Kirkby may well have been a genuine individual experiment. What followed, it is now clear, was centrally planned and centrally desired. It comes as no surprise to find that by April 1967 the unit beat system had been 'officially' shown to be a 'success'. The reported results were so extraordinarily good that one can only wonder why its general adoption did not instantly lead to a startling drop in the national crime figures.

The Accrington report showed that total crime in the area had dropped by 19 per cent over ten months. There had been a 30 per cent reduction in breaking and entering. The overall detection rate had risen from 36 to 49 per cent and the rate of detection for breaking and entering offences from 21 to 48 per cent. At Kirkby, there had been a 20 per cent reduction in all crimes with an increased detection rate from 27 to 42 per cent. These figures compared with recent national increases in crime of about 6 per cent. Officers also claimed a great improvement in the amount of information gained about the activities of known criminals.

The working party reports contained many other modernizing ideas which are now commonplace but that were then radical. More graduates were to be hired. There were also proposals for greater use of computers, with a national system as the goal. The abolition of police drill parades, more personal radios and more cars were suggested. Reducing the height requirement, then a minimum of five feet eight inches, and allowing constables to wear glasses were discussed but not agreed on. The issue was fudged with a proposal to recruit 'able and intelligent people who lack stature but could make a useful contribution'. The complete dismantling of the old requirements would come later, during the 1980s and 1990s.

The hiring of more non-uniformed staff, then numbering only sixteen thousand, was agreed in order to tackle paperwork and to include fingerprint experts and school-crossing patrols. The use of the expression 'civilian' to describe these workers has helped to undermine the idea that the police are civilians. It has encouraged them to consider themselves as a special body set above the rest of the citizenry. It has also nurtured the idea that the police are mainly a detective and record-keeping organization, rather than an active preventive force. A proposal to abolish the traditional helmet was rejected, although everything it represented was being jettisoned. It would instead be allowed to disappear slowly and quietly, the British establishment's favoured method of abolishing something that is popular. In another hint of the future direction of English policing, plans were revealed to start the experimental use of helicopters. The tests were not always successful and at least once had ludicrous results. In August 1967 six policemen were said to have been bitten, presumably by their captives, after three men wanted for questioning were run to ground by a police helicopter at a lonely farm at Ash, Surrey. The men ran from the farmhouse but the helicopter kept track of them as they waded through a canal and crossed a railway, only to be arrested, despite defending themselves with their teeth, by officers on foot. Nobody seems to have wondered whether they might have been arrested without the helicopter and without so much fuss.

In November the police began 'intensive helicopter training' over London. Officers dressed in militaristic berets and battledress-type uniforms with shoulder flashes marked 'Police'. The army provided the pilots. This was the first faint whisper of what would become a powerful trend among the police to abandon their 'citizen in uniform' appearance and kit themselves out in militaristic or stormtroop outfits which emphasized their separation from the rest of us.

In January 1968 police revealed that an experiment with closed-circuit TV had quietly begun in Croydon, following a similar scheme in Liverpool. Unknown to the public, the tests had been going on for several weeks. The cameras had mainly been used to film and arrest men spotted trying the doors of parked cars. A Chief Superintendent Hall said that the main advantage was that it saved manpower: 'I have just not got that number of men to cover the area effectively by policemen alone.' He said there was no moral difference between secret camera surveillance and being looked at by a man in plain clothes. At least, unlike most modern advocates of CCTV, he was aware that there might actually be a moral issue involved. Neither he nor anyone else dealt with the other disadvantages of this technology. First, to be at all effective, it requires somebody to watch it all the time. The more cameras that are installed the more people will be needed for even the most basic vigilance. Secondly, if it does not cover an entire area, then it will have the effect of driving crime into the districts where it does not exist – whereas if it is installed everywhere it will be at least as labour-intensive as the Peel beat system. Thirdly, CCTV cameras have serious technical limitations: they see poorly in the dark and cannot see through masks or round corners, which means that recorded tapes are often useless and even if a central control point 'sees' the crime nobody will be able to reach the scene in time to make an identification. As it happens, the monitors are often so distant from the scenes they are watching that, even if the police do react swiftly, they are bound to be too late to prevent crimes. Wrongdoers know all these things and behave accordingly.

These objections, clearly foreseeable, are at least as powerful as the working party's criticism of the beat system, which was scrapped at the same time that the CCTV network was founded. It is not clear from the reports whether the cameras were concealed or clearly visible. Scotland Yard said it was too early to make an assessment but results thus far had been encouraging, with thirty suspects stopped and questioned and eight arrests, although these were 'not necessarily a direct result of the existence of the television cameras'. The Yard asserted that there had been a considerable decrease in all types of crime. The claim is puzzling given that the experiment was secret.

It is fascinating to find that so many of the changes and concerns of the 1990s and today were prefigured in this hectic period of reform. The Police Advisory Board, in a thin bat's squeak of early political correctness, even noted that there was 'not nearly enough attention paid to the recruitment of women and there should be sustained effort in this field'. No doubt it would have mentioned institutional racism too, if it had been invented. The whirlwind of change continued to howl across the country. Many developments that would subsequently become the subject of widespread complaint and discontent began in this era. In Cornwall the police abandoned their Victorian whistles – which would be revived by some forces more than thirty years later when they turned out to be quite useful despite being unfashionable. In October 1966 the Devon and Exeter police pioneered the retreat from the countryside, introducing a new telephone system that allowed small police stations to be left unmanned. Installed at forty-one stations, it connected callers to an answering machine that gave them the number

ivisional headquarters or allowed them to leave a message if the
_tter was not urgent. Colonel R. B. Greenwood, Chief Constable
of Devon and Exeter said: 'The time has gone when policemen
should be waiting in police stations for something to happen.' It is
hard to think of a more misleading thing for him to have said. Such
methods were to lead to policemen spending more and more time
in bigger and more remote stations, waiting until after crimes had
happened before leaping into high-powered cars festooned with
sirens and lights. It would also lead to them arriving long after the
criminals were over the horizon. There would be a grave increase in
rural crime as professional burglars realized that large parts of the
English and Welsh counties now had no police presence at all.

The scythe of reform, which somehow never seems to have cut
state spending, has swept away many of the police stations which
once offered reassurance to city and countryside alike. Mighty
fortresses of policing, such as Rochester Row and Tottenham Court
Road in London, both located in active, inhabited and busy centres
of business and shopping, were closed and boarded up. While they
awaited their fate they were plastered with posters and graffiti, a
symbolic triumph of the new culture that governs the unpatrolled
streets. The scythe has swung far beyond the capital. The Victorian
network of police stations has been lopped as drastically as were the
railways by the half-witted Beeching cuts of the sixties. The rash
pruning has had similarly unpleasant and unintended results. The
effect of this policy on rural life, just at the time when new roads
made it possible for urban thieves to make swift raids on rural areas,
is only just becoming clear. Even the fastest response times will not
act as a deterrent when the nearest police presence may be thirty or
forty miles away.

In the years 1990 to 2000, according to Home Office figures,
England and Wales lost 630 police stations, mostly small ones in
country districts. Even those that remain are often working much
shorter hours than the nearby pubs which generate so much of the
disorder the police stations once deterred. The *Daily Mail* reported

in the summer of 2002 that one thousand stations, one in three, had closed their doors over the previous ten years, and conducted a survey that showed that six out of ten of those that remained in operation were open only during office hours and not at all at weekends. In small towns many police stations are in fact unmanned for much of the time. These closures are not popular and are frequently resisted by local people. A group of pensioners took over and started to man an abandoned station at Old Molesey in outer London in an attempt to reassure the inhabitants of the area. The gesture did not deter the modernizers.

Essex police closed forty-two stations in two years. Of the seventy-two that remain, a mere twelve are open round the clock. A look at the official tally of station closures shows that it is country districts that have suffered most from the cull. Between 1990 and 2000, Avon and Somerset lost forty-three of their eighty-two stations; Derbyshire thirty-two out of eighty-nine; Devon and Cornwall thirty-three out of ninety-eight; Gloucestershire twenty-four out of seventy-one; Hampshire thirty-two out of 126; Hertfordshire an incredible thirty-four out of fifty-five. London alone has almost the same number as before, having opened forty-three and closed forty-four between 1990 and 2000. The new stations, serving a different purpose, tend to be more remote from the high streets than the old ones. Greater Manchester lost twenty-two of its ninety-six stations in the same period; Merseyside nine out of fifty-three. Many more stations may yet close. There seems to be a general policy of abandoning the idea of a station as a physical and obvious presence. The new police service prefers the modern and remote headquarters, designed with custody suites and computer facilities to suit the post-Peel style of policing.

Like all such changes, this revolution has been carried out in the name of efficiency and economy. Those who criticize it meet the standard response of police chiefs to all such complaints: that it is all a matter of manpower and resources, that they just cannot cope, that to man a desk at a police station means taking officers off the eat. The embarrassing truth, that police manpower and non-uniformed back-up have increased by a third in the last thirty years, is seldom admitted.

Much of the thinking behind the closures was summed up in a report from the Audit Commission published in March 1999, although it is obvious that the ideas behind this document date from much further back. In the dreary Newspeak of modern government, it talks of 'improving the management of the police estate'. The buildings, it claims, are often in the wrong place to support police operations, or they are 'outdated and unable to cope with modern technology: 87 per cent are more than 20 years old'. It suggests that 'many stations are not conveniently situated for the public', which may be true but is an odd argument for shutting them down so that they are situated nowhere at all. Perhaps more significant is the appeal to the accountants, summed up in the words 'opportunities to generate income and reduce costs through rationalisation are being missed'. The report goes on to say that most public contact with the police now takes place by telephone. This is true out of necessity rather than public choice. The chance of direct personal contact with a helicopter two thousand feet overhead or a patrol car hurtling by is necessarily limited.

The Audit Commission urges 'strategic thinking', including asking the question 'Is there still a role for the traditional police station?'. While it admits that 'for many people, the traditional police station is a tangible reminder of the police's presence, a source of reassurance second only to the sight of a "bobby on the beat"', it seems to think that this is less important than the fact that many station buildings are not new. However, the real problem is explained in one brief paragraph of the Commission's document, which states: 'Policing styles have also changed, with a greater need for rapid response and an investment in "behind the scenes" intelligence-gathering.' Prevention, based on police stations in the hearts of towns or villages, has been abandoned in favour of 'rapid response' after the crime has already begun.

The idea of policing by remote control was closely connected to the abolition of the beat, which at last reached London, again through 'experiments' that mysteriously never failed, in March 1967. Pilot schemes were announced for unit beat patrols in Harlesden and Bromley, which, 'if they prove successful', were to be extended to all parts of the Metropolitan area. Cleverly, the innovation was sold as a return to a homely past and the car-based system was described in the press as a new form of 'old-fashioned village-type bobby'. Almost every future reform of the police would be portrayed in the same way, although the one change that no force would consider was a return to the regular beat. Chief Superintendent Stanley Hebbes set a rather low standard for the success of the tests, pronouncing: 'If after a year we find that this new scheme has cut down the amount of crime in this area by even 1 per cent we shall consider it a success.'

In the same month, *The Times* reported, under the headline 'More police drop beat system', that three British police forces were to scrap the traditional beat system and change to neighbourhood policing. Birmingham, it stated, had announced the decision the previous day. The unnamed reporter, obviously well briefed, added: 'I understand that Lancashire and Bedfordshire will also change this year.' The story asserted that one of the new method's chief advantages was improved contact between police and public, which would turn out to be the opposite of the truth. The changes were portrayed as 'part of a Home Office drive to reduce crime'. They coincided with an announcement by Roy Jenkins that crime had increased by 5.8 per cent during 1966, reaching a total of almost 1.2 million indictable offences.

This was a time of general turmoil and unprecedented change. A vast Criminal Justice Act had just been passed, introducing a series of profound reforms in the court and penal system. Parole, suspended prison sentences and majority verdicts were all brought into the English system in that year. The death penalty had just been abolished. The country had been dismayed and alarmed by the murders in August of three policemen in Shepherd's Bush: PC Geoffrey Fox (aged forty-one), DC Stanley Wombwell (twenty-five) and DS Christopher Head (thirty), shot dead in Braybrook Street outside Wormwood Scrubs prison.

This gruesome event led to angry confrontations between Roy Jenkins and rank-and-file police officers demanding the return of the gallows. Jenkins cut short his holiday because of the killings but said during a visit to the local police station that he would not make any changes in the law because of a wave of emotion caused by one incident. 'I will not change my policy in the shadow of recent events, however horrible,' he declared. Many officers saw his view as condescending and weak. Interestingly, Jenkins did then make changes in policy that suited him, including tighter gun controls. He also took the opportunity to suggest 'modifying' the right to silence, a favourite target of penal 'liberals', although this suggestion would have to wait until the Criminal Justice and Public Order Act of 1994 to find a House of Commons feeble and dim enough to enact it.

Public feeling about the killing of the policemen, who at the time were popular and generally well loved, was also bitter. The event was so shocking to a then-peaceful country that the three dead men were commemorated by a service in Westminster Abbey. There was a widespread feeling that the ground was shifting underfoot and that a stable and settled society was in the midst of uncertainty and confusion.

The police faced serious recruiting problems because of the high wages being offered to unskilled men by expanding production-line industries such as car manufacturing. This was still the era of 'You've never had it so good', when the old attractions of police work – including steady, guaranteed employment – no longer counted for much. Few young men used to a more relaxed world were now prepared to face the discipline and tedium of life on the beat. For every ten men who joined the police in 1964, nine left; 5512 joined and 4888 left during the first eleven months of the year. In early 1965 the government admitted that the police force was 15,000 under strength. George Thomas, then a junior Home Office minister, promised that the gap would be filled with up-to-date equipment and other measures. Such was the crisis that even the Monday Club was urging the recruitment of 'coloured' policemen, then the politically-correct term. This was widely seen as an outlandish and impractical notion. *The Times* quoted an unnamed officer as saying that this had not happened because 'the British public would not tolerate being arrested by coloured men'.

The problem was exercising many minds even before Roy Jenkins came to the Home Office. In May 1965 his forerunner, Sir Frank Soskice, told the Police Federation at Llandudno that he hoped the day would soon come when there would be 'coloured' policemen. Reg Webb, chairman of the Police Federation, responded by warning that every chief constable would have to ask 'will this man be able to fit into the force and be accepted by the general public… I wonder if the country has yet grown sufficiently used to the idea of being a multiracial society to accept the idea of coloured policemen'. The Federation's preferred solution was better pay, not a welcome idea to a Labour government wading through a severe economic crisis which would end in the humiliating devaluation of sterling.

Another enormous change was about to begin. The 1962 Royal Commission on the Police had urged, in the fashion of the times, that larger organizations were better than small ones. It proposed that the 127 English and Welsh police forces should be amalgamated into fewer larger ones. Nothing had been done about this at the time, but Roy Jenkins demanded action as soon as he took over from Sir Frank Soskice in 1966. Labour's general election manifesto in March of that year had been vocal on crime and policing, complaining of a rising crime rate, overcrowded prisons and many seriously undermanned police forces, all supposedly legacies of thirteen wasted years of Tory government from 1951 to 1964. It boasted: 'The slide in numbers has already been checked. Energetic action will now be taken to build up police strength.'

It promised the 'most modern scientific and technological equipment', and declared, without feeling the need to explain, that 'there is also an urgent need for fewer – and larger – police forces... we shall therefore press ahead with a vigorous programme of amalgamations.' It claimed, without evidence, that this was 'the form of organisation best suited to the battle against crime'.

Britain at this time was richer than it had ever been before, but it was also more uncertain and rackety. Trade union militancy was epidemic. Large-scale immigration was transforming many cities and, with a mixture of crude prejudice and baffled politeness, English people were adapting with various degrees of success to a multiracial society. Television and 'beat music' were creating a new youth culture. The comprehensive school revolution was beginning and the first new universities were opening. Millions of families were moving into new housing estates, council and private.

Taboo subjects, such as abortion and homosexuality, were being openly debated on TV and in the newspapers as well as in Parliament, in an age when many married couples had never even seen each other naked. Divorce had begun its sharp upward curve. The Shepherd's Bush police murders revealed a dangerous mood among the police themselves. It also widened the gulf of misunderstanding between the police and the new liberal elite, which many traditional officers saw as condescending and cut off from reality. The public clashes between Roy Jenkins and police officers were the first instance of open police militancy since the unstable years at the end of the First World War. In the midst of all this, reform seemed only natural and did not require much in the way of argument to support it. Change was generally seen as good in itself, new automatically better than old.

In May 1966 the government began the long task, the goal of which is only now becoming completely clear, of nationalizing the police under central control. Roy Jenkins brusquely told the 127 police forces of England and Wales that many of them were to disappear in a matter of months in forced mergers. The 1962 Royal

Commission had said that the optimum size for a police force was probably five hundred or a little more, but Jenkins went even further. His plans meant that the smallest force would be almost seven hundred strong. He also struck hard and fast to make sure that any small forces that wanted to keep their independence were cowed in advance. He threatened to use his powers under the Police Act 1964 to force mergers where there was resistance.

The parliamentary opposition did not appear to see any difficulties in a plan that blatantly undermined the independence of the police force. Their complacency might seem astonishing, given the huge debates that had preceded the initial founding of the police. They seem not to have been aware of the historic English opposition to the state gathering too much power into its hands. However, the Conservative Party of the day had decided to be more revolutionary than the revolutionaries. Many Tory lawyers, especially the Inns of Court Conservative Association, actually favoured a national police force at this time. So perhaps it ought not to be shocking that the shadow Home Secretary, Quintin Hogg, 'in principle gave general support' to a plan that was to break the century-old links between the police and their localities. In effect, the policy turned them into little more than branch organizations of the Home Office. Only the Metropolitan force came under the direct control of Whitehall. Until the mergers, most forces outside London were based on counties or the 'county boroughs' – towns or cities so self-contained that they were given their own independent local government, a simple and workable system which was, inexplicably, to be abolished in local government reforms at about the same time.

County forces were often controlled by chief constables from the local landowning gentry, often with military backgrounds. Borough forces were frequently run by long-serving chief constables, who had risen through the ranks. When the forces outside London were established, their chief constables had been made answerable to the Justices of the Peace, then much more powerful and independent figures than now. As the Justices' powers declined, the chiefs reported to local government 'watch committees' which gave them much freedom of action. Thus they had enormous independent powers of decision, powers of which the Home Office was obviously jealous. The mergers, by creating regional forces such as Thames Valley or Humberside put paid to that independence in several ways. They snapped the links between chiefs and their localities, not least because English people did not and do not have regional loyalties. What does Oxford have in common with Reading, or vice versa? They would now be rivals for resources within the new force, whereas previously they had had their own concerns and their own ways of meeting them.

The new enlarged forces – and their ambitious chiefs – were much more likely to look to London for guidance. They would naturally seek the favour of the Home Office and the national press and TV rather than that of local councillors or newspapers. Any chief of a major force knew that he might rise to become the Commissioner of the Metropolitan Police – a remote chance for most of them in the days before amalgamation. Technically, they were responsible to shapeless police authorities made up of local authority appointees and magistrates. In practice, the 'regional' character of the new forces, devoid in most cases of any recognizable common sense of place, made their chief constables more likely to follow national trends and respond to national pressures. Mr Jenkins explained that he had not chosen to create a national force because he valued the local connections and the relationship with the public formed by smaller units, but he also said that he hoped that by April 1967 there would be only forty-nine forces and stated that the changes did not exclude the possibility of a national force in the future. An interesting consequence has been that responsibility for the Metropolitan Police was later 'devolved' to the Greater London Authority and the Metropolitan Police Authority, without any real loss of central control. The Home Office would simply not have permitted this handover if it had had any serious fears that central government might lose real control the policing of the capital.

The first steps were also being taken towards the creation of a new police elite, selected from the most able mid-ranking officers and then imbued with the Home Office ethos at the Bramshill college. Soon, promotion to the higher ranks would be almost impossible without a spell at Bramshill, establishing an old-boy network of great influence which would come to dominate the Association of Chief Police Officers (ACPO) and create a national police officer class which was far closer to Whitehall than the retired military men, local squirearchy and experienced beat officers who had previously been in charge of operational policing. There was also a steady, increasing pressure on the police to recruit university graduates or to send their promising officers to university. This may have been meant to raise their educational level. It also meant that politically, socially and culturally conservative attitudes became confined to the lower ranks of the force. This has led to tension between the instincts of the rank and file and those of the officer class. The centralizing, socially-concerned ideology of Bramshill and ACPO has since become a potent, ever-present influence throughout the entire police service.

There was almost no open dissent from the view that the massacre of small independent forces was necessary and justified. Displaced chief constables were generally offered senior posts in the new merged forces. Only a Mr R. McCartney, Chief Constable of Hertfordshire, stood out in public against the change, arguing that there was 'still a lot of evidence' that small units were as efficient as, and sometimes more efficient than, larger units. He said, with some justice, that there was no guarantee that the proposals would achieve their aims. In the 1960s it was not yet fashionable for governments and officials to believe that small was beautiful. *The Times* said it was 'the greatest upheaval in policing since the time of Peel', which, in conjunction with the abolition of regular foot patrols, it certainly was. As with so many of the changes of that era, it was achieved mainly by elite action and never became an election issue or a subject of partisan debate in Parliament. Nobody mentioned the original constitutional objections to having the police under the control of central government.

By the time Roy Jenkins had left the Home Office to become Chancellor of the Exchequer in November 1967, the whole face and shape of the police in England had changed for good. A junior minister, Lord Stonham, told the House of Lords that month that half the programme of force mergers was already complete. After April 1968 there would be only forty-one police forces. For unit beat policing the Home Secretary had authorized the spending of an additional two million pounds (then a considerable sum) on small cars. By early in the next year two-thirds of the population would be covered by unit beat policing. By the end of the next year 80 per cent of the country and 90 per cent of the Metropolitan Police area would have lost their foot patrols, although the minister did not put it like that. Lord Stonham also paused to praise the TV programme *Softly Softly* and to reveal that six hundred detectives were now working in regional crime squads like the one portrayed in *Softly Softly*. As politicians so often do, he spoke as if the main concern of the police was major crime and organized dishonesty, rather than small and unbearable losses, insults, threats and slights. He announced proudly that there was at last to be a police national computer, with that touching faith in the magic of electronics that had by then infected industry, commerce and politics and which survives despite all the evidence that circuitry cannot replace human ingenuity or effort, let alone initiative and personal knowledge.

In general, Lord Stonham's speech bulged with optimism and the fashionable love of technology as the solution to all ills. He declared that the use of helicopters, computers, regional crime squads, amalgamations and the system of unit beat policing were keeping ahead of the criminal. And he claimed that any young man considering a life of crime would do well to think again. In words typical of the times, he said: 'Out-thinking a policeman is one thing but even an Al Capone might have had trouble with a helicopter-backed computer.' On the contrary, Al Capone would probably have made far more effective use of helicopters and computers than any police force ever has done or ever could do.

There were dark undercurrents in the debate hinting at the truth – that crime for most people does not take the form of Al Capone but of a slight, nimble and ruthless young man breaking into their house or snatching their wallet in a dark street. As if puzzled by his own hopefulness, Lord Stonham admitted that while under the welfare state there were thirty-five thousand people in prison, in the 1930s, when life had been much harder, there had been only eleven thousand. His fellow Labour peer, Lord Rowley, also mentioned the uncomfortable fact that while in 1937 there had been only 209 cases of robbery with violence in England and Wales, in 1966 there were 4474. The comparable figures for indictable offences were 216,000 in 1937 compared with 1,119,000 in 1966. Something had gone wrong out in the dark streets despite the radios, cars, helicopters, computers and modern, efficient management – but nobody seemed to know what it was. Even so, everyone seemed to think it was safe to retire Dixon of Dock Green and move into the age of *Z Cars*.

IV

The slow, bureaucratic death of George Dixon

The real significance of the unit beat system was that it ended the old foot patrols and undermined the idea that the main purpose of the force was to *prevent* crime from taking place. Thanks to unit beat, the constable ceased to be the embodiment of the notion that the law belonged to the people of England – one of the very few examples of a real 'People's Police' ever to have existed. As the police manpower working party had rightly said, the old method gave solid expression to the concept of the policeman as a citizen in uniform, freedom under the law made flesh. Had unit beat been applied as it was originally designed, it might well have worked in some areas as a preventive and a reactive system at the same time, preserving just enough of the old beat method to retain public confidence. As we shall see, things did not happen quite like that. For it arrived at the same time as the new merged forces and together with a shiny new set of mechanical toys. It came just as American law-and-order culture was gaining a grip on the public (and the police) through television.

Many of Eric St Johnston's innovations were American-influenced. Both the radio and the car were well suited to the enormous American cities where they were first used for police work in a completely different tradition from that of Britain. To an

THE DEATH OF GEORGE DIXON

extent that is still not really understood in Britain, much of America polices itself without much need for men patrolling on foot. Its prosperous suburbs are so distant from those who might want to rob or vandalize them that they are mainly trouble-free. American sub-urbanites can still leave their cars and houses unlocked in many areas. The USA's country districts are full of self-reliant people who expect to have to defend their homes and property, and are equipped and legally permitted to do so. In such areas the police are so distant that they could take hours to arrive – hours when any-thing might happen if householders did not hold the law in their own hands, from which it has never been taken. There are other differences, too. America's lawless urban areas, for historic and racial reasons, have seldom been willing to accept policing by consent. Police patrolling in such zones often takes a form alarmingly close to military occupation.

American law in many places permits the armed pursuit of felons by citizens, as well as the use of deadly force in defence of life and property. The patrolling officer on foot did once exist. In some places he still does, but not in the same way or to the same extent. In concentrated cityscapes such as Manhattan he can still be found – and is very effective, not least because he is not restricted by laws such as the Police and Criminal Evidence Act 1984. The Washington, DC Metro is superbly patrolled by officers on moun-tain bikes ready to pursue malefactors through its majestic vaults, although they rarely have to do so on a system that nowadays feels – and is – much safer than large parts of the London Underground. Manhattan is unique among US cities. Washington, DC is equally exceptional in a different way. All American police forces – big-city, suburban and rural – are armed, so that when they are called on to act they often do so lethally, but their weapons place an unseen barrier between them and those they guard.

So it may not be wise to copy their methods too slavishly in this wholly different country. One of the most striking things about modern English police methods is the way that American techniques are copied, as if directly from the TV screen. The British police car, once a sober and subdued affair with only a bell and a small illuminated sign to identify it, has become a highway patrol cruiser adorned with splendid coats of arms, slogans, reflective stripes, banks of multicoloured strobe lights and sirens which can be heard in the next county. Many are now more spectacular than the relatively modest vehicles used by American suburban forces. Newspaper reporters invited to go out on patrol with the police are almost invariably taken in such cars. It is clear that the officers are longing for the excuse to switch on the lights and sirens and fly to the rescue at speeds way above the legal limit. Who can blame them, with such machinery to play with and such inspiration from the many police programmes they have seen on TV, from the fictional dramas to the factual clips in *Police... Camera... Action*? Yet it is often the case that the crime they have gone to at such speed simply does not justify the effort, or the danger to officers and public of driving at speed through a built-up area.

Here is the problem. The machinery and structure of the English police have been designed since 1966 to react to crime instead of to prevent it before it happens. Its chief constables have become driven by targets, which inevitably concentrate on the major crimes that attract the most media attention. The mixed use of cars and foot patrols is ineffective against such crimes and poor at preventing more normal crime and disorder. It requires many men and women on duty if it is to work properly, and it has long been regarded with contempt by the new ambitious and star-struck type of policeman and woman. These types also tend to despise the community policemen who have sought to fill the gap left by the vanished beat officers. They are mocked as 'hobby bobbies' by their supposedly tough colleagues on the specialist squads and in the rapid-reaction cars. The real man's work, with status and the hope of promotion, is in those specialist squads, raiding drug-dealers, hunting down bank-robbers, catching paedophiles and tracking down murderers.

No doubt all these things are very necessary and worthwhile –

but the embarrassing truth is that most crime is amazingly triv
unless it happens to affect you personally. Then it is a grief and a.
outrage which can darken your life permanently or even shorten it
with worry and fear. Most crime is the kind of misbehaviour that
was never worth prosecuting but that was always worth preventing,
and still is. That prevention was, and could again be, achieved by a
uniformed police force on foot among us, which shared our fears
and hopes, gave us courage to stand up for ourselves and expected
support when it stood up for us. This sort of crime consists of
smashed windows, footballs kicked against houses, boys churning
up pensioners' front gardens, children riding bicycles on the pavement and knocking old ladies to one side, youths spitting on the
pavement and swearing at passers-by, the dropping of litter and the
scrawling of graffiti. It consists of shoplifting, bag-snatching, bicycle
theft, urinating in public, making unnecessary noise late at night.
Leave these things unattended, as a famous American study –
'Broken Windows', the seminal article in *Atlantic Monthly* of March
1982, by James Q. Wilson and George L. Kelling – showed, and you
move down to the next bitter stage of burglary, muggings, car-theft
and open drug-dealing on the street.

Much of this crime cannot by its nature be reported or recorded.
Much of it is not worth reporting, because in some areas insurance
rapidly ceases to pay out and even speaking to the police can
become a good way of bringing trouble to your home and misery to
your life. So while this book will mention crime statistics and cite
them where they show that the world has changed in important
ways, it is written in the belief that no figures yet published have
measured the sheer misery that has been caused by the retreat of
the police from the streets.

As for that retreat, let us look at some of the many studies of Eric
St Johnston's bright idea in action that are to be found in the archives
of Bramshill Police College. One of the earliest is 'Unit Beat
Policing: Reflections on the experiments and implications of a widespread adoption of the system', prepared by Chief Superintendent

E. Gregory in July 1967. Mr Gregory accepted that the Peel system was the foundation stone of the British system. He produced no reason why it should be generally abandoned and his paper did not seek to do so. It assumed that unit beat was going to happen and stated with some frankness who he thought was behind it: 'Beat patrolling is the basis of the British police service. It has generally changed little over the years and, in some forces, beats have remained largely the same for as long as 30 years.'

Although aware of the Kirkby pilot, Chief Superintendent Gregory did not think that it was the true beginning of the new model police. 'Unit Beat Policing (UBP) was first introduced by the Research and Planning Branch in Accrington, Lancashire, on 1st June 1966. Carlisle quickly followed and today there are over 30 schemes operating in the country. Other forces have stated their intention of trying the scheme as soon as the necessary personal radios and cars become available.' He revealed that 'the encouragement of the Police Advisory Board and the Home Secretary have furthermore made it likely that this or similar methods of policing may be used very widely in the near future.' He cited UBP's merits as greater speed of response to complaints and calls for help. It also helped overcome the shortage of officers at the time. Like most of its advocates, he recognized its drawbacks, namely that 'it is widely held that men in vehicles do not cultivate a better understanding with the public nor improve the information flow.' The favoured way of overcoming this was the use of clearly marked vehicles, plus resident foot constables to back up the car patrols. Another issue had already crept into the argument – what to do with the men no longer needed on the beat. There were going to be a lot of them: 'The saving of beat patrol manpower requirements produced by the scheme varies considerably from force to force and even from area to area. It is envisaged, however, that on average at least ten per cent of the men currently used for beat coverage could be saved from that type of work and made available for other duties. The question now arises of how best to use these men.'

Another view came in a study of the first big-city test of unit beat policing. Carried out in March 1968, this was titled 'Unit Beat Policing: Its application to a city of over half a million population (Birmingham)' and was the work of three experienced sergeants from varied forces, M. F. Bennison (York and NE Yorkshire), D. Flanders (Surrey) and J. C. Hoddinott (Metropolitan). The trio found that unit beat policing was not in fact the magic formula that had been suggested. They quickly spotted an obvious fault that would come to bedevil much police work in the years to come: police officers in cars cease to be part of society in general and become part of the traffic stream. The police had not had any cars before 1919, and even afterwards their numbers had grown quite slowly and they were mainly concentrated on patrolling traffic; now they all had to learn to drive – many forces suffered an embarrassing number of accidents during the early learning period – and cars were available to almost any officer with a good excuse. Naturally they begin to take a greater interest in the misdeeds of motorists than in those of pedestrians since they are in constant contact with other drivers. 'It is apparent that Car Beat Patrols and Resident Beat Officers spend a large proportion of their time dealing with traffic problems and accidents, whilst it seems to us that this scheme is essentially designed to deal with crime and public order.' They also spotted the natural tendency of almost every human being, offered the choice of going on foot or driving a car, to take the car. 'There are, however, areas of a city centre which are inaccessible to motor vehicles and require traditional policing on foot. Birmingham have recognised this problem but whether or not they have found the correct balance between UBP and traditional methods will require deeper research. There does however, appear to be a tendency to use available manpower primarily for car duties, rather than foot patrol duties.'

The officers perceptively warned of another difficulty which must have become commonplace over the last thirty years: 'With an increase in the number of arrests made by a force substantially the same in number, it follows that each individual prisoner will have proportionately less time spent on him in interrogation.' There will therefore tend to be a decrease in the number of TICs – previous offences 'taken into consideration', a device allowing criminals to own up to past offences when they are charged so that they cannot be prosecuted twice for them, which also allows officers to claim to have cleared up these crimes (perhaps these are not always wholly honest on either side, but most forces view them as important). 'We see little evidence that UBP will produce a saving in manpower under present conditions. There must be coverage in addition to UBP as we have mentioned. The system at present highlights exist-ing manpower shortages when not enough men are available to fill car beat patrols.'

And they saw very early on that the new kind of policing would have an odd effect on the crime statistics, pointing out that 'Since the introduction of UBP in Birmingham, whilst arrests for crime have increased, so has the amount of reported crime, and the per-centage clear-up rate for crime has slightly decreased.' This makes good sense. The new system encourages arrests rather than preven-tion, because it expects the police to arrive after crime has been committed. It encourages the formal reporting of crime, because citizens can no longer speak informally to a beat officer. It begins the process of turning the police from a preventive agency, linked to the public by friendship, common purpose and familiarity, into a distant bureaucracy whose main purpose is to function as a crime-reporting agency for government statisticians and insurance companies.

Reported crime, much of it impossible to detect or clear up, is bound to pile up on the logs faster than officers can get round to check up on it. So the gap between the reporting and the clearing up of crime is bound to grow. The old arrangement, under which crime was 'reported' by Mrs Robinson to PC Jones, who then went and had a word with somebody, produced almost no statistics. PC Jones, by plodding the streets, prevented a huge amount of criminal and antisocial behaviour but his effect could not possibly be measured in a Whitehall report. Most matters were dealt with informally and sometimes, it is true, quite roughly, without ever troubling the courts or the prisons. Sadly, this effect can only be measured now that it is no longer there, in the colossal differences between the crime figures of forty years ago and those of the present. You might think that these figures come from two different galaxies and that the streets of England are already boiling with disorder and brutality. This is an obvious exaggeration. The two Englands are recognizably the same place and, while conditions have grown a great deal worse, they have not grown *that* much worse. Had they done so, the cities would be smoking ruins.

There were crime and disorder in the past and, although there were significantly less of these scourges than there are now, that past was not a golden age of peace and order. By removing the risk of being disturbed by a patrolling officer, fire-brigade policing has given evildoers a new feeling of freedom from fear and so made the streets less pleasant and less safe. It has done something else too. By compelling the police to respond to incidents after they have occurred and encouraging the public to report them to a central authority, it has created a statistical monster, a demand that can never be met and a problem that cannot be solved, least of all by increasing the numbers of officers doing the wrong thing.

Some more early warnings were to be found in a June 1967 report on the original Accrington scheme, 'Unit Beat Policing: Accrington and a comparison with other schemes', by Sergeants G. W. Jones, (Gloucestershire), Banthorpe (Suffolk), Vine (East Riding) and Fullelove (Metropolitan). They noted that patrolling in cars made it harder to observe areas properly. However, they drew exactly the same wrong conclusion as many police forces since. They suggested that panda cars should have a crew of two, since 'The driver, if on his own, has little time for observation but a companion would remedy this and he would also provide assistance in times of emergency and on everyday police work.' This is perfectly true. But the widespread adoption of the two-in-a-car policy is a major reason why the police came, over the following thirty years, to view themselves as a special corps of men and women separate from the 'civilian' public. Anyone who has ever watched two police officers patrolling together will have noticed that they spend most of the time talking to each other and are, even if on foot, much less approachable than if they were on their own.

The Bramshill quartet obviously believed the current wisdom that the Accrington pilot was a sparkling success. However, their conclusion contained some interesting reservations: 'We realise, however, that the scheme is new, if not in concept then in practice, and there is therefore a tendency for keenness, devotion and persistence to assume a disproportionately high level, only to fall away after some time.' They balanced this sensible caution with words that sound like a Soviet propaganda bulletin from the Stakhanovite shockworker period. The modern reader cannot help wondering if this was not some model project that had been ordered to succeed at all costs. The sergeants said they regarded some decline in its success as inevitable,

> but accept the fact that whatever low level is reached it
> will be higher than it ever was under the traditional
> method of policing. The morale of the men is
> exceedingly high with a correspondingly increased desire
> to work – it is amazing how often the area constables
> volunteer to do night and evening and night as well as
> split tours of duty and overtime. There is no doubt that
> in Accrington and, we feel, in other areas, where the
> scheme is adopted, great advances have been and will be
> made and will continue to be made in the war against
> crime and in all other facets of police work.

More than fifteen years later the optimism had worn off. Eric J. Hewitt, in an MA thesis submitted in 1984 to the University of

Manchester and titled 'Preventive policing: An examination of the effectiveness of a form of directed patrol carried out by Greater Manchester's tactical aid group' took a cooler view. 'The strength of the police in England and Wales has more than doubled during the past thirty years,' he said, 'and yet crime continues to rise at an unprecedented rate. Moreover the number of "civilians" employed by the police in posts previously held by police officers has also grown at a corresponding pace, thereby enabling more and more police officers to return to "operational duties".'

Hewitt thought that the basic premise of patrolling had been adhered to up until the outbreak of the Second World War in 1939, but that it did not survive long into the post-war era. Hewitt blamed the scale of change on greater freedom and mobility of the individual, relief of poverty and ignorance, and extensive urban growth.

> The UB system, however, has not met with anything like the success hoped for it. At the time of its inception there could have been no idea of the extraordinary pressure to which UBP was to be subjected...
>
> Constant pressure on manpower has tended to devalue the role of the area man; he is the first to be pulled off his normal duties if there is a need elsewhere or if there is a man short in the station. Many policemen deride the area man and his job as they feel that 'drinking tea with old ladies' is not 'real police work'.

This scorn for the traditional form of policing was made worse by the separation of constables from their clients by boxes of steel and glass. They never met anybody except villains, strengthening the dangerous idea noted above that the police are a separate elite and everyone else is a civilian: 'The isolation of officers in heated cars with their windows closed was reinforced by the fact that they were limited to conflict situations, encounters with victims or criminals, sealed off from the rest of the community. This leads to insensitive policing and withdrawal of consent.'

Hewitt also noted the important truth, for a force where status is often measured by the number of 'collars', that car-borne officers are more likely to make arrests, so that the identification of area patrolmen as 'hobby bobbies' and car drivers as 'real policemen' is increased. And he quoted from R. Baldwin and R. Kinsey's *Police Powers and Politics* a senior officer who said: 'Unit beat policing was a good idea but it didn't work out because of the rising number of incidents they have to attend. The treble nine calls are stacked up now, three or four at a time, and you have to take the priority calls first. It's unfortunate. The pandas stopped being there to show the flag and went on to "fire brigade" policing just answering calls, one after another.'

Hewitt also highlighted two other fascinating pieces of research. One was a Kansas City experiment in 1974, where different levels of (car only) patrol made no difference to public feelings of safety. The other was J. A. Bright's *Beat Patrol Experiment*, a Police Research and Development Branch report published by HMSO, which found that the 'number of reported crimes on a beat decreased when the officers patrolling it increased from zero to one'. Further increases in numbers made no difference.

A few years earlier (its date is unclear) the Bramshill library received another professional assessment of unit beat policing made by experienced officers. It is strikingly different from the fresh-faced optimism of the early 1960s' studies. This was 'Unit beat policing: An assessment', by Sergeants Watson (Durham), Norris (Hampshire), Crew and Melvin (Metropolitan). They visited Manchester and Salford, which had adopted the system after the great Jenkins mergers took effect in April 1968, as did most forces. They were already concerned by 'The possibility that future young policemen will be car-orientated, having little foot-patrol experience'. In its early stages, unit beat policing in this area seems to have led to a huge increase in car accidents, as officers were forced to learn to drive for a job that had until then been pedestrian. Once again,

more crimes were being recorded. Vehicle crime had not been substantially affected. There was one huge and abiding change:

> Because so much time is necessarily spent by police
> officers in panda cars, and the public have less
> opportunity to put their problems to the foot patrolman,
> many more calls are made upon the police by telephone.
> In 1967 there were 52,030 '999' calls made to the
> Manchester and Salford police forces. In 1968 the number
> had increased to 69,971. The number is still increasing...
> The question must be asked: 'are we providing a fire
> brigade service?'

The answer, of course, was 'Yes, we are'. And to provide this service
a bulging bureaucracy of telephone answerers, controllers and
record-keepers was required: 'One disadvantage has been a necessary increase in the amount of staff, collators and communicators
etc., required to service the system.'

The curious thing is that the failure of the system has never
prompted any serious attempt to return to the practice that it
replaced. If the Peel method had been given the money, equipment, men and women that have been lavished on the failure of
unit beat policing, the streets and countryside would be in a very
different state. Those who dare to suggest this are told that it is
impossible or useless. A recent Audit Commission report, titled
'Streetwise – Effective police patrol' (February 1996), complained
about the public's appetite for 'bobbies on the beat', claiming that it
was unrealistic when set beside their requirement for fast response
times. It also revealed the shocking truth that only five per cent of
police strength is now out on patrol at any one time. This means
that out of the average 2500 strength of a normal English force, only
125 will be on the streets at any time.

Many of these will be in cars. The rest are swallowed up in the
ever-expanding number of specialist squads, the shift system, leave,

waiting to give evidence in courts, sickness (now a serious problem, quite probably connected with declining morale and discipline), training (much of which will be of the racial-awareness, sexual-equality or other politically-correct types, rather than aimed at making the police better at policing as such) and the activity known as 'need to spend time in the police station'. This is mainly a creation of the Police and Criminal Evidence Act 1984, a sort of legal tombstone placed on top of old-fashioned policing to make sure it can never rise again.

James Bartholomew, writing in the *Daily Telegraph* in July 2001, described the bureaucratic cobweb through which an officer must struggle if he dares to do so much as issue a caution to a suspect. After making the arrest, he must 'call up transport', then queue for space in the station 'custody suite', with an average wait of twenty-five minutes. Then there is 'booking in', the reading of rights, and logging of possessions – another twenty minutes. Then a solicitor must be found, a process that can take hours. If the suspect is drunk or injured, he must be seen by a 'forensic medical examiner'. These are not instantly available. If the suspect is a juvenile, an adult must be found who can accompany him. The suspect must be read his rights again in the presence of this 'appropriate adult'. No medical examination or interview can take place until the adult is there.

The constable must also write up the arrest according to the elaborate codes of practice in the Police and Criminal Evidence Act 1984, knowing that any error could rebound on him in a career-wrecking complaint. The process is still not over. The case must again be referred to senior officers for their judgement on whether a caution is appropriate. Bartholomew concluded:

> the police officer, knowing that five hours of his time
> could be taken up with bureaucracy if he makes an arrest,
> has a strong incentive to ignore minor crimes. That
> means that there is no chance of getting the much touted
> 'zero tolerance' policing in Britain. The police just have

not got enough five hours to arrest people who write
graffiti, vandalise telephone booths, cycle on the
pavement and so on. They have only got time for the big
stuff. The small stuff is 'completely tolerated'.

This is one of the reasons why, as the Audit Commission concluded,
working a beat of any kind is 'close to the bottom rung of the police
status ladder'.

'Unrealistic public expectations and rising demands mean that
the police are at a crossroads; they will have little time for foot patrol
unless they match their responses more closely to the seriousness of
incidents,' the Audit Commission said. Its argument that you
cannot have Peel's police and *Z Cars* at the same time is perfectly
true. But they did not see where this leads. Like almost everyone in
the police business since the introduction of unit beat policing, they
did not grasp that preventive patrolling and response policing are
two different and mutually exclusive systems, based on different
views of human nature, law and crime.

Even so, they knew which side they were not on. They favoured
what they called 'well-directed patrolling', the special concentra-
tion of police on areas where trouble is likely and concern is high.
Such 'well-directed patrolling' is used in busy city centres and on
estates where order has broken down. It is mistaken by the public
for a return to the beat. Perhaps it is meant to be mistaken for it.
The officers involved are dressed in reflective yellow jackets to
make them stand out, presumably as a counter to claims that the
police have become invisible. However, like 'fire-brigade' policing,
it is deployed in response to crime and disorder, not in an effort to
stop these happening in the first place. And it is seldom if ever permanent, being withdrawn once the crisis has passed as resources are
shifted to new fronts.

The enforcement of the law has become a concession granted by
the authorities from time to time, not a right enjoyed equally by all.
The Audit Commission's strictures also revealed that it shared the

politicians' and chief constables' obsession with 'major' crime. It also shared their lack of interest in the small-scale wrongdoing that really blights lives. Its original version, leaked to the *Guardian* newspaper, was even more critical of foot patrols than the published text, which appeared to have been toned down as a result of public criticism. Modern chief constables, too, often argue that patrolling officers almost never interrupt a crime in progress. This assertion reveals a complete failure to grasp the beat's deterrent purpose. You might as well criticize the British nuclear submarine fleet for never having fired its missiles. It is just a variant on the more usual claim that there are simply not enough officers to provide the sort of cover that was available in the 1950s when, according to the great manpower falsehood, there were so many more officers available for a smaller population.

A similar failure to grasp the reality of life was shown in the Commission's attitude towards 999 calls. It pointed out that they had risen by 150 per cent between 1980 and 1996 but that only 30 per cent of such calls were about what it considered to be crime. Many, it declared, concerned 'nuisance or anti-social behaviour'. Others were inquiries about late-night chemists and football scores. It is perfectly true that some 999 calls are trivial, stupid and wasteful. Similarly, doctors and nurses in hospital casualty departments are sometimes asked to examine cases of dandruff. Other calls are an effect of the mass slaughter of police stations or the fact that it is difficult to reach the police on their normal phone numbers and all but impossible to speak to an individual officer. However, 'nuisance or anti-social behaviour' is a source of grave unhappiness to millions. It is also the very thing that the old Dixonian police force was very good at controlling, discouraging and preventing.

So why, given all the problems that have followed, has there never been a counter-revolution to restore the Peel system, which, for all its faults, appears to have worked much better than what replaced it? There seems to be some sort of psychological block. 'We can't go back to the old ways,' say chief constables, as if this were an unalterable truth. But why ever not? And why is the ment conducted with such dishonesty and ignorance?

The manpower shortage theory – demolished above – i widely accepted and so wholly untrue that its constant use is itself part of the mystery. It requires an explanation. There must be another reason for the obstinate clinging to 'fire-brigade' policing and to the Kafka-in-reverse rules that ensure that the individual constable is actually afraid to arrest anyone because to do so will spoil his, the constable's, whole day.

Of course, there was a desire to cut costs, and especially wage bills, but this cannot possibly still be the problem that it was in the thin days of 1966. Police equipment, spending and manpower are all financed by rivers of public gold beyond the dreams of the 1960s. The Britain of the mid-1960s was sunk in economic failure and pessimism. There was a prevalent belief that we simply could not afford to be what we had once been – which now looks remarkably foolish given the huge mountain ranges of money we were to spend on new schools that could not teach, new local authorities whose names nobody could remember, new courts that could not cope with crime and new roads that swiftly became more clogged than the ones that had gone before. However, it was what people thought at the time. The affluence of the Macmillan era was beginning to fade and the shadow of the coming devaluation of sterling lay across the country. Wages and salaries are always the most expensive part of any public service. It made sense of a sort to paper over manpower shortages with capital spending on cars and radios. Unit beat policing was policing on the cheap. Then there was the 1960s' mania for gigantism. Big companies, big factories, big hospitals, big schools, big local authorities and big government all came into fashion then. Most have since fallen out of fashion, especially in the private sector, as their boasted 'economies of scale' have turned out to be illusory. These changes can be explained by the pressures of the day. When they have obviously failed, why not change back, now that we are in an age of vastly greater wealth?

Other interesting questions demand an answer. Why was Roy Jenkins so keen to merge smaller police forces into bigger ones? Why did his Home Office encourage Eric St Johnston, with the fervent support of Harold Wilson's Downing Street? Why was unit beat policing adopted so swiftly and without being given time to reveal its failings? How was it that so many innovations, from police helicopters to crown courts, majority verdicts and suspended sentences, came under his stewardship? Regrettably the late Lord Jenkins can now never answer these questions more fully than he did at the time in his Commons speeches or later in his charming and fascinating autobiography. Even so, it is not unreasonable to seek for some sort of pattern. A different sort of society came into being after these changes. It could be said to have resulted from them. Was it the sort of society that Mr Jenkins intended? Consciously, subconsciously or even unconsciously, could he have seen in the Peel system of policing an important pillar of the old conservative state?

There is something worthy of Edmund Burke in the method of policing adopted by the Victorians. They were reluctant to have a police force of any kind on English soil. Peel's 'Blue Locusts' were initially denounced as 'an insidious attempt to enslave the people by arbitrary and tyrannical methods.' The police were to be employed, it was said, as the instruments of a new despotism, the enlisted members of a new standing army. English conservative thinkers at the end of the eighteenth century hated the idea of a Continental type of force, originally proposed in the days of Pitt the Younger. T. A. Critchley, in his *History of Police in England and Wales*, details the difficulties the reformers had in getting the idea past a hostile Parliament, which viewed the very concept as foreign and repressive, despite the very high levels of disorder in the England of those days. William Shenstone had complained in 1743: 'Pickpockets, formerly content with mere filching, make no scruple to knock people down with bludgeons in Fleet Street and the Strand.'

The terrifying Gordon Riots of 1780 caused William Shelburne, who was to become the first Home Secretary, to praise the French police system and recommend something of the kind in lawless London. William Pitt's Solicitor-General, Archibald Macdonald, introduced a radical Police Bill, anticipating Peel by thirty years. The City of London saw its provisions as a threat to its ancient liberties and the bill was withdrawn, not to be discussed again for decades. Like many other radical ideas, it became unacceptable because it was associated in the national mind with the enemy. The French revolutionary tyranny, by making everything French stink in the nostrils of freedom-loving Englishmen, closed all such discussions for years to come. Parliamentary committees in 1816, 1818 and 1822 rejected police proposals as incompatible with British liberty. The very word 'police' had a sinister ring to most English people then and for long afterwards, and even a hundred years later there were many who remained suspicious of the idea and the practice. The 1818 parliamentary committee said that a Continental type of police would be 'odious and repulsive, and one which no government would be able to carry into execution. It would be a plan which would make every servant of every house a spy on his master, and all classes of society spies on each other.' The 1822 committee said:

> It is difficult to reconcile an effective system of police,
> with that perfect freedom of action and exemption from
> interference which are the great privileges and blessings
> of society in this country; and your committee think that
> the forfeiture or curtailment of such advantages would be
> too great a sacrifice for improvements in the police, or
> facilities in the detection of crime, however desirable
> themselves if abstractedly considered.

The chairman of that committee was Sir Robert Peel.

Eventually, Peel and the Duke of Wellington came to believe that there had to be some sort of police system controlled by the government. The 'Peterloo Massacre', the disastrous use of mounted troops against a peaceful crowd in Manchester, helped convince the Duke that it was foolish to rely on soldiers to support the civil power in time of trouble. Their own doubts, together with the long hostility of the political class to such a foreign idea, meant that they introduced something unique.

The Peel police force was deeply influenced by the English past, restrained by law and custom. The unadorned, far from majestic or overbearing constable, patrolling alone and on foot, was the outcome of the struggle between the need for some sort of force and the wise mistrust of a Continental gendarmerie. It was a cunning compromise, imposed by men who did not really want a police force at all and suspected that it would become a monstrous tyranny if not closely watched and constantly restrained.

That suspicion was still alive in the early twentieth century, as revealed in the entry on 'police' in the eleventh edition (1911) of the *Encyclopaedia Britannica*. While most modern reference books rejoice at the technical prowess and efficiency of various police departments, the *Britannica* at that time was still able to envisage a society without any police at all and to doubt whether the idea of a police force was a wise one. It noted that Charles V of France is said to have been the first king to invent a police force in order to increase the happiness and security of his people, but that it had developed into 'a horrible engine of repression'. This is not because the *Encyclopaedia*'s authors were complacent about the levels of crime in the years before Peel's Metropolitan Police Act. They wrote:

> …crime was rampant, highwaymen terrorized the roads, footpads infested the streets, burglaries were of constant occurrence… the watchmen appointed by parishes were useless, inadequate, inefficient and untrustworthy, acting often as accessories in aiding and abetting crime…
>
> At the commencement of the 19th century it was computed that there was one criminal to every 22 of the population…

In those days victims of robberies constantly
compounded with felonies and paid blackmail to thieves,
promising not to prosecute on the restitution of a portion
of the stolen property.

Despite all this there was much opposition to a police force. This
hostility was based on the idea that the price being asked for controlling crime was higher than any free Englishman ought to be
willing to pay. It would place in the hands of the state a power it had
not had since the hated days of Cromwell's Major-Generals. Peel's
scheme was denounced as 'an insidious attempt to enslave the
people by arbitrary and tyrannical methods'. The police were to be
employed, it was said, as 'the instruments of a new despotism, the
enlisted members of a new standing army'. Fear of such a standing
army was still alive and dangerous in English politics less than two
hundred years after Cromwell's death.

Huge care was taken to limit the powers of the police, to prevent
them from acting too haughtily or arrogantly or becoming the state's
private army. As a result of that care, they came to symbolize in practice the Englishman's belief that the state was beneath his feet,
supporting him, not above his head, oppressing him. The early
police also had the good luck to arrive at a moment when the remoralization of society was well under way, and to spread across the
country at the same time as Victorian morality and Christian self-
restraint. Even when, in later years, the police were sometimes
used as strike-breakers or to restrain legitimate demonstrations,
these actions were seen as exceptional. Their powers remained
strictly limited, and it is nowadays astonishing to read official reports,
such as the 1929 Royal Commission on Police Powers, which make
this plain. It declared that 'It is desirable to avoid any questioning at
all of persons in custody', and it dwelt at length on whether the
police had any right to question anyone at all, although the semi-
official 'Judges' Rules' of 1912 implied that some sort of right to do so
did exist. The Commission quoted Mr Justice Hawkins, who said

in 1892, 'Neither Judge, magistrate, nor juryman can interrogate an accused person. Much less then ought a constable to do so.' Hawkins was also the author of the once-famous maxim that a constable 'ought to keep his eyes and ears open and his mouth shut'.

The 1929 Royal Commission also reasserted Peel's principle that a policeman is not a special official but 'a person paid to perform, as a matter of duty, acts which if he were so minded he might have done voluntarily'. A policeman, it believed, possessed few powers not enjoyed by the ordinary citizen, and 'public opinion has shown great jealousy of any attempts to give increased authority to the police.' These pieces of conventional wisdom from the Victorian era would have made sense to a 1950s officer. They are outlandish to anyone used to the vastly increased powers of the modern English police. A police veteran or lawyer from that era would be shocked by the change in character the police have since undergone. They have developed into something much more like examining magistrates, who can grant bail and are permitted to interrogate, unrestrained by a full right of silence. To confuse things further, they must do so under rules that seem designed to aid the unscrupulous, who can all too easily use the complex rules of procedure to avoid prosecution.

Police forces, too, were highly independent of central government as late as the 1962 Royal Commission. While admitting that Whitehall was now interfering more than before, it could still say of the individual chief constable:

> [He] is accountable to no-one and subject to no-one's
> orders for the way in which, for example, he settles his
> general policies in regard to law enforcement over the
> area covered by his force, the disposition of his force,
> the concentration of his resources on any particular
> crime or area, the way in which he handles political
> demonstrations or processions and allocates and instructs
> his men when preventing breaches of the peace arising

from industrial disputes, the methods he employs in
dealing with an outbreak of violence or of passive
resistance to authority, his policy in enforcing the traffic
laws and in dealing with parked vehicles, and so on.

Arthur Scargill's unprecedented use of mass pickets in an effort to
thwart an elected government through industrial power was mainly
approved of by the supposedly democratic political left. The
equally unprecedented government response to it, restricting the
picketing miners' freedom to travel, was a dubious and possibly
unlawful extension of police powers and of government powers
over the police. There may have been a good excuse for it, but it did
permanent damage to the neutrality of the police. It also provided
an excuse to withdraw officers from many duties to which they
seem never to have returned. Given this bending of the rules of
democratic behaviour by both sides, and the New Labour assault on
the constitution that followed it, the views on the certainty of
liberty expressed by the 1962 Royal Commission seem complacent.
However, they were the views of most at the time. It is hard for
those born later to realize how secure England felt before 1965.
'British liberty,' the Commission proclaimed, 'does not depend and
never has depended, upon the dispersal of police power. It depends
on the supremacy of Parliament and on the rule of law. We do not
accept that the criterion of a police state is whether a country's
police force is local rather than national.' But immediately afterwards they thought it wise to add that there was 'a fundamental
contrast: between the continental principle of placing responsibility
for the maintenance of law and order upon the executive government, and arming it with powers of direct enforcement; and the
British principle that it is the right and duty of each citizen to preserve the peace and bring malefactors to justice, with its corollary
that the police are merely paid to act on the citizens' behalf'.

Reading these words in the age of David Blunkett and Alastair
Campbell, it is necessary to wonder how important might be the

dispersal of police power if the supremacy of Parliament were to dwindle and the rule of law be called into question. In such circumstances, the dispersal of police power might become considerably more important. The announcement, in February 2004, of a new national force to deal with 'serious and organized crime' worried many who felt that such a force could easily become political in character, as its chiefs sought to please their Whitehall and Westminster masters. The wise lawmaker, like the drafters of the American Bill of Rights, takes precautions against the apparently unlikely as well as the obvious. The Victorians, who ensured that no national police force was created, seem to have taken the view that there might one day be circumstances in which this would matter. They also thought that nothing important would be gained by having a single force. At the back of their minds was the completely different character of the English state from those on the Continent. The 1962 Royal Commission again expressed this point with great clarity. For its members, the new post-war democracies of Western Europe were young and untried. Their historical memories stretched back to earlier eras when the difference between the two sides of the Channel was more marked: 'The contrast, in this view, is seen in the big things and small things alike: the British police are unarmed but most policemen on the continent carry arms; and political and secret police appear to flourish on the continent, for their role as agents of the state leaves them a prey to political extremists.'

They were unimpressed by the arguments of those who sought a national force on the grounds of greater efficiency against that useful bogey, organized crime. Speaking of the 'basic soundness' of the existing system they concluded: 'the police forces of this country should not be brought under the direct central control of the government.' Some members even argued that higher efficiency, as well as more scope for the exercise of initiative, was attainable within a system of local forces. As for the 'serious and growing problem of organised crime', they accepted that reported cases of robbery with violence more than doubled between 1950 and 1960. They noted that a high proportion of these robberies occurred in London which already had a large-scale police force – but in reply to those who argued that big was better, they pointed out that the Metropolitan Police CID had a detection rate lower than almost anywhere else in the country. They concluded: 'The great bulk of crime is still local, in the sense that it is committed by local people operating near their homes. We have no doubt that crime of this kind is best tackled by detectives who form part of the local force, enjoying the continuous interchange of information with the uniformed branch which daily association affords.'

Once again, all the arguments were on the side of small forces – just as they had been on the side of the beat system. Yet the Jenkins era chose to ignore the fears and experiences of the past and press ahead with changes that reduced police independence, strengthened the power of central government and gave no obvious benefits in return. Public dissatisfaction with remote forces has grown every year since they began, and a dwindling number of people now even know that things were ever done differently or that the arguments for change were feeble and have not been borne out in practice.

Actually, there are several reasons for the obstinate refusal of government and police to consider that they may possibly have been mistaken. Some of them will be dealt with elsewhere at more length. One is simple: in the age of Railtrack, one should never rule out stupidity as an explanation for anything in modern English government and administration. There is no doubt that some foolish things have been done by a Parliament that was not paying attention. Many of them have been the work of the 'Conservative' Party, which was supposed to be protecting us against the more adventurous elements of the liberal elite. However, it is not the only explanation, or a complete one.

The Police and Criminal Evidence Act 1984, the establishment of the Police Complaints Authority and the setting up of the Crown

Prosecution Service (created by the Prosecution of Offences Act 1985) might have made sense in some Arcadian society of well-behaved and self-effacing folk who also happened to be extremely rich. These measures effectively destroyed individual initiative in the police force and demanded a perfection in action that few could attain. They bore no relation to the reality of crime and disorder, or to human nature as displayed in twenty-first-century Europe. They also ignored the social breakdown caused by the cultural revolution, the permissive society, the abolition of the married family, the abandonment of corporal punishment in schools, the dropping of the principle of any punishment at all in prisons and the scrapping of the death penalty. Our leaders seem to have believed that modern English society would just stay up by itself once all its foundations, props, guy-ropes and buttresses had been removed. More unworldly still, they seem to have decided that one of the few forces in society that still stood for conservative morality and discipline should be systematically transformed into the uniformed army of social liberalism. Yet their actions were in tune with most of the legislation and reform of the last half-century, based on the idea that government has supplanted God and can solve all dissensions, bind up all wounds and wipe away every tear from every eye. There is a utopian pattern here: the modern secular belief that if society is run by an elite of perfect, civilized and brilliantly able mandarins, people will no longer have to be good, because the machine will compel them to be.

The plodding, unarmed constable in his dull blue tunic and helmet, proceeding slowly through the night streets with his lantern, was the creation of sceptics who mistrusted human nature and suspected that men would behave badly if not watched and restrained. They applied this rule to governments as well as to criminals, by making sure that this mild police force could not be turned into a tool of tyranny. They had the great good fortune to inherit very ancient and beloved Anglo-Saxon ideas of 'every man his own constable' and of the law as the treasured possession of the common people. They trusted the constable to kick the right back-side, apply fist and truncheon where necessary to the right suspect and to show respect to the respectable of all classes.

Let us not be in any doubt that the old police force was the army of the respectable (though *not* the army of the wealthy) and that it was often unscrupulous in its methods. All societies are imperfect. Most people, asked to make the choice, would choose this imper-fection rather than the one we currently suffer from – that the police are almost entirely powerless against wrongdoers. Yet although our grandfathers trusted the constable to fight rough battles with the criminal classes, they did not trust him with powers of forced entry or interrogation, or unlimited detention. Almost by accident they conceived a scheme of great brilliance, which defended and enforced the law, and contained crime and disorder without threat-ening liberty in general. This, the original English police force, embodied morally conservative notions of right and wrong. It there-fore offended the new liberal religion of benevolent government, welfare state and human rights. Instinctively, the new elite knew that the 1829 police system was an obstacle to what they wanted. Without really knowing why, they knew the bobby on the beat was the enemy of what they stood for and what they wanted. He had to go – and they got rid of him.

V

Making bad people worse

Modern prisons are the result of idealist projects to improve the world, like most other human mistakes and disasters. Those forbidding towers and walls are in fact temples of the Enlightenment. This truth is largely ignored because most people prefer to forget that such horrible places exist at all. Yet for much of the last two centuries prisons and penitentiaries have striven incessantly to improve those who were sent to them. No matter how many times they failed in this task, the utopians tried and tried again. Solitary confinement, ludicrous as it seems now, was supposed to save the prisoner from contamination by his fellows. A Tory Home Secretary, David Waddington, delighted the penal reformers by remarking in a 1990 White Paper that prison was 'an expensive way of making bad people worse'. How this would have shocked the French revolutionary Mirabeau, who was fond of describing prisons as 'Houses of Improvement' (Maisons d'Amélioration) and pioneered the ideas of labour, separation of prisoners from each other to curb bad influences, rewards for good behaviour and aid to discharged convicts.

Prison had been formally introduced as a punishment, rather than simply as a place where punishment happened or where people were held while they waited to be punished, in the French penal code of 1791, which had itself been inspired by the Declaration of the Rights of Man of 1789. This distinction – between detention and reformation – is still made in the American system, where a jail is simply a place where the accused are held. The word is never used to describe a penitentiary, where inmates are supposedly punished or reformed after the courts have convicted them. The first American colonies did not, to begin with, use imprisonment as a punishment at all.

In England, where the prisons were stinking and diseased dungeons mainly used for holding people on their way to transportation or the noose, the idea of prison as reformatory had its first flowering remarkably early. The original Millbank Penitentiary, built in London after the Napoleonic Wars, was intended to reform its inmates. Fully operational by 1817, it was initially dedicated to rehabilitation. Its inmates were carefully chosen as being the most likely to respond to such generous treatment. The work they were to do was intended to be useful in the world outside – tailoring and weaving for men, sewing and laundering for women. While the punishment cells were subterranean and lightless, the normal accommodation was, by the standards of the time, comfortable. The cells had glazed windows, were furnished with a bed, table and stool and were warmed by flues. All went badly. Within a few years the model gaol suffered from disease caused by its poor site on low-lying land near the Thames. It also experienced malnutrition and full-scale riots. Flogging was introduced to keep control of increasingly riotous prisoners, and the reconviction rate for ex-inmates was found to be over 50 per cent. In 1844 the whole experiment was written off as a failure and Millbank became a reception centre for the hulks and the new youth training centre that had just opened at Parkhurst.

The hulks, dismasted former warships moored permanently in dreary locations such as the Medway, and familiar from the opening scenes of *Great Expectations*, were disgusting hellholes with no social purpose. They were miserable beyond belief for the poor and weak but tolerable for the richest, hardest and most lawless. To that extent, they bear a disturbing resemblance to the pointless, anarchic warehouses we have today. They had bribable officers. Prisoners who knew the ropes were able to get hold of pornography, drink and tobacco, and had free association up until 10 p.m. In another curious prefiguring of our times, it was the mentally ill who suffered most in these places. Conditions for them were especially savage, squalid and unspeakably cruel. There are fearful accounts of men in chains literally rotting in puddles of their own urine.

Of course, it was not officially meant to be so. Sir Samuel Hoare, great-great-nephew of Elizabeth Fry, would in 1938 praise the early nineteenth-century reformers, especially Robert Peel, for their revolutionary act in bringing to an end the medieval conception of punishment – that is, 'the system under which imprisonment played a very small part and in which punishment depended almost entirely upon sentences of death', or mutilation or confiscation. The old dungeons had been places of abandonment, disease, chaos and lawlessness while the accused or condemned waited for trial and execution. In the hulks, where the law was supposed to prevail, the government's rules stated: 'Every person belonging to the Convict Hulk establishment is on all occasions to treat the convicts with humanity and to lend a willing ear to their complaints and grievances, whether real or imaginary.' English prisons, it seems, have always been fond of notices exhorting everyone to behave well. Judged by the end results, the cynics and brutes had not done all that much worse than the enlightened reformers.

The next experiment was at Pentonville, which was at first intended to fit convicts for freedom in the colonies, by subjecting them to a long period of solitary confinement. It was built after William Crawford, a Home Office delegate, had visited the then-famous Eastern Penitentiary in Philadelphia, which was seen as the most advanced prison of the day. The plan was for eighteen months of complete seclusion before transportation. There was to be no contact whatsoever with other prisoners. Each convict's cap had, grotesquely, to be pulled down over his face if he met another prisoner in case they should communicate or recognize each other. This experiment, too, was abandoned gradually in the 1850s, thanks to its failure as much as to its inhumanity. Although the idea of reform never entirely died, the Victorians eventually settled on something much less ambitious and, as it turned out, much more successful. Robert Peel, when not creating the police, developed the first modern English penal code, which replaced barbarities such as the gibbet (unpopular with the middle classes because they did not like rotting corpses being displayed in cages near their homes) with graduated prison terms. Great victories were won against physical and moral squalor.

The notable humanitarians, Elizabeth Fry and John Howard, fought with courage and ferocity against the cruelty, filth and moral depravity of the eighteenth-century system and the hulks, and they are strikingly commemorated in bas-relief sculptures on either side of the gates of Wormwood Scrubs prison in London – a startling reminder that this place, when it was built, was a triumph of the most modern and advanced penal thinking. Every cell had its own plumbing, the cell-blocks were light and airy and easy to keep clean. Pass through the gates and the ugly new fencing that bounds the secure interior and you will find a majestic Victorian chapel which would grace a fair-sized town, its chancel decorated with accomplished paintings done on old mailbags, symbolizing the moral improvement the Victorians hoped to achieve among prisoners.

The faces of Fry and Howard are the only comforting things about the exterior view. As Giles Playfair wrote in his *The Punitive Obsession*, the Victorians thought that prison architecture should make the beholder afraid: '[Jeremy] Bentham believed that the very sight of a penitentiary from outside should fill all who beheld it with such dread of what might await them inside that they would never dare take the risk of being put there.' The government architects listened to this view and did their worst. Castles of doom sprang up in prominent sites across the country, although, as it turned out, none of them ever quite matched the sheer raw, stark representation of penal servitude achieved by the dismal cell-blocks of Dartmoor Prison at Princetown, which were originally put up to house French prisoners of war in Napoleonic times. Even so, they left a lasting and permanent impression and it was a deliberate one. As Major H. S. Rogers, the Surveyor of Prisons, remarked in 1910: 'It appears that a prevailing view on prison construction was to provide heavy, massive and gloomy structures, giving an impression of donjons, bars and chains; small, heavily-barred windows, with obscure glass, dark passages etc.'

English prisons, like English policemen, still look much the same from the outside as they did in a previous age. There are many new jails (though nothing like enough of them) mostly buried in the countryside or remote suburbs where few see them. However, it is hard to miss Pentonville, Armley, Leicester and many other nineteenth-century monuments to stern retribution, hard labour and penal servitude, glowering over the Victorian cityscape. You might even think that Victorian ideas still survived within. However, the paradox of English prisons today is that these imposing outsides hide a rather pathetic secret on the inside. Perhaps that is the way the government wants it to be. We, the public – victims and poten-tial victims – can deceive ourselves that there is still a penal system of grim fortresses where cowed convicts in arrow-flecked suits live on porridge and do hard labour. Meanwhile our rulers, weakened by generous social consciences, know the truth – that the nineteenth-century battlements conceal well-intentioned warehouses of futility where a little social work is attempted but not zealously pursued.

There are powerful national myths about prison. In newspaper cartoons convicts still wear arrowed uniforms and are often depicted in chains or even shown breaking rocks. Their heads are shaved. They can see visitors only through wire-netting. They eat porridge. It is entirely false. There is also an opposite myth, with some truth in it, that of the pampered prisoner, allowed out to go to the pub or the shops, or even home for the weekend, playing snooker, watching TV, bribing the warders to bring him gourmet food and wine, taking and dealing in drugs which are passed to him by mouth-to-mouth contact during poorly supervised visits. And there is a third myth, a dark one of prisoners beaten up, stabbed, forced to smuggle drugs and robbed by fellow inmates, of gangs running whole wings after dark. This is, regrettably, the closest to the truth, although the Inspectors of Prisons do not often dwell on it. They see it as their job to criticize the official running of the prisons, not the unofficial regimes.

One rare exception to this rule was the investigation into Wymott Prison in Lancashire before and after a disastrous riot there in 1993. The then Chief Inspector of Prisons, Judge Stephen Tumim, had found that the jail had been subject to 'a reign of terror by prison gang leaders' which 'reduced a model jail to a burnt-out shell'. Staff as well as inmates were intimidated by drug barons who ruthlessly exerted control similar to the 'paramilitary influence in Northern Ireland prisons'.

> In the run-up to September's riot [in 1993], Wymott was 'close to anarchy'. Prisoners, who lived in student-style rooms rather than cells, had their own keys and did as they pleased, within their locked wings, for hours at a time, particularly at weekends. Judge Tumim believes that the free-and-easy, university-style regime was one of the main reasons for the troubles. However, it was the drugs rackets that gave the gangsters so much power. Inmates returning from home leave were forced to strip by racketeers and searched for narcotics, the main currency inside. The judge criticised Wymott as 'no more than an open prison with a fence around it and wholly inadequate for the majority of young and volatile inner city men it was receiving'. About 100 inmates were actively involved in the riot, which caused at least £20 million worth of damage.

Judge Tumim was reported as saying: 'The majority of prisoners were left to the mercy of the activists. They were placed in a vulnerable position which could have resulted in death or serious injury.'

Less than a year before the riots, the Prison Inspectorate had produced a report that uncovered drug dealing, violence and evidence of no-go areas at Wymott. They said that Manchester's gangland culture had been re-created inside the jail and that drugs, including heroin, were easier to obtain inside the prison than outside. Staff were said to be unable to reimpose order. Wymott had been built in 1979, optimistically intended to hold more than eight hundred low-security prisoners on short sentences. It quickly filled up with far more serious criminals than had at first been intended, making a nonsense of its idealistic buildings and regime. There were riots in 1986 and claims of reform and improvement in 1990. By 1992 the inspectors were warning: 'It is hard to imagine a more corrupting environment in which to place an offender.' Inspectors on a night visit 'confirmed that inmates appeared to be completely in control behind secure gates'. Prisoners were said to have appeared amazed that anyone should trespass on 'their' territory. During the visit, heroin worth £2000 was thrown over the wall. After the report the Home Office said security had been strengthened. Judging from what was to happen there later, they either strengthened it too much, or not enough – in the prevailing atmosphere it is hard to know which is which.

So what really does go on in English prisons, places where the inmates can actually be allowed to take over the buildings at night? What does not go on is punishment. The official view, repeatedly expressed, is that being locked up is punishment enough, that convicted criminals are locked up *as* punishment, not *for* punishment. While they are inside, which is often not for very long, some sort of attempt is made to turn the criminals into good citizens. It does not seem to be very successful. All figures agree that huge numbers of ex-prisoners rapidly reoffend.

At a time when violent crime is at its worst in living when no property is safe from the thief or the vandal, y think that the unfashionable idea of punishment might be reconsidered. You might think that the social-work approach would at least be questioned, since its results have been so bad. At the very least, you might think that there are many people now on our streets who ought to be locked up for the good of the rest of us. You might think that our experts would look enviously at America's achievement – serious crime down 16 per cent in four years, violent crime down 20 per cent in the same period. They might be interested, too, to know that this achievement followed the building of nearly five hundred new prisons and a general ban on light sentences and early releases. There is no sign of it, though. Lord Woolf, the Lord Chief Justice, said in January 2001 that judges should send far more criminals on 'vigorous' community projects instead of locking them up, although not long afterwards he started demanding long sentences for people who stole mobile telephones. The Home Office has let thousands of prisoners out early with tags on their ankles. By contrast, the US prison system has vacuumed the wicked and the ill-behaved off the streets, so that two million now languish behind American razor-wire.

However, among the narrow-minded elitists who take the real decisions on criminal justice in this country, the only prison debate is about the conditions inside. Almost monthly some new Chief Inspector of Prisons denounces one jail or another for its squalor, hopelessness or failure of management and discipline. There is a fuss, the Chief Inspector demands action, the Home Office promises action and the same problems then happen again elsewhere soon afterwards. A new, still more liberal, Inspector of Prisons is appointed, who begins the same cycle of frustration. Nobody ever adds up these reports and wonders if prisons, as they are currently run, are as certain to be nasty as the sea is to be wet. Of course we should be concerned about prison conditions. But are we concerned in the right way? Squalor, neglect and casual cruelty are signs of barbarism. They are also signs of a complete lack of serious purpose in buildings intended for one thing and now used for an utterly different aim.

In 1910, Winston Churchill, then Home Secretary, urged 'a constant heart-searching by all charged with the duty of punishment, a desire and eagerness to rehabilitate in the world of industry all those who have paid their dues in the hard coinage of punishment, tireless efforts towards the discovery of curative and regenerating processes and an unfaltering faith that there is a treasure, if you can only find it, in the heart of every man'. Churchill's words are often quoted by modern prison reformers. However, they usually omit the vital words 'the hard coinage of punishment'. While deprivation of liberty is nowadays considered to be punishment in itself, it was not so when Churchill was Home Secretary. Ninety years ago the English Prison Commissioners described their task as 'the due punishment of fully responsible persons', a mixture of retribution, deterrence and reformation, in that order. They explained that 'the penalty of crime is in the dishonouring circumstances which must accompany loss of liberty; in the deprivation of what liberty permits in the way of indulgence and self-gratification; in compulsory labour; in the loss of self-respect'. Even then, the Commissioners already sensed that the elite's resolve was weakening. They criticized 'loose thinkers and loose writers' for reversing the order of things so that prison would be 'altogether reformatory, as little as possible deterrent and not at all retributory'. They might also have said that, if there is no punishment, there will be no reform either.

Early in the year 2000, I visited Her Majesty's Prison at Wormwood Scrubs in London to see what the Home Office hoped for in a modern prison and to write about it for the *Mail on Sunday*. Unlike Her Majesty's Inspectors, I was not able to choose the prison I wished to see, nor the time at which I saw it. They told me when I could go and they chose it for me – from a list of current and former 'hellholes' named in a recently-delivered speech by Martin Narey, the director general of the prison service in England and Wales – so it is reasonable to assume that they are fairly happy with the way it is.

I was puzzled. It seemed odd that the man in charge of the prison system should be able to criticize his own empire in public in such terms. Was this bravery, or a public refusal to accept responsibility for a system imposed on an enlightened elite by the crude punitive demands of a supposedly stone-age electorate?

As soon as I stepped through the gates of the prison I struggled to discover what its true purpose might be. It was plainly more civilized, in simple physical terms, than it used to be. Criticisms of dirt and crude discipline made by the inspectors had been heeded. But were they the right criticisms? Was it better in the right way? Behind the great, gloomy gate, the stern, overbearing towers and the tall, thick walls that the Victorians built, you might almost be in a university hall of residence. Everywhere there were politically-correct notices denouncing discrimination of the usual forbidden kinds. There were table-football sets, payphones, showers, the everyday echoing noise of pop music. The cells, each with its own TV and en suite lavatory, might almost have been study bedrooms. Even the bars were disguised by window frames in a cheery blue, the panes of which could be opened. Most people were in tracksuits or jeans, trainers or slippers. The only inhabitants in a recognizable uniform were the warders but, without tunics or peaked caps, they had less physical menace than the average parking warden. Nobody really had to work, although they could earn up to £30 a week in some jobs and spend as much as £15 of that on little luxuries in the prison shop.

No one sewed mailbags any more. A typical job was repacking headphones for airlines. There was even 'unemployment pay' of £2.50 per week for those who did nothing at all. Those who could not read – and many prisoners were very bad at it – got a chance of a proper education. Here, thanks to the threat of losing pay, there was some of the discipline they never experienced at school, and they were taught to read by traditional methods which are seldom used in the sort of schools they attended. It is odd that you have to commit a serious crime before the British state is prepared to grant you the boon of a disciplined education at the taxpayer's expense.

Wormwood Scrubs had its own branch of the Citizens' Advice Bureau. Copies of the European Convention on Human Rights are everywhere. Perhaps somewhere in a cell nearby was the prisoner who would take the government to court and win the cases that everyone knows are inevitable under our new law – conjugal rights for the married and unmarried prisoner, clean needles for heroin addicts and, almost certainly, the right for transsexuals to dress as women. No doubt the modern prison service will learn to cope with convicts in tights. The kitchens had already adapted to the twenty-first century's fads and necessities, with two kinds of vegetarian and one vegan menu, and rice for those who would not eat potatoes. Islam was catered for with both halal meat and Friday prayers.

Even so, it would have been foolish to describe this place as any kind of holiday camp. There was an air of unstated, intangible menace and a feeling that, after dark, this is no place for a weak or gentle man. The pastel-painted walls are plastered with warnings against 'bullying', as if this were Wormwood Lane Comprehensive. However, bullying in a place like this, where you cannot go home, has a much more sinister meaning. 'Are you a bully?' asked one such placard, giving away more than it intended to about the real nature of the establishment:

> Do you intimidate or threaten prisoners who are weaker
> than you? Do you force others to join you in drug taking
> or other subversive activities and make them feel weak if
> they don't? Do you persuade other prisoners to smuggle
> contraband through visits? Do you think it's OK to
> intimidate or assault sex offenders? Do you think it's
> OK to intimidate or assault other prisoners who have
> been labelled as 'grasses'?
>
> If you do any of these things then you are a bully.
> Bullying is antisocial and destructive. It destroys lives
> and can lead to self-harm and suicide. So don't do it!

This all seems terribly worthy, like an appeal for subscriptions in a youth club. However, in a prison apparently run by an unofficial consensus between officers and inmates, calls to 'Stop it!' are unlikely to have much effect. Authority seems to rule with a deliberately light hand, not wanting to provoke trouble from fit young men in a confined space where the guards are usually outnumbered. There were still plenty of places where a vulnerable prisoner might have been pushed into an unseen corner and threatened. Who would take the risk of reporting this and being denounced as a grass, a marked man for the rest of his time inside? (Judging by private telephone calls I received from former inmates and officers after the *Mail on Sunday* article was published, my suspicions are justified.) But officially all is relatively well.

It is even more difficult to tell how much drug abuse goes on here. The men are locked away for nearly twelve hours each night. There is drug testing but it is not frequent. Physical contact at visiting times (not allowed in the American prison system) means that parcels of dope and heroin can be – and certainly are – exchanged while kissing. Prisoners asked about this do not even try to pretend that there are no drugs available. Sometimes outsiders throw packages of narcotics over the walls in tennis balls, hoping or knowing that the delivery will be passed on.

Drugs or no, a fortune has obviously been spent on rebuilding, redecorating and civilizing the 114-year-old cell-blocks. A lot of trouble has been taken to keep them clean. There is no stink of sewage, not even the normal jailhouse aroma of stale food and dried sweat. Fresh paint and bright lights make the fortified walls and armoured doors seem almost picturesque, their original hard intention obsolete. However, the yards outside are scattered with litter flung needlessly from the windows, a warning that spiteful, damaging anarchy is never far away and that improving conditions does not necessarily win either appreciation or co-operation. Until recently it was undoubtedly a place of ill-repute, neither Victorian jail nor twentieth-century penal laboratory, just a slum. When the then governor, Stephen Moore, first arrived in 1998, it was so squalid, overcrowded and dismal that, as he put it to me, he wondered if he had been put in charge of a prison in Romania or Albania. No civilized person could want that. However, should a civilized person want the sort of place Mr Moore then created, a kind of ideal, liberal prison where everything flows smoothly and nobody is made to do anything much, except be locked up? Here is the problem: Mr Moore had no official duty to punish those he was guarding. 'The courts punish people by depriving them of their liberty for some time. We are in the business of using that time as constructively as possible.'

How constructively is that? In a special unit I met a well-spoken and personable young murderer who, while high on heroin, had knifed his victim to death. With every appearance of sincerity, he said he was determined to stay off drugs. He had good reason to do this since, if he did not, he would never get out. In the modern fashion of 'confronting your crime', he had been persuaded to re-enact his deed, to imagine himself the victim, to realize what he had done. Does he really? A murderer who really knew what he had done might not think it was right that he should be released, ever.

In another special unit were the miserable figures of the mentally ill, moaning and slumped in their cells, bewildered, pitiful yet probably dangerous. It is likely that many of these people had come to this state because they had taken illegal drugs and permanently damaged their minds. The prisons have become the final destination for many such people because of the demolition of the mental hospitals under the shameful Care in the Community programme. Their presence is a terrible burden on prison staff, who ought not to be asked to do this. These people are dangerous to themselves and to others and should not be in prisons at all. Their presence is undoubtedly the cause of much grief and trouble, and, like all aspects of Care in the Community, it is a national disgrace that ought to be reversed and whose advocates should in some way be punished for what they have done.

Inside this place it was easy to see why staff thought that their main job was to help the prisoners become better people. When you see only the criminal, never the victim, it is easy to forget that at least part of your job is the reassurance of the wounded and the robbed, and the discouragement of wickedness. You may be inclined to become confused about which one you are supposed to be helping. Common humanity, where it can, seeks to avoid cruelty and assuage misery, and it is right that it should be so. Dirt, brutality and gloom are never good. But much of what passes for kindness is also a form of appeasement, driven by the permanent fear of a new outbreak of prison riots, cell-blocks ablaze, warders perhaps kidnapped or worse, TV cameras camped outside as the government hesitates between negotiation and a SWAT team.

It is certain that the TVs in the cells – something that most victims of crime and many others besides think is quite wrong – are there as an electronic cosh to keep the prisoners quiet and contented. It is also possible to wonder if authority's blurred, if not quite blind, eye to the flow of drugs has something to do with the same fear of trouble. If dope helps to keep the cell-blocks quiet, then it is easy to see why the authorities might be tempted be relaxed about its supply and use. Then there is the way in which warders have been turned into social workers, sticking up notices telling everyone to be good. Warders do not need to act like prison-camp guards. Many have distinguished themselves over the years with a wise mixture of humanity and firmness. But the relationship between them and the prisoners is now strangely equal, symbolizing the elite state's neutrality between victim and offender.

The idea of private prisons is repellent to many because of the total absence of moral disapproval from the commercial contract. Imprisonment is not a business. It is a stern public obligation. However, such morality is now just as absent from the state sector. Most people who have suffered at the hands of criminals would think that mere deprivation of liberty was not punishment enough. Nor would they want those criminals to be able to use the telephone or play pool, to wear an outfit designed not to look like a uniform or to choose what they eat from seven different menus. And no one in his right mind would think it acceptable that illegal drugs, the cause of so much crime in the first place, should circulate in places supposed to be completely under the control of the state.

There is another aspect of this new regime that ought to worry the gentle and thoughtful. As the authorities have relaxed control of the prisons, the inmates have not become any more free. They have swapped one oppressor for another. Where governors and warders no longer rule, the hierarchy of criminals asserts itself. A violent, ruthless, strong and selfish person has little to fear in this sort of jungle. The weak and non-violent, who do most certainly end up in our prisons, have much of which to be frightened. Most unbearable of all is the likely fate of any innocent person locked up and abandoned in a snakepit of tattooed career criminals. As the prison doctor, Theodore Dalrymple, has written, we owe a great deal to the prison officers who are prepared to offer at least some protection to the vulnerable in prison. It is wrong in principle that a man in prison should be more afraid of his fellow prisoners than he is of the law.

Once, long ago, when Wormwood Scrubs was new, it had a clear, hard and frighteningly grim idea of its purpose which prevented many of the abuses we see today, even if it had abuses of its own. Realistically, we cannot go all the way back to that time. We would find it hard enough to cope with the lives lived by free and prosperous Englishmen of a hundred years ago, let alone the Edwardian prison regime. As the violent and the dishonest laugh and sneer at a criminal justice system that holds no fear for them, vegetarian diets, anti-bullying campaigns and therapy cannot be the right answer. As the old and the weak and the vulnerable live in growing fear, their lives in many cases more confined, dangerous and restricted than those of convicts, has the government forgotten its first duty to defend the gentle and punish the wrongdoer? If so, the process has been a long, slow one, winding along that primrose path, paved with good intentions, which always leads to the same place. How did we get from there to here?

The most explosive event in the history of modern British prisons was the publication in 1922 of *English Prisons Today*, edited by the prominent and clever liberal reformers, Stephen Hobhouse and Fenner Brockway. This book, a respectable middle-class person's view of the penal system, was the consequence of two foolish mistakes by the government. The authorities used prisons designed for transgressors to attempt to crush women and men who were essentially political offenders. They persecuted the suffragettes and then soon afterwards imprisoned those who refused to serve in the trenches after conscription was introduced in 1916. They exposed educated, articulate and normally law-abiding people to the harshness of a world they had not even known existed. (There would be a faint echo of this in the 1960s, when rough police treatment of left-wing protestors – especially the Challenor case where an unhinged detective planted a brick in the pocket of a pacifist cartoonist – was to turn the radical middle class of the day against the police. This had grave and lasting consequences on relations between the thinking classes and the police, still felt to this day.)

Brockway was one of those imprisoned for refusing to serve in the trenches. His experiences allowed him to write with authority on the hitherto undiscovered territory behind the thick high walls. He was no crude propagandist. He and Hobhouse produced a book that had the scope and authority of a Royal Commission, and which influenced prison policy for years to come. It must have been welcomed by at least some of the Prison Commissioners themselves, who were already trying to lessen the rigour of the regime. It was and remains an impressive piece of work, a fascinating description of things as they were as well as a coherent plan of reform.

They quoted what would now be called the 'policy' or 'mission statement' issued by the English Prison Commissioners in 1900: 'the principle of the English system is to deter by an exact though

THE ABOLITION OF LIBERTY

not a severe discipline, inculcating habits of obedience and order, and at the same time to reform by labour, education, and religious ministration.' The Commissioners were also clear that at least part of the point of the prison system was the effect that it had on those who had not yet offended, a point nowadays almost completely forgotten. Prisoners must suffer not only for their own good but also so that others would seek to avoid the same suffering. The Report of the Directors of Convict Prisons 1873 had proclaimed: 'When everything has been done to deter from crime or reform the criminal there will still remain a certain class whom it is hopeless to influence and who must be dealt with in course of law, not for much result on themselves but to carry out the principle of justice and mainly to deter others.'

This was a modernized version of the early nineteenth-century remark by a judge who told a condemned man: 'You are sentenced to be hanged not because you stole the horse but in order to prevent others from stealing horses.' Halsbury's *Laws of England* similarly stated: 'The object of punishment is the prevention of crime, and every punishment should have a double effect, namely to prevent the person who has committed a crime from repeating the act or omission, and to prevent other members of the community from committing similar crimes.' Few would have dissented from what would have seemed at the time to be a rather obvious statement.

Hobhouse and Brockway describe in gloomy detail what this policy involved for those who were convicted. The facts they revealed to a surprised and disquieted middle class were of course well known to the criminals of England, who had for decades seen such things as the risks of their profession. They were also known, by rumour and repute, to the classes most likely to turn to crime. Cells, all for individual occupation, varied from ten feet by seven, by nine feet high, to thirteen by seven by nine where they were supposed to be used for labour. Windows varied from fourteen to twenty-one panes measuring eighteen inches by four, with one or two panes designed to be opened. Winter temperatures were fifty degrees Fahrenheit (ten degrees Celsius) or lower, so that in the coldest weather inmates were only able to keep warm by walking around or wrapping themselves in blankets. The floors were of stone, tile, concrete or asphalt. 'It is difficult to convey an impression of the hope-destroying, forbidding aspect of prison buildings,' they wrote. 'They embody architecturally the repressive characteristics of the prison system. Many of our witnesses, drawn from both officials and ex-prisoners, express the view that the only reform to which the buildings can be usefully subjected is dynamite.'

They set out the reception procedure and prison life for a man sentenced to the 'Third Division', then the commonest type of sentence. Those who have read the description of the arrival of Paul Pennyfeather in prison in Evelyn Waugh's *Decline and Fall* will be familiar with much of it, although it must often have lacked the humour that Waugh managed to give it. The new arrival's name was entered in the 'body-receipt book', presumably a reference to the law of habeas corpus ('habeas corpus' translates literally as 'you have the body...'). He was then locked up in a reception cubicle (often dirty), ordered to strip and examined nude, a shocking and degrading experience for men of the period. He was made to wash in nine inches of warm water in a compulsory bath. Then he was ordered to dress in the prison uniform of collarless coat, waistcoat and buckled trousers stamped with the broad arrow marking them as 'government property', a cap of the same material, heavy shoes, socks, cotton shirt, a coarse handkerchief, pants and flannel vest. Clothes were allocated with 'little regard for height and girth'.

The convict was given a Bible, Prayer Book, small towel, brush and comb. During this procedure conversation was forbidden. He was handed the prison rules on a printed card with 'a formidable list of possible offences'. After buttoning on an unsightly yellow badge giving his cell number, he was conducted to the cell, the furniture of which was a wooden table, a small backless stool and a bed-board. The window was 'so high up that it is necessary to stand on the stool to look out of it', which was probably a punishable offence. What view there was, was reduced by several heavy iron bars fixed from outside. The cell light was often not switched on until after darkness fell. The whitewashed walls did not hide 'pathetic and often objectionable inscriptions'.

The description continues with details of the sparse and dispiriting furnishings. The bed-board was two or three planks fixed on a low support, six feet wide by thirty inches broad. During the day it had to be leant against the wall along with the thin mattress (hard labour prisoners had to sleep without a mattress for the first fourteen days of their sentence) and the hard stuffed pillow. A little shelf contained a white, glazed pint pot, salt jar, knife and spoon; soap and lavatory paper; slate and slate pencil; religious books, a wooden rack (permitted only after the first eight weeks) to hold monthly letters from home, and three or four pictures of relatives. A collection of printed cards hung on a nail, including some prayers and a notice threatening the prisoner with punishments for 'a number of activities that would be quite innocent in normal life'.

There are also details of the 'system of progressive stages' through which a prisoner might obtain privileges and some remission. He could earn a target of fifty-six marks for labour and good conduct, which led to 'associated labour' in the workshop, more frequent books, letters or visits. Visits took place through a wire grille or double row of bars, without physical contact. Some prisons were also equipped with an arrangement known as the 'meat-safe', two small compartments similar in size to phone boxes, separated by two screens of wire-gauze about a foot apart. Visits were not permitted more often than every four weeks and lasted no longer than half an hour (modern prisons generally allow weekly visits, where physical contact is allowed, and these can last for some time, since many governors do not believe in strictly enforcing time limits). A letter was often an alternative to a visit. Remission of up to one sixth of the sentence was possible if conduct was good enough (compare this with the automatic remission of half the sentence granted today).

Looking round his cell, the newly arrived convict would see a number of dreary and dutiful objects. On the floor was a metal water can covered by an enamel plate, an earthenware chamber pot (much of the original nineteenth-century plumbing had been removed because the piping was used by prisoners to tap out messages between cells) with a metal top, and a small tin basin. There was also a dustpan and brush, a scrubbing brush, some cleaning rags and a box containing brick dust and whitening for scouring. Each prisoner had a small towel and a dishcloth. Each cell contained a bell handle for emergencies. There were sewing or other implements for his work.

The daily routine of prison life was as follows:

> Rising bell at 6.30. Dress, clean and tidy cell and make requests or complaints.
>
> Stitching mailbags.
>
> After an hour pint pot filled with porridge, plus six oz of bread.
>
> Three times a week given bucket of cold water to scrub floor. Must polish tins.
>
> At nine bell rings for chapel.
>
> 15–20 minute service, go to and from in silence, under watchful eyes of warders.
>
> Hour's exercise on concentric tracks. Warders watch from raised platforms.
>
> 10.15, march back to cells, mailbag sewing until noon, or to workshop.
>
> At noon dinner trays, 40 minutes allowed, work until 4.15, followed by delivery of cocoa and bread and two to three ounces of 'some relish'. Door does not open again for 14 hours. Lights went out at nine.

Hobhouse and Brockway note: 'The man who is expert and diligent enough to complete his task by supper-time can, in some prisons at any rate, spend most of the evening hours in reading his Bible or other book, in pacing round his cell, writing rhymes or blasphemies upon his slate, or occupying his vacancy in any other of the very limited means that a cell affords.' They quote E. W. Mason's gloomy description, from his 1918 book *Free in Prison*, of the night hours within prison walls: 'Outside the prison wards are bare and silent and dark except for a beam of light at every cell lamp hole. They are unfrequented, save for the night-warder, who moves in felt slippers and peers in at the cell spyhole as he works his way up the long landings from cell to cell. From the inside of the cell one hears nothing of him except a click of the spyhole shutter and the dry dragging sound of the slippers.' There were very few solaces. Tobacco was strictly forbidden, although plans to allow its limited use by privileged prisoners were under discussion.

Many things were to change as a result of the Hobhouse and Brockway report. Even so, more than ten years later prison life was still austere and hard. In *The Modern English Prison*, published in 1934, L. W. Fox detailed the daily diet for a man in the punishment cells: 'No. 1 diet is 1 lb of bread per day with water (which could be imposed for a maximum of three days at a time).' By this time, prisoners held for four years or more had facilities for smoking, which was allowed at set times in a prescribed room. Women, for whom smoking was still banned, were allowed to make tea. The close cropping of prisoners' heads had been abolished and the use of broad arrows to mark their uniforms seems to have disappeared in the late 1920s, although W. F. McCartney's prison memoir *Walls Have Mouths*, which deals with the late 1920s and early 1930s, records their use at Parkhurst. With or without these unpleasant and humiliating features, there was little sign that the prisons were deterring those already used to them.

The report of the Persistent Offenders Committee recorded that of the 39,000 sentences of imprisonment in 1930, 28,000 were imposed on culprits who had previously been found guilty of offences. Many had been dealt with through the fines and probation introduced by Winston Churchill before the First World War, which drastically reduced the numbers in prison and eventually ended the era of strictness recorded by Jose Harris. In 20,384 cases the offenders had already been in prison and plenty of them had served repeated sentences, as is shown by the following list:

4740 had served 1 previous sentence.

1949 had served 3 previous sentences.

1499 had served 4 previous sentences.

1115 had served 5 previous sentences.

3382 had served 6–10 previous sentences.

2622 had served 11–20 previous sentences.

2125 had served over 20 previous sentences.

These figures create a picture of a small, slowly circulating group of more or less incorrigible crooks and troublemakers, going in and out of prison despite its dismal conditions. Undoubtedly, among them were a small number of vagrants who committed minor crimes at the beginning of winter so as to have food and shelter during the cold months.

The important figures, however, are the unrecorded ones for people who might have committed crimes but chose not to because they knew what to expect if they did. These, it is reasonable to guess, are the people who have since swelled the prison population, despite the determination of the authorities not to send them there if they can possibly help it.

Another weapon still in the hands of the authorities at the time was flogging, the subject of relentless campaigns for abolition by penal reformers. It was not to be formally abolished until the Roy Jenkins years. The courts still felt able to use it despite growing public disapproval. Leo Page in his 1937 book, *Crime and the*

Prison population of England and Wales (ten-year intervals)

1900–01	17,435
1911–12*	19,797
1920–21	11,000**
1930–31	11,346
1940–41	9377
1950–51	20,474
1960–61	27,099
1970	39,028
1980	42,300
1990	45,636
1999	64,770

During 2002 the total passed 70,000 for the first time.

* Figure for 1910–11 not available.
**Strict liquor laws and conscription are thought to be the reasons for the sharp drop in prison population during and following the 1914–18 war.

Community, examined the use of the birch and the cat-o'-nine-tails during the years 1926 to 1935. He found that it was used mainly to punish robbery with violence – a total of 235 sentences. Its other uses in this period are curious and interesting for what they tell us about the attitudes of a past era:

other offences of violence 1

living on earnings of prostitute 1

male soliciting 2

indecent exposure 4

malicious damage, arson and larceny
by boys of fourteen and fifteen 10

Total 253

Page felt that this made a strong case for using it more often, again for the effect it had on others rather than for any good it might have done the flogged robbers. 'In the ten years before the war [corporal punishment] was not used with any freedom (61 times 1904 to 1913) as a penalty for this offence, and there were 1,414 convictions for this crime (robbery with violence); in the last period of the same number of years it has been used with far greater frequency (235 times 1926 to 1935) and the number of convictions has fallen to less than half (656).'

A rather different view of inter-war crime problems is found in *The Lawbreaker*, published in 1933 by Roy and Theodora Calvert. They opposed flogging and attacked as a myth the idea that the nineteenth-century epidemic of garrotting had been stamped out by the introduction of flogging to deal with it. Believably, they said that garrotting had actually ceased before the 'Garrotters' Act' was passed in a parliamentary panic by the Commons after an MP was a victim. They also produce this interesting account of crime for the year 1930: that year there were 122 murders; ninety-one attempts, threats or conspiracies to murder; 178 manslaughters or infanticides; 178 woundings; 289 other offences of violence; 648 'unnatural offences or attempts'; 2524 sex offences; 374 bigamies; 25,937 burglaries or housebreakings; 311 robberies or extortions; 10,019 aggravated larcenies; 84,697 simple and minor larcenies; 11,296 obtaining by false pretences; 2045 other frauds; 2102 receiving stolen goods; 185 arsons; 166 other offences against property; 857 forgeries; 215 coinings; 168 perjuries; 3053 attempted suicides; 311 other indictable offences.

Most of these figures would represent a huge improvement on those of today. At the time, there was some disquiet about them. The Calverts claimed it was unjustified. 'The impression, widely fostered by the sensational press, that violent crimes against the person have increased to an alarming extent, is quite erroneous,' they said. 'There has actually been a steady decrease in murder from 4.7 per million during the five years 1900–4 to 3.7 during 1925–9 and 3.1 in 1930.' Attempted murder was also down and the increase in manslaughter cases was a by-product of the bloodshed on the roads as motoring offences began to climb. 'The highest published figure [for robbery] since the war, viz. 7.8 per million in 1930, is lower than the average figure for the ten pre-war years 1900–9, when the country was not confronted with an unemployment problem comparable with that of the last few years.'

They also recorded a reduction in assaults, cruelty to children, liquor law breaches, prostitution, begging, cruelty to animals and truancy. Their most fascinating finding, for those who believe in a crude link between poverty and crime, was that crime did rise with unemployment. It did so, however, in a complicated pattern which cuts to ribbons the crude 'poverty = crime' equation. In the North, it was true that theft offences had risen (though to nothing like as much as in the period of full employment thirty years later). What they called 'downright lawlessness' was more common in the South, where unemployment was much less of a problem. They wrote: 'The ordinary unemployed man does not drift into crime; he has generations of moral principle behind him and stands with his back to the wall fighting the demoralizing influence of enforced idleness year after year without resorting to crime.' And while they accepted that the great majority appearing before the courts were poor, they rightly added that so were the great majority of those who did not appear before the courts.

Seen from the early years of the twenty-first century, this era of the broad arrow and the exercise yard may seem like one long, chilly epoch of harshness. In fact, it was under constant pressure to change from within and without and was frequently reformed and humanized from mid-Victorian times onwards. One of those pressing for change was Sir Evelyn Ruggles-Brise KCB, who became chairman of the English Prison Commission and set down his thoughts in his 1921 book, *The English Prison System*. He is mocked as Lucas-Dockery, a gullible and well-meaning sort, in Waugh's *Decline and Fall*. But in fact he was no fool. He believed that the imprisonment of suffragettes and conscientious objectors had helped to weaken discipline and undermine the entire penal structure. He wrote:

> Our prison system has, in recent years, been subjected to a very severe test by the fact that, of necessity, penal treatment in prison, primarily designed for the criminal class, has been applied to thousands of individuals in no way belonging to that class, whom it has been necessary to commit to prison under the Defence of the Realm Acts, either as conscientious objectors to military service, or otherwise, for the safety of the realm.
>
> Prison rules and regulations press hardly on men and women who, under normal circumstances, would never have become the subject of those punitive and repressive conditions which are inseparable from the deprivation of liberty by the State... To persons of refinement and education (as many were), the many restrictions necessary for the safe custody of criminals would naturally seem harsh, unnecessary and even unnatural. No doubt their experience has given an impulse to the prison reformer who, in his honourable zeal to soften the lot of the unfortunate captive, is apt to overlook the necessity for strict rules and regulations in dealing with a class to whose habits and instincts he is himself a total stranger.

He was right. The law was unleashed with fury and without mercy on the middle-class protestors. Despite the great issues involved and the undoubted courage of the far greater numbers who went to the front, the government's zeal against the pacifists now looks like a serious error of judgement and failure of justice. We are paying for it still in the lasting effect it had on prison discipline. More than six thousand men were arrested after refusing to be conscripted. Of these, seventy-one died in prison or after release on medical grounds. 'The imposition of solitary confinement, bread-and-water punishment and the silence rule were commonplace.' Among those imprisoned was the philosopher Bertrand Russell, who was convicted after writing a pamphlet condemning the treatment of a conscientious objector. The outcome of all this was the Hobhouse and Brockway report and a growing, and mainly misconceived, demand for reforms from the post-war left where many of the objectors had become prominent and respected figures (Brockway and Russell would both end their days, full of years and garlanded with honours, in the House of Lords, one by hereditary right and the other by political favour).

Much had already been done to lessen the nineteenth-century harshness of the system, mainly by trying to keep harmless people out of it if possible rather than by making the experience any pleasanter. Churchill's introduction in 1908 of probation and fines for many offences that would otherwise have ended in imprisonment was then considered bold and enlightened. Few had time for social explanations of wrongdoing, since this was an age of falling crime despite social provisions that were minimal by the standards of today. In his book *Criminals and Crime, Some Facts and Suggestions*, Sir Robert Anderson (barrister, JP, Home Office adviser, Assistant Commissioner of the Metropolitan Police and head of CID 1888–1901) urged an attack on professional crime, which he thought could then be utterly defeated. He pointed out that in 1868, the year after transportation had been abandoned, London property felonies had totalled 22,083. In 1905, they were significantly lower, at 18,515, a drop that was even more significant when set beside the fact that over the same period the city's population had risen from 3.5 million to just over seven million.

However, while ordinary crimes against property were decreasing, professional burglary was increasing. Anderson urged a pitiless response: 'The true professional is an advanced disciple of Hobbes. He is not embarrassed by either twinges of conscience or a sense of shame...' He added: 'The humanity-mongers are so lavish in their pity for the criminal that they have none left for their victims.' Sir Robert also took the view, common at the time, that the prisons had been successfully reformed and were emphatically no longer nurseries of crime. Prison, in short, worked and was widely believed to work. The authorities were confident that they had both morality and practicality on their side. Secure in these beliefs, they were happy to allow a surprising amount of reform.

Between 1895 and 1921 Ruggles-Brise made great changes in the local prisons, where most minor offenders then served their terms. When he took charge, convicts still had to turn useless cranks, slowly grinding stone to powder, in their cells. These cranks could be set tighter or looser by a screw on the outside of the cell – hence the name 'screw' still given to prison officers. This practice along with oakum-picking, the pulling to pieces of old rope to form mattress-stuffing fibre (and the origin of the expression 'money for old rope'), was abolished. Ruggles-Brise also scrapped the treadmills, the main purpose of which had been to exhaust the prisoners as they tramped endlessly upstairs. In 1899, the dehumanizing convict crop so much beloved of cartoonists was also dispensed with in local jails, although it would last another two decades in the long-term convict prisons. The rule of total silence was officially abolished in 1898, although talking was still a privilege to be granted by the authorities and withdrawn by them as well.

Ruggles-Brise was followed in the 1920s as 'chief prison reformer' by the energetic Alexander Paterson, a man of great personal courage who had twice been recommended for the Victoria Cross. Paterson was an old-fashioned liberal reformer who believed that unless the wealthy energetically helped the poor, state socialism would follow. He was the force behind many of the softening reforms after the First World War, partly in response to the Hobhouse and Brockway report. He already believed that the regime was too harsh and hopeless. After a visit to Dartmoor as a young man he had written in obvious dismay:

> The drab uniforms of the prisoners were plastered with broad arrows… their heads were covered with a sort of dirty moss… hair that a pair of clippers could not remove. The prison regime, determined to minimize the chances of violence or suicide had succeeded in making human beings into objects of ugliness and contempt. As they saw us coming, each man ran to the nearest wall and put his face closely against it, remaining in this servile position until we had passed him by.

Like many others who have seen prison in action, he began to feel a keener concern for the piteous object the prisoner had become than for his unseen victims, and to think in terms more of reforming the individual criminal than of deterring crime at large. He wrote: 'If a prison is merely a cloakroom, in which the enemy of society is duly deposited till called for after a fixed period, or a kennel in which he is safely caged until on the appointed day he is let loose on society again, then indeed the protection afforded is of a temporary nature and it may well be that, after the security of a few months or years, society will be at the mercy of an enemy more bitter and implacable than before.' However, he was not blind to the dangers of too much relaxation of discipline, warning presciently that: 'A sloppy and unthinking sentiment may rush us into forms of association far more injurious to those concerned than any evils of solitude.'

In a way, Paterson created the modern English prison system, which would certainly have coped much better with inmates such as Fenner Brockway and Bertrand Russell than what went before. The problem is that, for the most part, its inhabitants were, and always have been, more like Reggie and Ronnie Kray than the great philosopher Russell or the high-principled conscientious objector Brockway. Under Paterson's influence, the total separation of convicts from one another was suspended in 1923 and abolished in 1930. In 1924 compulsory chapel attendance was abolished. Until then, chapel had been one of the few places where news could be passed on, under the cover of hymn-singing or other chants, as wittily described in *Decline and Fall*. This example of a mangled 'Magnificat' is given by W. J. Forsythe in his *Penal Discipline, Reformatory Projects and the English Prison Commission 1895–1939*. The lines on the right are sung to the rhythm of those on the left:

And behold from henceforth	What are you in for?
All generations shall call me blessed	I'm in for shoplifting
For he that is mighty hath magnified me	How long have you got?
And Holy is his name	Six months hard labour

Disciplinary floggings with the cat-o'-nine-tails fell to nil in mid-1920 (although the milder birchings continued). In 1922 raised platforms in chapels to allow officers to keep watch on the praying prisoners were removed. Prisoners could now be released on licence after serving three-quarters of their sentence. In March 1922 conversation was allowed in workshops. From 1924, potential escapers were no longer forced to wear the clownish particoloured uniform and heavy leg chains that had until then been their lot. Such uniforms, though not the leg-irons, have since been reintroduced.

In 1921 visiting-boxes were introduced, where husbands and wives could embrace without netting to separate them. From then on, prisoners were transferred between prisons in civilian clothes – to avoid the sort of humiliation bitterly recalled by Oscar Wilde in *De Profundis* where he described the misery of being exposed to public mockery on Clapham Junction station, an experience so foul that he wept every day at the memory of it, at the exact time when it had happened. Paterson was also responsible for the removal of the broad arrows from the prison uniform. Under his influence, earnings were introduced and smoking more generally allowed. Many fictional treatments of prison written much later than this still assume that pre-1914 conditions continued far longer than they actually did. Waugh's *Decline and Fall* was out of date before it was published, and probably when it was written.

Forsythe concludes that this period was a successful one, during which an unloved and unwelcome duty was done remarkably well:

> English prisons were severe, regimented and disciplinary
> in the early twentieth century. Notwithstanding,
> provision of the basic necessities of life, freedom from
> widespread institutionally legitimised violence by staff
> and an effective recognition that prisoners of the state
> have the right to some dignity and protection were
> characteristic of the English prison system between 1895
> and 1939. Such features were not typical of many prison
> systems in the world, then or thereafter.

He also touches on one of the fascinating might-have-beens, had the Second World War not inflicted a vast social revolution on British society which reduced all previous attempts at change to insignificance. He believes that 'overall in England the inter-war years witnessed a significant growth in the liberal ameliorative approach to prisoners. Advocates of this attitude managed to retain their advantage despite such setbacks as the Dartmoor riot' (a savage outbreak of violence that began over the serving of a cold breakfast to the convicts on 24 January 1932 and had to be quelled with the aid of regular troops; Dartmoor at the time housed 440 prisoners, mostly murderers and violent robbers). Even the great buildings that now seem certain to survive for another century might have disappeared under this benevolent scheme for reform. Impelled by an optimistic approach to crime and its control, in the late 1930s the commissioners were 'preparing an assault on the great architectural monoliths bequeathed to them by the Victorians and intending to move further towards modern, open prisons for men and women'.

The broadly successful prisons of this period were a reflection of the extraordinarily stable and contented society that they served. They continued to follow the same path, towards gentler conditions and less discipline, well into the post-war period. Quite possibly, conditions could have continued to grow significantly softer without any serious growth in crime. However, the war and the welfare state, not to mention the permissive society and the great consumer boom, were to create a world in which prisons ceased to be the last destination of a small knot of incorrigibles. Instead, they became one of society's few weapons against a wave of unrepentant wrongdoing. As levels of crime grew in the brave new world that was created after 1945, the prisons certainly could no longer claim to be successful.

Just when the prisons needed to make a greater impact on those sent to them and on the new criminal class, a more relaxed outside world undermined old-fashioned discipline. This is well-illustrated by the story of Roger Keith Maxwell. The last disciplinary birching of a prisoner in England was approved (as it had to be before being administered) by R. A. Butler, the Conservative Home Secretary, in 1962. Four years later, Roy Jenkins refused to approve the birching of Maxwell. This was a perfectly reasonable decision. Birching was unacceptable in modern England because it was, simply, too cruel and demeaned those who had to inflict it. But no more civilized punishment was available to replace it.

Maxwell had been sentenced to life imprisonment in March 1966 after murdering Derrick Lambert, a guard at Portland Borstal, with an iron bar during an attempted escape. He was the ringleader of a race riot at Maidstone Prison, attacked several officers there and was sentenced to six strokes of the birch. His parents were constituents of Ted Heath, then Leader of the Opposition, and petitioned him against the punishment. Jenkins ruled on 5 October 1966 that he would not confirm the sentence. Nor did Maxwell get the alternative sentence of solitary confinement. Instead he underwent psychiatric testing and was later diagnosed as a psychopath. Psychopath or not, he was freed in 1982, with many years of life still ahead of him.

The Prison Officers' Association was incensed by his initial offence, saying it had resulted from the abolition of the death penalty. The POA leader, Fred Castell, said, quite correctly, that the Jenkins decision meant birching was effectively at an end in England. 'I will be surprised if Maxwell does not get a medal next. He has killed one prison officer and assaulted four others and I feel very angry.' His anger had no effect on policy.

Hugely increased prison numbers around this time produced overcrowding and squalor not seen since the days of the hulks, especially the insanitary and unsettling cramming of several prisoners into cells meant for one. The disgusting practice of slopping out, never attractive, became unbearable. Prisoners often simply wrapped their stools in paper and flung them from their cell windows in nasty parcels. Sometimes the authorities were forced to house convicted criminals in disused army camps or to keep them in police cells. The pressure on the courts meant a grave increase in the numbers of remand prisoners, in spite of ever-laxer rules on granting bail.

The closure of mental hospitals forced prisons to house the insane as well as the wicked. The growth of the drugs menace outside spread inside, as did greater readiness to use violence. The ending of the death penalty increased the numbers of very long-term prisoners serving so-called life sentences and requiring special treatment to make their lives bearable. A number of embarrassing escapes compelled the spending of millions on greater security, at the expense of treasured rehabilitation projects and badly needed new prisons. Yet the real problem remained the fact that England simply did not have enough prisons to hold its new wave of criminals. Worse, it had no idea what to do with them once they were locked up. This pressure and confusion made nonsense of both rehabilitation and retribution, because it resulted in unending efforts to reduce the prison population through suspended sentences, parole and dishonest sentencing.

The extraordinary Criminal Justice Act 1991 compelled judges to pretend that criminals were going to jail for twice as long as they really were. Next came the introduction of 'tagging', early release accompanied by ineffective electronic monitoring. This led to a serious number of offences committed by men who would otherwise have been in prison. In March 2002 it was disclosed that prisoners freed early under the tagging scheme had committed 1400 crimes when they would otherwise have been in prison. Those crimes, between January 1999 and December 2001, included four rapes, thirty-eight serious woundings and eighty-two serious assaults. About eighty released convicts went missing after cutting off their tags, which were supposed to restrict their movements. The figures, which may themselves be misleading because of the difficulty of obtaining convictions, were released by the Home Office to a Member of Parliament, but not made generally available until after they were published in newspapers, probably because of their sensitivity.

From 1986 to 1990 a succession of ugly riots, accompanied by expensive and spectacular destruction of buildings, led to a nervous improvement of conditions, which looked like appeasement, mainly because that is what it was. In 1986 alone twenty-two prisons exploded into riots and in 1990 Manchester's monumental Strangeways Prison was subjected to a lengthy, televised uprising which cost £130 million and left 147 officers injured. The next year's riot at Moorland Prison in Doncaster, a new prison, exploded any idea that Victorian conditions and buildings were to blame.

The relationship between prison conditions, prison population and crime is difficult to work out. Between 1909 and 1938, probation as a substitute for prison, coupled with the introduction of allowing time to pay fines (dating respectively from 1908 and 1914), resulted in a drop in annual prison receptions from 205,216 to 40,430. These Churchillian reforms ended the era of rigorous social discipline described by Jose Harris. This was also a time of generally low or stable crime figures. However, the average daily figures for the prison population underwent such an astonishing increase in the post-war period that full-scale moral panic would be a reasonable response. Look back at the table earlier in this chapter and the scale of the change is clear. It is not just a matter of larger numbers, but of a wholly different size and shape of criminal class. At the end of the war the figures were still comparable with the 1930s, at just under thirteen thousand (the highest pre-1939 figure was 20,757 in 1903–4, the highest inter-war figure 12,986 in 1933–4). By 1950–51, the total was at 20,474. By 1960–1, it stood at 27,099. By 1971 it had reached 39,708. By 1991 it was still climbing, at 45,817. By 1999 it had reached 64,770. By the autumn of 2002 the prison population was 72,000, its official limit. It continues to climb.

Under present moral and legal conditions, any future fall will not be the result of a decline in the level of crime. It is much more likely to follow yet more measures to make it difficult to get criminals into prison and easy to get them out once they are inside. As the early releases of tagged prisoners have shown, many of those allowed to go free under this policy are violent and dangerous. There is simply no comparison with Winston Churchill's pre-First World War reforms, which benefited only the most minor and harmless of offenders. These likely measures will be taken at a time when criminals are already less worried than ever about being sent to jail. What makes this especially hard to accept is the continued pretence that the existing system serves any positive purpose. These crammed and disorderly holding pens may occasionally achieve miraculous successes of reclamation. There are isolated stories of such heartening events. If so, it is in spite of their nature and ethos. They are unpleasant and frightening, but in the wrong way.

The rule seems to be that the more violent the criminal, the less he has to fear from prison. It is true that child-molesters can seek special protection from their fellow inmates. This is, of course, absolutely necessary, although the best precautions can sometimes fail. However, it says much for the balance of power in the cell-blocks that this has to be so. Many who are not child-molesters also need protection but do not get it. Pressure to get involved with drugs and drug-smuggling, for example, is a serious problem for vulnerable inmates. Many decline special protection because they fear association with the despised 'nonces' on the sex-offenders' wings more than they fear the brutality of the normal wings. Once classified as a 'nonce' or a 'grass', a man is forever in danger inside or outside prison in our depraved and chaotic society. While the establishment and the law have long abandoned the use of physical punishment and fear in dealing with offenders, the criminal classes and successful terrorist groups still clearly believe in both, applying them with vigour when they get the chance. This suggests that criminals and terrorists alike would be deterred by fear and punishment if they were used against them by the state, contrary to current penal and political theories.

What can a modern society do? We cannot re-create the conditions described by Fenner Brockway, even as reformed by Evelyn Ruggles-Brise and Alexander Paterson. That does not mean we should do nothing at all. The combination of comparative austerity, discipline and work, and rewards for consistent good behaviour, could be reintroduced to suit the modern age. A building programme to ensure one cell per prisoner and a recruiting programme for new officers would greatly reduce the risk of riots. The rebuilding of vanished mental hospitals, in any case an urgent national need, would remove the mentally ill from a system in which they should not be placed. The remoralization of society, the end of the state campaign against marriage and the reintroduction of preventive policing would all have their own impacts. The convicted criminal should suffer for his crime and be known to suffer.

Once in prison, he should long for release. Every day and hour of remission should be earned by positive acts of goodness and self-discipline. Once released, he should wish never to go back and should advise others to stay out. He should do hard physical work. He should wear a recognizable uniform which is distinctly unfashionable and that marks him out for what he is. Under certain circumstances he should be made to work in public places on penal tasks designed to reassure the law-abiding public, such as removing graffiti, picking up litter and repairing the damage done by vandals. He should not have access to television or radio or be allowed to play pool or table-football. He should certainly not have access to the telephone. His visits should be controlled so that there is not the slightest chance of visitors passing drugs to inmates. The use of drugs should be unfailingly and rigidly punished by loss of remission. Almost every normal liberty should be a privilege to be earned by good behaviour, cleanliness, self-discipline and obedience. Remission should be reserved for those who undergo proper education and training, which should be either basic or vocational. It should not be designed to help gangsters to write self-serving sociological epistles to the newspapers. There should be punishments, tangible and telling, which can be imposed by governors, usually involving the deprivation of liberties and privileges. These are illustrations, not an exhaustive list of measures.

Criminals do not offend against their fellow human beings because they have too little self-esteem but because they have too much. The guiding words should be those of Winston Churchill, with his 'hard coinage of punishment', and of the old Prison Commissioners, who talked of the 'due punishment of responsible persons' and stated some important truths when they declared: 'The penalty of crime is in the dishonouring circumstances which must accompany loss of liberty; in the deprivation of what liberty permits in the way of indulgence and self-gratification; in compulsory labour; in the loss of self-respect.'

Our mistake has been to reform our prisons so that they might suit Bertrand Russell and Fenner Brockway quite well. However, the kind of people who actually dwell in them are seldom either philosophers or pacifists.

VI

Evil drug-dealers

The war on drugs, if it was ever fought, was lost in the late 1960s when the authorities stopped disapproving of them. The struggle against narcotics is a moral crusade or it is nothing. A morally literate people would not want to stupefy themselves. The only thing that the law can do about drug-taking is to encourage and reinforce a generally accepted moral message, that this action is wrong and wicked. It can disapprove and by doing so strengthen the will of the individual tempted to buy. It can punish and so reinforce the message of parent and teacher that this is one of the things the wise person should not do.

The liberal elite, however, has never really felt that it is wicked to seek chemical oblivion. Many of its members have used illegal drugs in the past. Many have children or friends who use them now.

The ruling class has tried, not very hard, to discourage an activity that it does not really think of as wrong. In doing so it has helped to spread the idea that narcotics are not wrong in themselves, that those who take them are innocent victims of wicked persons who sell drugs to them. This means that, increasingly, great forces are deployed to attack the suppliers of drugs, while few or none at all are mobilized against the people who buy them. The product is vile and the traffickers in it viler still, but the buyers who obtain these vile substances from these villainous people are to be pitied and exonerated.

However, many citizens do persist in thinking that drug-taking is wrong, making it difficult for the elite to legalize what many of its members see as a normal pleasure. The state is also bound by international treaties to prevent the legal sale of many drugs. To make matters more complicated, some drugs are so unpleasant and devastating in their effects on those who take them that even social liberals disapprove of them. The difference between these drugs and the ones of which they approve is hard to see, except by an ill-defined scale of horror and disgust. Cannabis is supposedly 'soft', although in some genetically-engineered versions it has as potent an effect on the brain as heroin. Heroin is supposedly 'hard', though even this substance has its defenders. Cocaine is halfway between the two but, in the form of 'crack', it becomes 'hard'. Ecstasy pills, widely regarded by teenagers as harmless pleasure tablets, suddenly appear dangerous when, as they occasionally do, they kill those who take them. Their long-term effects are as yet unknown, but they are likely to be significant. Far more public concern is voiced about the possible ill effects of mobile phones.

Much anti-drug propaganda brackets legal alcohol and tobacco with illegal cannabis. This (unintentionally?) makes it hard for a generation who smoke tobacco and drink beer, wine and whisky to tell their children to stay away from marijuana. The comparison is false. While some people drink to get drunk, most do not, whereas nobody smokes cannabis for the taste. All of them smoke it to become intoxicated. And tobacco, although harmful, is hardly a powerful mind-altering substance. Then there is the campaign for the 'medical use' of cannabis, winning the sympathy of millions who would never otherwise listen to campaigns for drug legalization.

Without a clear moral objection to drug-taking as such, or to law-breaking as such, the law and its enforcement do not make sense. As a result, the 'war against drugs' has often been reduced to hysterical slogans, ludicrous advertising campaigns, bizarre self-defeating actions and comically misplaced efforts. In more recent years it has begun to offer the young instructions on how to take drugs 'safely' – an approach for some reason not tried in the official campaigns against cigarette smoking or driving while drunk. And it has utterly failed, to the great cost of the country. As the Royal Navy and the SAS churn the seas or slip through the Colombian jungle in pursuit of drug-smugglers and producers, the Metropolitan Police publicly announce that they will look the other way if they see people openly smoking illegal cannabis and the Home Secretary legally downgrades cannabis to the law's lowest possible danger level. How long before they do the same with the cocaine which the SAS and the Navy try so hard to interdict and suppress?

This feeble approach to the drug issue is yet another result of the elite's rejection of absolute right and wrong. A system based on clear moral choice would condemn all kinds of deliberate intoxication. Interestingly, the same elite state has done much to relax England's alcohol laws over the same period, allowing longer opening hours while claiming, absurdly, that these have had no effect on behaviour. Conventions governing alcohol advertising have buckled so that many drinks are now openly promoted purely because they are strong. The only form of drunkenness that is either officially or unofficially discouraged is drunken driving.

Much of this relaxation is the result of a thoughtless selfishness among the elite themselves. Parental control is now so weak and the fashion for drug-taking so strong that the sons of a Home Secretary and of the heir to the throne have been revealed to be involved with cannabis. No parent, however exalted or morally well equipped, can confidently assume that his teenage children will not do the same. Those who privately believe cannabis to be harmless gravely increase this risk. They themselves have led successful and prosperous lives, and they believe that because such drugs did not harm them they will not harm others. To remove the fear of prosecution from themselves and their offspring, they seek to weaken the law for everyone. In doing so, they forget the many millions who cannot cope so well with such things and the many more millions who must live alongside them and suffer from their behaviour – especially the epidemic theft of portable goods to pay the price of narcotic pleasure.

Enormous amounts of 'petty' crime are linked to drug-taking. The theft of small saleable items, preferably electronic, is the quickest way of raising money to pay a dealer. Aggressive begging, which often comes close to mugging, is another. Mugging itself is, of course, a third. This resort to theft is quite logical. A drug habit, which is a selfish and arrogant form of behaviour in itself, increases the need for money while reducing the inclination to work for it or to care about the consequences of so-called 'petty' crime.

In some poorer parts of the country, boys of eleven and twelve are stealing to pay for cannabis. Measured on the moral scale of the elite, this is unimportant compared with the risk that the child of a media figure might get a criminal record for possessing a few ounces of cannabis. It is considered too much to ask the children of the ruling class to obey the law, but perfectly reasonable to condemn huge swathes of society to lawless dishonesty. Once, this would have been called class justice, but since class is now based on power and celebrity rather than wealth or moral standing, such expressions are no longer used.

It also does not seem to occur to those who argue this position that a strongly enforced law against cannabis would actually protect their children from pressure to join the drug-culture. If there were a real chance of arrest, conviction and prison for doing so, many would have a good, permanent excuse for refusing to buy or smoke cannabis. Instead, elite commentators complain that enforcement of the existing law would 'criminalize' their young. This view, often advanced by people who consider themselves to be conservatives, reveals an extraordinary attitude to the law. The fact is that users of illegal drugs criminalize themselves by breaking the criminal law. They have the freedom to keep the law or to break it.

Perhaps the most eloquent denunciation of modern England's long, lazy and self-deluding weakness in this matter is to be found in the first volume of Malcolm Muggeridge's autobiography, *Chronicles of Wasted Time*. He recalls his time as a teacher in Egypt in the 1920s and the efforts then being made by the authorities to try to stamp out hashish in an attempt to bring about modernization and national revival, in imitation of Turkey's reforms under Ataturk. After describing the listlessness and sloth of students addicted to hashish smoking, Muggeridge wrote:

> Russell Pasha, the head policeman and the last Englishman to hold the post, was particularly active in trying to prevent hashish getting into the country, and in reducing indulgence in it. At the League of Nations, too, the suppression of the traffic in hashish was one of the few things the member states unanimously agreed about. If anyone then had suggested that all this endeavour was misplaced because hashish did little harm, and was anyway non-addictive, the suggestion would have been received with incredulity and derision. To the best of my knowledge no one at all reputable, or for that matter disreputable, ever did make such a suggestion. I had to wait forty years to hear it made, and then not just by crackpots and wild libertarians; but by respected citizens, clergymen, purported scientific investigators and other ostensibly informed and enlightened persons.
>
> When I hear or read their apologies for hashish, I recall the Zaffaran Palace [seat of Cairo University at the time] and the stupefied faces and inert minds of so many of the students there; the dreadful instances of the destructive effects of this drug on bodies and minds which any resident in the Middle East was bound to encounter. I know of no better exemplification of the death wish at the heart of our way of life than this determination to bring about the legalisation of hashish so that it may ravage the West as it has the Middle and Far East.

This should be coupled with Allan Bloom's denunciation of rock music and its accomplice, the drug-culture, in *The Closing of the American Mind*:

> Rock music provides premature ecstasy and, in this respect, is like the drugs with which it is allied. It artificially produces the exaltation naturally attached to the completion of the greatest endeavours – victory in a just war, consummated love, artistic creation, religious devotion and discovery of the truth.
>
> Without effort, without talent, without virtue, without exercise of the faculties, anyone and everyone is accorded the equal right to the enjoyment of their fruits. In my experience, students who have had a serious fling with drugs – and gotten over it – find it difficult to have enthusiasms or great expectations. It is as though the colour has been drained out of their lives and they see everything in black and white. The pleasure they experienced in the beginning was so intense that they no longer look for it at the end or as the end. They may function perfectly well, but dryly, routinely. Their energy has been sapped, and they do not expect their life's activity to produce anything but a living, whereas liberal education is supposed to encourage the belief that the good life is the pleasant life and that the best life is the most pleasant life… as long as they have the Walkman on, they cannot hear what the great tradition has to say. And after its prolonged use, when they take it off, they find they are deaf.

Both men have understood what our political leaders have failed to grasp: that drugs are the enemy of the moral society in which effort is rewarded by exaltation and success in this world. Oddly enough, rock musicians and those who surround them immediately understood that the implicit message of narcotics was the same as theirs – a challenge to the hated suburban work ethic. By providing exaltation without effort, while making success an empty matter of cash and possessions, they strip the striving classes of their motivation to be good and to work hard.

The striving classes are not only what is usually called the middle class. They include all those who, in modern economies, have worked hard to better themselves or to maintain a respectable and honest place in the world. Drugs and rock music, in contrast, cause people to stay in the same place or even to sink, and encourage their dependence on the state. Political discontent and criticism of the existing order are rare among the children of the middle class, who have found inner contentment in a culture of easy intoxication, rock music and sex. They are even rarer in what used to be the working class. Heroin is on easy sale in Manchester, Merthyr and Grimethorpe, where it blurs the minds of the losers in the industrial conflicts of the 1970s and 1980s. As for the new generations, uneducated, unemployable, illiterate and yet exposed to all the blandishments and temptations of modern advertising, dope and pills are a double salvation. They make the dull world shine and they offer fast, tax-free income to those prepared to deal and trade in them.

Another argument ignored by the authorities is the one that says that we owe a responsibility to those who nurtured us not to throw the gift of life back in their faces. Given that the effects of narcotics are still only dimly known, no wise or intelligent person should risk such an important part of his body – if not for his own sake, then for the sake of his parents, brothers, sisters and friends.

However, a sternly moral society is needed to reinforce such views with law. Modern England is not such a society. Only the dimmest young person could have failed to notice what happened in 1967 when several members of the Rolling Stones were charged with various drugs offences. At this distance it is pointless to delve into the details of the charges. The truth about the long-ago evening at a farmhouse in the incongrously cosy Sussex seaside village of West Wittering will remain elusive and disputed. What is important is that, given an opportunity to make an example of several prominent rock stars, at a time when rock stars were well known to be dabbling in drugs and their actions were influencing the young, Britain's governing classes deliberately missed that opportunity. Mick Jagger was charged with the possession of four amphetamine tablets for which he had no prescription. Nineteen police officers surged into Keith Richards's house where, among other things, they found Marianne Faithfull clad only in a fur rug which kept slipping from her shapely form.

The atmosphere at the time, as viewed by one hormonal fifteen-year-old schoolboy (the author), was of a war between the generations. The dreadful cliché is for once absolutely accurate. The beliefs and morals of those who had been through the war were losing their grip. The giant commercial and emotional power of rock music had harnessed the great flood of self-pity and self-important angst of millions of teenagers. It had turned it into a sort of immoral force. Things that were not important at all, such as the length of a man's hair, were suddenly crucial. Jagger was said to have told the *Daily Mirror:* 'Teenagers are not screaming over pop music any more, they're screaming for much deeper reasons. We are only serving as a means of giving them an outlet. Teenagers the world over are weary of being pushed around by half-witted politicians who attempt to dominate their way of thinking and set a code for their living. They want to be free and have the right of expression, of thinking and living without any petty restrictions.' It sounds remarkably like Anthony Blair's speech in Stevenage thirty years later, in which he spoke of being part of the rock-and-roll generation. Mr Blair's award of a knighthood to Sir Michael Jagger in June 2002 neatly closed a political and cultural circle.

Instinctively, the authorities knew that those four apparently insignificant pills were enormously important. The arrest of Mick Jagger, hero of the teen delinquent and the waking nightmare of the teenage girl's respectable mother, was like the sound of gunfire in the hills outside the city. The rebels were approaching the suburbs. Did what was left of the grown-up establishment have the strength and will to stop them?

When Jagger's trial began on 27 June it seemed as if they did. For a war between generations, it was exceedingly polite. Judge David Block dealt briskly but fairly with such matters as the curious clothes worn by Keith Richards and with the lady in the fur rug, yet the contrast between the judge and the defendants remains astonishing. Block, who was to die in 1980, was a distinguished and decorated former naval officer. He had survived the Japanese sinking of the aircraft carrier HMS *Hermes* in the Indian Ocean in 1942 and was present at the destruction off North Cape of the German raider *Scharnhorst* in 1943. What must he have felt about the people appearing before him, whose liberty to behave in this way he had personally defended at such risk to himself? What did he think when Keith Richards said: 'We are not old men. We are not concerned with petty morals'? Yet he still sought to be fair. 'Put out of your minds any prejudice you may feel about the way Richards dresses, or his observations about petty morals,' he told the jury. 'Disregard the evidence as to the young lady who was alleged by the police to have been in some condition of undress.' Whether they obeyed him or not, the jury found Jagger and Richards guilty and the judge sent Jagger to prison for three months. Despite claims that a mysterious interloper may have brought drugs into the house, Richards was imprisoned for a year. A poll in the *Daily Mail* found that 56 per cent of the population aged between twenty-one and thirty-four thought the sentence on Jagger was not harsh enough. Only 12 per cent thought Judge Block had been too severe. In the end it was the middle-aged establishment, not the supposedly rebellious young, which came to their aid.

For the pair were not freed by an enraged mob of teenagers. The walls of Brixton Prison were not torn down by the bare hands of the rock and roll generation. Their salvation came from *The Times* newspaper, supposed to be the voice of the establishment, in words penned by a conservative Roman Catholic, William Rees-Mogg. He managed to compare Jagger to Oscar Wilde in a leading article surmounted by Alexander Pope's words: 'Who breaks a butterfly on the wheel?' Perhaps the comparison was actually unfair to Jagger. Wilde had brought his persecution on himself with a stupid libel action and disdained several chances to save himself. Jagger was also in the throes of a libel action against the *News of the World* (later dropped), but had most certainly not sought his troubles as keenly as Wilde had done. Wilde's offence was loathed by almost everyone, including many of his friends. It would be nearly a century before he would become a hero, except to other outcasts. Jagger's alleged offence was viewed as harmless even by many of his critics. He would be a hero before his appeal was heard.

Rees-Mogg's leader minimized the drugs involved and suggested that the star was suffering from strain and exhaustion. Then he argued against what has always been one of the main purposes of the criminal justice system – to make an example of those who come before it: 'It should be the particular quality of British justice to ensure that Mr Jagger is treated exactly the same as anyone else, no better and no worse. There must remain a suspicion in this case that Mr Jagger received a more severe sentence than would have been thought proper for any purely anonymous young man.' He added: 'There are many people who take a primitive view of the matter. They consider that Mr Jagger has "got what was coming to him". They resent the anarchic quality of the Rolling Stones' performances, dislike their songs, dislike their influence on teenagers and broadly suspect them of decadence.' Indeed they did.

However, decadent or not, the Rolling Stones could afford excellent lawyers. Jagger was rapidly bailed and his appeal was heard with great speed. Davin Seay, in a biography of Jagger, quotes the rock star's counsel, Michael Havers, as saying: 'It was imperative that I get those convictions overturned or Mick and Keith, with drug convictions on their records, would not be able to enter the United States to perform their concerts.' On 31 July, Richards's conviction was overturned on appeal by Lord Parker, the Lord Chief Justice of England, in person. Richards was absent from the courtroom owing to an attack of chickenpox which he said he did not wish to give to anyone else. Jagger, wearing jacket and tie (albeit a mauve, blue and yellow one) for the occasion, stood to attention when the judge spoke to him and actually bowed to the bench at one point. His conviction was turned into a conditional discharge and his prison sentence cancelled. Interestingly, Parker directly contradicted the great Rees-Mogg editorial, saying to Jagger: 'You are, whether you like it or not, an idol of a large number of the young in this country. Being in that position, you have very grave responsibilities and, if you do come to be punished, it is only natural that those responsibilities should carry a higher penalty.' However, he felt that testimony from Jagger's doctor, saying he had verbally approved the sort of pills Jagger was found with, was 'the strongest mitigation there is'. And he said the tenuousness of the evidence against Richards meant that his conviction should be quashed altogether.

Teenage troublemakers everywhere rejoiced. So, presumably, did those who hoped that the Rolling Stones would continue to be profitable, especially in the USA, that largest of all markets for British rock music. The rebels had fought their way out of the hills, taken the outer suburbs and would soon be marching through the streets of the capital. The establishment had suffered a total and unmitigated defeat, although few of its then members could have imagined that thirty-five years later Jagger would become a Knight Bachelor and that neither he nor the public would find this event especially ludicrous.

After his release, Jagger was almost immediately flown by helicopter to an Essex stately home (the property of Sir John Ruggles-Brise, nephew of the great prison reformer) to meet his saviour, Rees-Mogg. The editor of *The Times* then informed the rock superstar: 'You are often taken as a symbol of rebellion.' The heir of Sir William Haley went on to ask the singer of 'Let's Spend the Night Together': 'Do you feel that society has a great deal in it today that ought to be rebelled against?' The truly rebellious answer to that question would have been: 'No, I am a member of one of the luckiest, most prosperous, safest, most pampered generations ever to have lived, growing up in one of the freest countries on earth under the benign rule of law. Why should I complain or rebel?' It did not come, for, while it might have been true, it was not what Jagger was expected to say or what he had been encouraged by adulation to think. Nor was it what the producers of Granada TV's *World in Action* – or Rees-Mogg, for that matter – would have wanted to hear. They believed that Britain as it had been was finished. They were only too happy to sit and be chastised for their reactionary fustiness. They liked being congratulated for their open-minded acceptance of the exciting new age. It would be wonderful to know what Jagger actually thought during this absurd exchange. But we probably never shall.

The defeatist attitude of such people as Rees-Mogg was shared in the official world. During the Jagger affair a great band of worthy and fashionable persons had signed an advertisement in *The Times* calling for changes in the cannabis law. Even before they had done this, a Whitehall committee was at work on undermining that law. It was to be the first of many such committees, all determined to establish that the narcotics laws were too fierce, all unmoved by the enormous increase in narcotics use that accompanied their verdicts. On 1 November 1968 the committee, under the leadership of Baroness Wootton of Abinger, reported. They concluded:

> We think that the adverse effects which the consumption
> of cannabis in even small amounts may produce in some
> people should not be dismissed as insignificant. We have
> no doubt that the wider use of cannabis should not be
> encouraged. On the other hand we think that the dangers
> of its use as commonly accepted in the past and the risk
> of its progression to opiates have been overstated, and
> that the existing criminal sanctions intended to curb its
> use are unjustifiably severe.

Witnesses to the committee included R. D. Laing, the ultra-radical and fashionable psychiatrist, William Levy, editor of the counter-culture magazine *IT* (*International Times*), Martin Sharp, a 'representative' of the equally counter-cultural magazine *OZ*, and the radical journalist Peter Laurie. They recommended that there should be no use of imprisonment to punish possession of small quantities of cannabis. They also urged that the use of private premises for drug consumption (which had been an issue in the Keith Richards case) should be excluded from legal penalties. They called for a review of police powers on search and arrest, and said that the law should be recast to give Parliament greater flexibility of control. They urged, too, that the law should separate cannabis and heroin as soon as possible. These recommendations would all eventually take effect in one form or another. Once again, anyone wondering what were the authorities' true feelings towards drugs would have been filled with doubt about their resolve.

In the following years, as the law against cannabis was weakened, its enforcement weakened as well. Quietly, police forces began to ignore the possession of small amounts of the drug. Quietly, the rhetoric of politicians shifted from condemnation of drug-taking to denunciation of drug-dealing. Drug-dealers were constantly described as evil.

By the 1980s it was plain to any thinking person, and to many unthinking ones, that the government did not really know what to do about drugs. A poster campaign warning of the health risks of heroin – 'Heroin Screws You Up' – not only failed to persuade anyone but its artwork, showing tragic, hollow-faced people in dark and desperate circumstances, became a rare collector's item. A programme was launched to offer heroin addicts the supposedly less harmful methadone instead. Many then sold the methadone to buy heroin. Others found that the substitute was a potent drug in its own right. By early 2002 more than a million prescriptions for methadone were being issued each year. Projects for the treatment of drug-addicts sprang up everywhere. A fashionable doctrine of 'harm reduction' was widely adopted. This assumed that the young would inevitably take illegal drugs and offered them advice on how to do so safely, or at least more safely.

At first this was semi-official, carried on by privately financed organizations. It soon began to be the official view, and was confirmed as such in January 2002 when the government sponsored an advertising campaign urging club-goers to consult the Drugs Helpline for advice on narcotic safety. The helpline, run by a private company but paid for out of taxes, took a 'non-judgemental' view of drugs. Its website described their properties and their effects, often in terms that made them sound quite attractive. At no point did it try to say that drug-taking was wrong in itself. However, it did reveal the legal classification of drugs and state which were illegal. This step had been foreshadowed some years previously when a Tory government bill licensing dance clubs in Scotland had stipulated that they should provide 'chill-out' rooms where users of the illegal drug ecstasy could drink water and rest after taking it. In March 2001 similar advice was offered by the government to clubs in England, and a Home Office minister, Robert Ainsworth, said that society had to recognize that illegal drug use had become an integral part of a clubber's night out.

Meanwhile the assault on respectability and the ethic of sobriety continued. An independent charity grandly calling itself the Police Foundation (which actually had no direct connection with the police) produced a report calling for the effective decriminalization of cannabis and ecstasy. The report was taken seriously in some highly conservative quarters. Few noticed that the group of people who had prepared the report contained not a single person who believed that drug-taking was morally wrong.

The Dutch government's experiment with relaxing cannabis laws in Amsterdam has been widely and one-sidedly praised by the British media. In fact, the project has had many problems and is widely disliked by many people in the Netherlands, who object to the easy availability of drugs and the large number of cannabis cafés that have opened near their homes. The reform was followed by a 250 per cent rise in the use of cannabis by Dutch adolescents and a 22 per cent increase in the number of registered hard-drug-addicts.

Interestingly, almost nothing has been heard of another experiment with legalization, in the American state of Alaska. The experiment, significantly, was imposed by the State Supreme Court and overturned by democracy. From 1975 to 1990 Alaskans could legally possess four ounces of cannabis for private use at home. Crime, welfare dependency and health problems all increased during this period. The argument that making a drug legal reduces its glamour for the young also proved false. Use among Alaskan teenagers rose to triple the USA's national average. In 1990 the state's citizens organized a 40,000-signature petition to hold a referendum on the law. Despite being outspent ten to one by the pro-cannabis lobby during the campaign, they restored the anti-cannabis law by a vote of 55 to 45 per cent. If decriminalization is such a good idea, so free of problems, this result is hard to explain. Rather than seek to explain, however, cannabis legalizers generally either do not know about it or prefer not to discuss it, referring instead to Amsterdam which they misleadingly represent as a pure triumph of enlightenment.

The sobriety ethic has also come under attack from those who claim that cannabis is a useful medicine. They have been given a kindly hearing by academics and the media as well as a government research project to test their claims. This is absurd. The University of Mississippi has literally thousands of research papers on the medical effects of cannabis, all of them critical. The evidence for the miracle properties of cannabis is scanty, to say the least. For instance, a glaucoma sufferer would have to smoke cannabis every two hours to obtain relief (that is, four thousand times per year), and would be too intoxicated to make sense of any improved vision that might result. Many promising drugs, which do not need to be smoked and are available in easily measured quantities, never make it to the market because of much smaller problems than this. It is also inter-

THE CAUSES OF CRIME

esting that the powerful and wealthy pharmaceutical industry, which could make a vast fortune out of a pill that provided euphoria without harmful side effects, has yet to produce any such product. Perhaps euphoria always exacts a price.

Because of the way it is smoked, cannabis causes disfiguring mouth, tongue and lip cancers. It is also more dangerous to the lungs than tobacco. Modern versions of the drug, intensively cultivated, are vastly stronger and more dangerous than Beatles-era marijauna. Cannabis can trigger latent schizophrenia and wipes out the effect of anti-schizophrenia drugs. It remains active in the body for days, and is found ever more frequently in the corpses of dead drivers after accidents. Any prescription drug that had one-tenth of these effects would be withdrawn from sale amid a national panic.

One rare opponent of cannabis among the liberal elite has been the Oxford Professor, Susan Greenfield, who, as she launched her TV series about the brain, told liberal pro-drug campaigners they were fools. 'You've got this beautiful, lovely thing that's evolved, and it's all yours, and then along comes this drug and it goes... splat!', she said graphically. Knowing how the brain works, she could not understand drug-takers: 'They wouldn't go about slashing up their muscles. Why on earth would they want to damage their brains?' Professor Greenfield's opposition is rare among her generation. So is detailed knowledge of the working of the human brain, her speciality.

The main ingredient of cannabis, tetrahydrocannabinol (THC), has been available for years on hospital prescription in the UK as the anti-nausea drug nabilone, which can be given in proper measured doses and is sometimes supplied to patients undergoing chemotherapy. However, it cannot provide a euphoric 'high', which is perhaps why campaigners for medical cannabis prefer to forget its existence. In fact, the whole 'medical use' argument is consciously false, as was unwisely admitted by the leader of America's pro-legalization campaign, Keith Stroup. He told an audience at Emory

University in 1979 that the pro-cannabis campaign would use the medical marijuana argument as a red-herring to give pot a good name. This was recorded in the campus newspaper, the Emory *Wheel*, of 6 February 1979: 'We are trying to get marijuana reclassified medically. If we do that... [we will] be using the issue as a red herring to give marijuana a good name.' In which case it must be one of the most effective red-herrings in history.

The alternative approach to the British one has been partly tried in America: strong moral and cultural resistance supported by decisive prosecutions and police hostility. For years the US federal government campaigned resolutely against drug abuse and backed its moral arguments with legal punishments. The number of illicit drug users dropped from 24.3 million in 1979 to 11.4 million in 1992. In the following years, crime of all kinds also began to fall. Researchers are still arguing about the reasons for this decline. It is at least possible that reductions in crime were the result of reduced drug abuse.

Strangely, many conservatives in Britain (and America) would not be interested in that fact if it were the case. To the delight of the liberal elite, who would not relish a proper debate on this subject, these conservatives have adopted what they believe to be a 'libertarian' position on drug abuse. This allows them to support the dismantling of the laws against cannabis. Presumably, in the future it will permit them to attack the laws against other drugs as well. (An article to this effect by the noted conservative pundit, Bruce Anderson, was published in the *Spectator* in March 2002.) They contend that drug-taking is a private decision in which the law has no business. They also say that the law, by persecuting suppliers, does nothing but encourage the growth of crime. They suggest that keeping the existing laws against drugs is the equivalent of American alcohol prohibition in the 1920s and 1930s, doomed to fail and a boon to gangsters.

The parallel is false, since alcohol was already well established in the USA, and especially among Italian, German and Irish immigrant groups, before prohibition was attempted. Drugs, even cannabis, are not yet accepted as part of British culture and remain a minority pursuit. They could become part of the culture, but only once all legal and moral sanctions against them have been removed. The problem of gangsters benefiting from the illegal nature of their goods is more difficult. Such people have always profited from evading the law, under many different circumstances. No doubt the rewards of drug-smuggling are increased by its legal prohibition. That would not in itself be an argument for relaxing controls. If the substance involved is dangerous and unwelcome, this kind of thing will happen during the effort to banish it. If the effort is successful, the problem will be temporary. The real difficulty is that controlling the supply while effectively encouraging demand is bound to fail. If the suppliers faced severe penalties for smuggling and a diminishing market as well, then they would eventually abandon their efforts.

But the main foundation of the 'libertarian' argument is in some ways more insidious. It is a folly that paralyses conservative democracies faced with an assault on the culture of effort and reward. It has captured influential journals, including the *Economist* magazine, where Frances Cairncross recently cited an argument of the great libertarian John Stuart Mill – that the individual is sovereign over his own mind and body – in support of the legalization of cannabis, and explained that the *Economist* would in future support that cause. Her arguments, however, were elegantly answered by Norman Dennis, Director of Community Studies at the Institute for the Study of Civil Society. Dennis, in an article published in the *Salisbury Review*, points out that Cairncross bases her case on only one of Mill's positions and retorts: 'That does not mean, for Mill, either that other people must accept that the sovereign individual is right, or that his free choice must be costless to him. Other people can properly display their dislike and disapprobation of the sovereign individual's choice. They can properly offer him advice and employ persuasion. They can legitimately shun him.' Dennis continues:

The sovereignty of the individual is not Mill's only
principle. He says just as firmly that 'whenever there is
a definite damage, or a definite risk of damage, either to
[another] individual or to the public, the case is taken out
of the province of liberty and placed in that of morality
or law.'

It is true that he comes down against the legal
prohibition of the only drug he deals with, alcohol,
while fully admitting that the mischief a person does by
intemperance can seriously affect those nearly connected
to him. In reaching all his concrete policy conclusions,
Mill makes it clear that the application of his two
principles depends on the circumstances of the time.

He says there are some times and some places where
there is no advantage at all in people breaking the rules.
At other times there is an advantage in them doing so,
namely when they act 'not only differently but better'.
He was specifically concerned with an increasingly
powerful Victorian public opinion, demanding and
securing more and more elevated and rigid moral
controls from the community and the state.

For this reason, Dennis says, it is an anachronism to use Mill's arguments against oppressive Victorian morality to support the case for
drug legalization in twenty-first-century Britain:

Oppressive morality scarcely exists and British teenagers
are now the heaviest drinkers, smokers and drug-takers
in Europe. The most effective argument today for
freedom to take drugs is that it is impossible for either
public opinion or the police to do anything to diminish
drug taking, and that therefore the moral and legal towel
should be thrown in, in defeat and despair. That is the
complete opposite to Mill's argument for liberty in 1859.

Dennis quotes Mill's warning that civilization can become 'so degenerate that neither its appointed priests or teachers, nor anybody else, has the capacity or the will to take the trouble to stand up for it'.

Failure upon failure – the failure of a free country to recognize a peril, the failure of an elite class to understand the moral basis of its own influence and power, the failure of the criminal justice and police systems to support their own laws, and now the failure of conservatives to distinguish between liberty and licence – have together combined to make narcotic drugs effectively legal in England. The consequences of this have only just begun to be felt. As the resulting selfishness, indolence and theft spread through the country many may come to regret it. As the resulting separation of effort and reward destroys sobriety and the work ethic, all these problems will be doubled and redoubled so that what used to be an efficient and functioning civilization stumbles down the staircase into a condition of Third World confusion and squalor from which only the rich will be able to escape.

During 2001 and 2002, many senior police officers openly supported the relaxation of laws against cannabis and, with government approval, publicly abandoned any effort to enforce the law against this drug in Brixton, one of the most crime-stricken areas of the capital. This 'experiment' was swiftly classified as a success and extended to the rest of the country. The excuse was advanced that this would free officers to fight other sorts of crime – an excuse that appeared particularly feeble when crime, and especially robbery, immediately increased sharply in the same district. In July 2001 the number of street robberies in Lambeth reached 760, a 56 per cent increase over the previous year. Later, it would be claimed that street crime had diminished following the introduction of the softer approach to cannabis and that this was a beneficial result of the switching of resources. In fact, there were widespread complaints from residents that dealing in all drugs had become more intense. As for the reduction in street crime, it was not what it appeared. In

February 2002 the number of street crimes was 556, slightly below the 562 of February 2001. However, at this time Lambeth was one of nine London boroughs specially targeted by the Metropolitan Police in an attempt to combat street crime, by diverting officers from their 'normal' duties to patrolling the streets. Reductions in street crime were recorded everywhere that this strategy was introduced, not only in Lambeth. The idea that the drop in street crime was the consequence of the softer approach to cannabis was, to put it mildly, questionable. Yet it was claimed by the policy's supporters that it was so. The abandonment of proper law enforcement was alleged be a rational use of resources. On closer examination, it looks much more like the degeneration of civilization.

VII

Twelve angry persons

The jury is more noble in theory than in reality. There is nothing especially elevating in the sight of twelve people crammed into a room trying to decide whether to ruin a fellow human being's life. Yet for once, the idea *is* more important than the practice. As long as these strange committees continue to exist, governments are less powerful and citizens are more free.

Two things happen to trials when a jury is present. First, there is an element of doubt about the outcome that is quite beyond the control of the state. This turns the presumption of innocence from a mere slogan into a real possibility. Some on the jury may actually be prepared to believe that the police have the wrong man. Secondly, the prosecution's huge advantage over the defence is greatly reduced. The defence is not an interloper among officials but one of two contestants before a panel that owes nothing to either side.

Regrettably, this arrangement can help some criminals escape justice, although it is certainly not bound to do so. This is the price we pay for its benefits to freedom of thought and speech. It is why it is better, not just in general but for human liberty, that a hundred guilty men should go free than that one innocent man should be imprisoned. The question 'better for whom?' is often asked. The answer must be 'better for everyone'. These freedoms have until recently been considered so valuable that wise people accepted the painful cost. Now, however, that wisdom is repeatedly overruled on the grounds of expense or convenience. Governments constantly make it easier for wrongdoers to mock the law or escape justice by changing the rules of evidence, by weakening the police, by seeking to empty the prisons and reducing penalties to the point where they are meaningless. The same governments become piously self-righteous about plans to remove or reduce jury trial, claiming that restricting this right is a 'crime-fighting' measure designed to strengthen the law. They even claim that jury trial is not a right at all. The blazing hypocrisy of this attitude is matched only by its sheer nerve, its oppressive brutality and its small-mindedness.

Without a jury, the legal process is like any other government action. Strip the process of arrest, trial, conviction, sentence and appeal down to its basic parts and it is quite simple. A series of state employees, few of them especially brave or intelligent or percep-tive, are asked to approve the original decision of another state employee. The chances are strong that they will do so at every stage, and will feel that this is what they are paid to do.

Police, prosecutor and judge are all representatives of power, reluctant to admit that they might be mistaken. There is a danger that the defence lawyer will become the state's advocate to the defendant, rather than the defendant's advocate to the state. In fully totalitarian countries, lawyers are either too afraid to act for the defence, or accept their client's guilt and do no more than plead for a lower sentence. In those without juries but with a measure of freedom, the defence starts at a disadvantage and the defendant is required to co-operate in the investigation of his own alleged offence long before he comes to trial. And when guilt is assumed, habeas corpus and other protections against long pre-trial detention seem idle.

In short, jury trial is a grave nuisance to the authorities, especially to governments which believe they have a moral purpose, as the

Blair administration does. It is constantly under attack because of the benevolent state's instinctive impulse to take absolute power so as to be more effectively benevolent. Even where juries exist, they can face severe intimidation from judges and governments. Their right to exist at all, let alone to act freely, is not always guaranteed. When, as in the USA, they are part of the holy writ of the constitution, they can still be avoided by such methods as the use of military tribunals under the excuse of a 'war against terror'.

When, as in England, they are supported by nothing but ancient custom, they can be attacked on the grounds of incompetence, delay and cost, and gradually removed from the courtroom. All too many democrats and libertarians will not come instinctively to the defence of juries. Totalitarians, quicker to see their true purpose, unfailingly recognize them as an enemy and attack them on sight. French juries were abolished in 1940 by the German National Socialist occupation authorities. Dictators fear not only what juries do now but what they might do in a tight corner. However, it is not only naked tyrants who mistrust them. All governments do so, and when France was liberated and the republic reborn, juries did not return.

The assault on juries in England has been far more subtle than on the Continent where, after a brief vogue following the French Revolution, jury systems were established and later suppressed or abandoned in several countries, including Prussia, Hungary and the Netherlands. In England, and in a different form in Scotland, they simply continued uninterrupted. However, thanks to a series of changes and reforms, the institution is now significantly weaker in England than it was at the start of the 1960s. It is soon likely to become weaker still.

In the 1950s, an innocent person might well have been convicted of a crime, but only through the incompetence of the police or the courts, or very occasionally through the malice and dishonesty of individual officers. A guilty person might well have walked free, but only through the incompetence of the prosecution. The danger came from imperfections in the justice system itself, not from a state machine with a desire to increase its power at the expense of its citizens. By the start of the twenty-first century, England was slowly approaching the point, unknown for centuries, where an innocent person could in theory be convicted *at the wish of the state*. At the same time, and for connected reasons, acquittals on the grounds of class prejudice and hostility to the prevailing ideology were also slowly becoming possible.

The first whisper of approaching danger came with the report of the Departmental Committee on Jury Service, chaired by Lord Morris of Borth-y-Gest, set up by the Tory Home Secretary, Henry Brooke, in May 1963. It reported to a Labour government almost two years later, and although it took some time for its recommendations to gain government support, they came to pass in the end. The England of the time simply could not cope with the idea that middle-class, property-owning people were the best source of juries.

As it turned out, the committee could not come up with a better scheme. However, in the fashion of the time, change was deemed to be good in itself. It did not have to be for the better, as long as it acknowledged the growing fashion for egalitarianism. The inquiry began respectfully at the beginning. It took the view, preferred by traditionalists, that English juries dated from Magna Carta and replaced trial by ordeal, rather than that Henry II had brought them into being. It also accepted that juries had often been overridden by naked power and needed to be strong to be effective. The courage of jurors and judges alike had won juries a measure of true freedom by the end of the seventeenth century. The great confrontation of 1670 known as 'Bushell's case' involved the acquittal of two prominent Quakers, Penn and Mead, accused of taking part in an unlawful assembly. The crown was furious at the verdict. The jury were kept without food or drink for three days until they almost starved. Then, when they still refused to alter their verdicts, they were marched into prison. In a revolutionary judgement, however,

Lord Chief Justice Vaughan released them on a writ of habeas corpus, ruling simply that the law of England forbade the punishment of jurors.

This, combined with the astonishing English reverence for the law which had been so greatly reinforced by the dictatorial behaviour of the Cromwell regime, changed the history of the world. By liberating jurors from the fear of oppressive judges, it made possible the defiant acquittal of the 'Seven Bishops' which destroyed the autocracy of James II. It was the free jury, as much as any other power, that made possible the Glorious Revolution of 1688 and the limited constitutional monarchy that followed. Otherwise, the course of the seventeenth century, so decisive in the history of England, France and America, would have been utterly different. The freer England of the late eighteenth century gave still more independence to the jury. The 'Fox Libel Act' of 1792 provided juries with an invaluable weapon in the defence of freedom. This law took away the power of judges to order juries to convict in cases of criminal libel, a charge then often used to persecute political dissenters.

It is clear from this history that the main effect of independent juries was to prevent the prosecution of *political* cases, although the Morris committee, deliberating at a time when political freedom was taken utterly for granted, did not dwell on this. The benefits to those accused of ordinary crimes were incidental, though important. The existence of independent juries so completely prevented the use of the courts to pursue political matters that the idea of a political offence became absurd in the eyes of most Englishmen. Directly political trials likewise became almost unthinkable. The suffragettes were prosecuted for public order offences, and the First World War conscientious objectors for defying the conscription laws. Opinions differ about compulsory military service in a free society, but these people were imprisoned for their actions rather than their opinions.

The privilege of jury trial has benefits for the criminal justice system, especially in promoting the belief that most of those in prison have been rightly convicted rather than arbitrarily locked up. It also has a much greater importance in the national constitution. Jury trial for those accused of common crimes is the price society pays for freedom of thought and speech. The same could be said of the rule preventing anyone from being tried twice for the same offence. There will always be criminal cases where it will be tempting to break this rule. However, if it is broken for criminals, it is broken for everyone that the state may come to view as a criminal, and so it leaves dissenters open to the danger of state harassment by repeated prosecution. It also weakens juries by giving the state another method of overturning verdicts it dislikes.

The Morris inquiry did not seem to be challenging any of these fundamentals. At that time a largely peaceful society could reasonably feel confident that its institutions were safe and permanent. Now, many of the props of English liberty are threatened from all directions because of the grave rise in crime that has since occurred. Then, the government was simply seeking a way to get rid of what was seen as an archaic and unequal method of selecting juries.

The main purpose of the inquiry was to look into qualifications for jury service, which since 1825 had been based on property. It was careful to set out the reasons for the existence of juries, and treated the history of the jury with interest and respect. It quoted the potent words of Blackstone: 'The trial by jury, or the country, *per patriam*, is also that trial by the peers of every Englishman which, as the grand bulwark of his liberties, is secured to him by the Great Charter', which promised that no free man should be deprived of life or liberty or property save by the judgement of his equals and by the law of the land. The original Latin sealed at Runnymede thundered across the centuries: '*nullus liber homo capiatur, vel imprisonetur, aut exulet, aut aliquo alio modo destruatur, nisi per legale judicium parium suorum, vel per legem terrae*' (No free man shall be arrested, imprisoned, exiled or otherwise punished, unless by the judgement of his peers or by the law of the land).

The inquiry report approvingly cited Blackstone's description of the jury as the 'strong and two-fold barrier between the liberties of the people and the prerogative of the Crown', thanks to 'the unanimous suffrage of twelve of his equals and neighbours, indifferently chosen and superior to all suspicion. So that the liberties of England cannot but subsist so long as this palladium remains sacred and inviolate.' Its development here as a defence of liberty seems to have been a fortunate accident which only became truly important many years after the jury system was first instituted. In fact, it is hard to believe that any state would intentionally have invented or encouraged such a restraint on its own power. No wonder so many governments of all complexions have since sought to rescind the concession they had so unwisely made.

Juries were first used as a form of inquiry or inquest on the Continent under the Carolingians. They were brought to England by the Normans, who used them not to try cases but to compile the Domesday Book. Henry II brought them into civil and criminal law. After the prohibition of trial by ordeal in 1215, judges turned to juries as the best available alternative oracle. At first the distinction between the Grand Jury of Presentment, which decided if there was a case to answer, and the Petty Jury of Inquest, which decided the outcome, was not clear-cut, but in 1352 it was enacted that no accuser should be put on the petty (or trial) jury. Since then the role of jurors has been transformed from that of witnesses chosen for their expert local (and therefore far from impartial) knowledge and qualifications, into their present role as independent arbiters who come to a case without any previous knowledge of the facts.

The all-powerful Court of Star Chamber, not abolished until the reign of Charles I, often punished jurors who had in its view corruptly returned a verdict of acquittal. Star Chamber, not surprisingly, tended to treat as 'corrupt' any verdict that *it* considered to be against the weight of the evidence. The original function of jurors, as experts knowledgeable about the case and the accused, had faded away when it became difficult to find juries who were personally well informed about the case. This was dealt with at first by introducing additional jurors brought in for their knowledge, but in the end juries became judges of fact and fact alone, with the law being decided by the judge. There seem to be no historical reasons for keeping jurors in ignorance of the previous convictions of the accused, or for the extraordinary measures taken nowadays to keep them from knowledge of the background to the case before them. The original juries would certainly have known a great deal more.

The Morris committee did not openly seek any major changes to the powers of juries, to their secrecy or to the right of defendants to appear before them. In fact, they flatly stated that their purpose was based on the 'need to maintain the system of trial by jury as one that both merits and commands public respect'. Rather movingly, they explained the ancient words used in the old form of pleading at assizes: 'Q: "How wilt thou be tried?" A: "By God and my country."' They said: 'When in a criminal case an accused pleads not guilty, he "puts himself upon the country". The jury are "the country".' This feeling that a man convicted by a jury has been sent to prison not by the state but by the people is one of the reasons for the general popularity, until recently, of the English criminal justice system.

The committee assumed that all this would continue. Lord Morris himself was an experienced judge who had at one time been a Liberal parliamentary candidate. They were, however, unhappy about the way in which jurors were picked solely on the basis that they were householders. In practice this meant that juries were chosen from the lists of those who paid the rates, the council tax of the time, generally levied on the head of the household. In most families this was the husband, ensuring that the majority of jurors were male, although sometimes a husband and wife were jointly registered. In some parts of the country it excluded those living in blocks of flats and council accommodation, because they did not pay rates directly. The age limits were then from twenty-one to sixty.

The committee complained that the property restrictions belonged to 'a period in which only those who possessed property were considered to have a sufficient stake in the country to justify their being allowed to take part in public life'. They did not suggest any other measure of responsibility and solidity that might be better. If anything, there was evidence that the pool from which juries were drawn was becoming wider, rather than narrower. They estimated that there were 7.15 million names marked as eligible for jury service, 22.5 per cent of the 31.77 million names on the registers. A series of property revaluations had recently produced steep increases in the number of people qualified to serve. In February 1955 there had been just 1.51 million, a year later 3.71 million and by February 1964 there were 7.15 million. Yet even this modest expansion of the jury-serving classes was affecting verdicts.

The Metropolitan Police Commissioner, Sir Joseph Simpson, complained that there had been 'a marked deterioration in the quality of jurors'. The Association of Chief Police Officers said that the quality of rural jurors had stayed high while that of urban juries had declined, perhaps because of middle-class movement to the countryside. This presumably meant that rural juries were readier to convict than urban ones. An unidentified (but non-police) witness was quoted as saying that price inflation in the property market had widened the basis for selection and so led to 'an ever-increasing number of men and women of poor education who are ill-equipped for such service... the position must be expected to deteriorate still further'.

The committee dithered over whether there was any serious problem, saying: 'We do not feel able to express an authoritative view of our own... the majority of witnesses have expressed their confidence in the ability and determination of juries.' One thing on which all agreed, already seen as an issue even in 1964, was that far too few women served on English juries. One way of dealing with this would have been to adopt the Scottish system of the time, which allowed 'women with heritable property' to qualify. In practice, this resulted in a near-equality between men and women on Scottish juries, and it could easily have been adapted to English law.

The inquiry admitted: 'there is perhaps some force in the argument that to be a householder, or the spouse of a householder, is to some extent at least an indication of maturity and responsibility.' However, they turned away from the conclusion to which this might have led them, adding hastily: 'We have received no convincing evidence to the effect that householders would necessarily make better jurors than non-householders.' And they sought to use hard cases to make bad law by citing a problem that they had not actually shown to exist on any scale: 'It would be difficult to defend a system under which a householder and his spouse were eligible, whatever their standards of intelligence, education or integrity, while a lodger in their house, who might be a person of outstanding qualities, was nevertheless ineligible.' It would, in fact, have been quite easy to defend it so long as such a case was rare and the system as a whole served the interests of justice. It would also have been possible to devise a system of educational and other qualifications to overcome the problem. The committee, however, did not think in this fashion.

Instead, they seem to have been anxious to dispense with the property qualification altogether, rejecting any plans to change its levels or extend it to women. 'We do not see how property values, laid down in 1825, can be related, 140 years later, to any rational principle whatever,' they insisted. The fact that the existing system was working reasonably well – and that an extended franchise was already worrying the police – did not deflect them from their chosen reform, the abolition of almost any selection at all. They sought to replace the old method with another far less rational system, one that excluded nobody from the jury box save criminals and lunatics. This was their logic, as they dressed up their surrender to unthinking egalitarianism. They resorted, as people tend to do when they are unsure that they are right, to lofty gibberish: 'Our view is that jury service should be regarded as a duty which is a counterpart of the privilege of being a citizen. From this view it follows that citizenship should be the basis from which the duty to serve arises.' Unless you believe that everyone is equally qualified to serve on a jury, which the members of the Morris committee plainly did not, this sentence does not make sense.

The committee raised perfectly sound arguments against their own ideas, saying: 'The householder qualification, whatever its other defects, does have the advantage of being to some extent at least a guarantee of the maturity and sense of responsibility of young jurors.' Surely, if maturity and responsibility were desirable, some sort of selection was required that would exclude the immature and irresponsible?

They could not have foreseen just how young future juries would be, once their recommendations came into effect. They admitted that juries would be younger but argued that this would not be a bad thing in itself: 'We recognise that unless the present lower age limit is raised, the effect of our other recommendations will be to increase the number of young jurors, but we recommend nevertheless that the qualifying age should continue to be 21.' The committee took the view 'that there is a greater measure of maturity in people between the ages of 21 and 25 than some of our witnesses were prepared to concede', and that 'while such people may have less experience than their elders they may nevertheless possess experience which is relevant to the duties of a juror'. By the time their ideas were put into practice, a government in love with youth culture would have lowered the age of majority, and so of jury service, to eighteen. Few of the Morris committee's witnesses in 1964 or 1965 would have argued that there was much maturity to be found in citizens aged between eighteen and twenty-one.

The Morris committee also conceded one of the most valued benefits of the householder qualification: 'Although we can find no compelling justification, in principle or practice, for the retention of the householder qualification, it is only right to say that it probably does at present serve the purpose of excluding a significant proportion of the criminal classes.' They even quoted from Lord Devlin's

Trial by Jury, with its prescient warning that a wider selection system might lead to pressure for majority verdicts: 'If unanimity is insisted upon and the narrow franchise is preferred, it is no doubt right that juries should be taken from out of the middle of the community where safe judgement is most likely to repose.'

There might have been another way of achieving this. The committee studied American methods of jury selection, which at that time involved searching literacy tests and other inquiries to ensure that jurors were fitted for the task. 'We would expect such a procedure to produce jurors of high calibre,' they concluded, but then they made it plain that they wanted nothing to do with such a scheme: 'Although it would be possible to devise ingenious tests for prospective jurors, we do not think that they would be appropriate or acceptable here. We have already rejected any proposal that there should be an organised basis for making up a jury on the recommendations of some selecting body.' Such an exhaustive process would take some time. If the test were rigorous, the selecting officer would have the task of telling large numbers of people that they had failed it. If it were simple, it would be useless. So in the committee's view there could be no test.

Nor could the property qualification be modified in some way to suit the times.

> The proposal to retain even a limited form of property qualification would be resented, and justifiably so, by those who consider that jury service is a right as well as a duty and that they should not be deprived of this right by the accident of not being a householder, any more than they are for that reason denied the other rights of citizenship…
>
> If our view is accepted that a jury should be a cross-section of the community as a whole, it would seem somewhat curious to draw jurors exclusively from those who are householders or the spouses of householders.

How strange this sounds now, when home ownership is so much more common. If they had simply left things alone, most of the unfairness and the anomalies of the old method would have disappeared. The property qualification looks far less snobbish and rigid than it did in 1965. With the sensible Scottish rules on spouses extended south of the border, it would also have meant women had an equal chance of jury service. The Morris committee seem to have been quite determined to choose the system of random selection from the entire electoral roll, not because it was best, or even better, but because it was the most egalitarian and so politically the least troublesome. The committee's proposals eventually became law in the Criminal Justice Act of 1972 and were confirmed by the Juries Act of 1974, which opened jury service to anyone registered as an elector and aged between eighteen and seventy. This did not come into full force until April 1974, and its effects took some time to be felt.

In the years in between, however, an equally important change had been imposed on juries, in one of those all-too-frequent episodes that make Parliament look like the easily-wielded tool of the executive. On the pretext of 'jury-nobbling' by criminal gangs, for which the evidence was vague and elusive, Roy Jenkins greatly altered the courtroom balance of power in favour of the state by introducing majority verdicts. It was a heavy blow, but like many such blows, not much felt at the time. Yet its significance was known and understood by experts. Lord Chief Justice Hewart had ruled in 1922 that the value of a jury's verdict lay precisely in its unanimity, not in the process by which it was reached.

No research has been permitted into juries, for fear that it might call their verdicts into doubt, but it is quite plain that a tough-minded individual can sway a jury in either direction by force of argument and personality. He can take courage from the knowledge that he has a complete veto. If he holds out to the end he can at least force a new trial – no mean threat. Even so, the bravest and most determined individual is likely to fail in such a lone stand if he does not have right on his side. This is the plot of the famous American film about a deadlocked jury *Twelve Angry Men*. Such a drama could still take place in most of the USA, but not in Britain where ten angry persons can now overrule two equally angry persons who refuse to join the majority. Here, a juror who swims against the stream can be dismissed as a tiresome nuisance, quite possibly at the exact stage where he might once have been on the verge of winning converts. And not just one individual but two can now be overridden.

Without the protection of their all-or-nothing unanimity, juries – like any other group of fallible humans – are far more easily divided and conquered. The change is colossal. A unanimous verdict and a majority verdict are not two different degrees of the same thing, but two quite different things. Yet the change passed through Parliament with very little protest or controversy. And, in an age of demonstrations and protests, there do not seem to have been any marches through the streets urging that England should Save the Jury. Vietnam was more important then, as veal calves and genetically-modified tomatoes would be later. The modern English have an extraordinarily unselfish inability to protest against anything that actually menaces their own liberty and well-being.

There *were* sharp protests from acute and knowledgeable people. Lord Denning told the House of Lords on 6 June 1967 that majority verdicts undermined the whole idea of guilt being proved beyond reasonable doubt. As usual, he struck at the heart of the thing. If one juror has doubts, let alone two, then how can guilt have been proved to the high standard demanded? In an earlier debate, on 10 May, Lord Morris of Borth-y-Gest, who, thanks to his inquiry, had become one of the greatest experts on the subject, had told the Lords that the majority verdicts proposal was 'retrograde'. Lord Denning said on that occasion that it was a fundamental part of the constitution that the jury should be unanimous. Among those who thought the principle of unanimity should be maintained, he said, were some of the wisest and most experienced judges. Lord Brooke, a former Tory Home Secretary, favoured majority verdicts

THE ABOLITION OF LIBERTY

but doubted if Roy Jenkins had enough evidence to prove his case for the change. Lord Stow Hill, formerly the Labour Home Secretary Frank Soskice, urged the government to reconsider its plan. Interestingly, the Lord Chancellor, Lord Gardiner, said that the main reason for majority verdicts was 'cranks on juries', only later adding the official line that there was also a risk of jurymen being bribed or intimidated. To the prosecution-minded, or the tidy-minded government servant, any nonconformist is a crank.

When Roy Jenkins introduced his enormous and far-reaching Criminal Justice Bill on 12 December 1966, with all its changes to court procedure, sentences, parole and gun control, he said of his plan for majority verdicts that 'in the present state of the crime wave we can feel less equanimity about the acquittal of the guilty'. Yet he made modest claims for the immediate practical effect of the change, saying the new procedures 'are not likely to result in different verdicts in many cases, but these few cases may well be crucial from the point of view of law-enforcement and the breaking-up of big criminal conspiracies'. At that time, he said, about 35 to 40 per cent of cases that went to juries resulted in acquittal. In about 3.5 per cent of cases there was jury disagreement that could not be resolved by the ordinary process of argument and persuasion. At the Old Bailey this had affected forty-nine out of 1180 cases in the previous year, hardly an enormous crisis requiring a radical change in the standard of proof. He spoke of an unidentified bank-robbery trial in the previous January where there had been repeated peremptory challenges and attempts to bribe jurors. In the end, four out of the five accused in the case were acquitted.

It seems likely that there were such problems at the time, but that they were confined to small areas and could have been dealt with by prosecutions for perverting the course of justice. The question again arises as to why Roy Jenkins and the Home Office were so insistent on a change the main effect of which would be to weaken jury independence and, while leaving the jury in being, gravely reduce its ancient power to stand in the way of the state.

Here it should also be mentioned that at about this time the old institution of the lay magistracy, another independent part of the system, also began to be weakened. By dispensing with the requirement for evidence to be heard before the lower courts, the Criminal Justice Act 1968 greatly reduced the power of magistrates to throw out a charge at the committal stage. In 1973, to protests from Lord Denning, Lord Hailsham, then Lord Chancellor, first introduced full-time, paid, 'stipendiary' magistrates into rural areas. He promised that the numbers involved would be very small, but in later years this promise has been broken. Many local courts have also closed, usually on the grounds of economy or lack of disabled access. Between 1996 and 2001, 108 magistrates' courts, mainly in rural areas and suburbs, were shut, thus weakening the link between Justices of the Peace and their localities, and making justice more remote in general. In 1973 the Home Office also began to talk about limiting jury trial to certain types of case.

It is hard to chart the effects of these changes. Official figures conceal as much as they reveal. But if they were intended to strengthen the prosecution they have not so far succeeded. In recent years prosecutions have been failing at about twice the rate of thirty-five years ago. By 1999 the number of unsuccessful prosecutions approached the politically important level of 25 per cent. Many other prosecutions fail at an earlier stage thanks to the Crown Prosecution Service's unwillingness to risk cases that do not have a good chance of success. In the most recent year for which figures are available, almost one in eight (12.3 per cent) of cases intended for the crown courts were dropped before trial by the CPS.

However, changes may run far deeper than this, and further detailed research is needed to establish the full truth about the past. Figures produced in early 2002 by the Lord Chancellor's Department suggest that the difficulty of persuading a jury to return a guilty verdict is increasing at an alarming rate. Figures on the outcomes of *contested* jury trials are available only back as far as 1990. They exclude cases where the jury acquitted on the judge's direction, where the trial collapsed or the defendant died. They therefore deal with a significantly smaller number of trials. They are, however, a better guide to the actual mood of juries when faced with a choice.

These figures show that in 1999 38.7 per cent of contested jury trials in England and Wales resulted in acquittals, while in 2000 the figure was 36 per cent. This percentage had changed remarkably little since 1990, the earliest figure obtainable from the Lord Chancellor's Department, when it stood at 37.7 per cent. Regrettably, no statistics of this kind are currently available for the 1960s, 1970s or 1980s, when the effects of majority verdicts and the abolition of the property qualification would have first been felt. Almost as striking is the variation between different parts of the country. The acquittal rate in 1999 in Salisbury, for instance, was 21.1 per cent. In Liverpool it was 61.9 per cent (the 1990 figure was 45.7 per cent), in Caernarvon 66.7 per cent (30.9 per cent in 1990), and at the Old Bailey 34.5 per cent (39.0 per cent in 1990). The results in 2000 were much the same, and in some cases the number of not guilty verdicts was higher. When judge-directed acquittals are added in, 79 per cent of defendants in contested trials in Liverpool were acquitted despite the best efforts of the prosecution in the year 2000.

The immensely complicated guidelines and codes of practice that now beset the police obviously have something to do with this. Any procedural slip-up or delay can kill a prosecution even before it gets to the point where the evidence would be weighed. Meanwhile, the willingness of juries to disbelieve the police and to treat prosecution evidence with suspicion has obviously greatly increased.

The author visited Liverpool Crown Court in March 2002 and found a near-breakdown of respect for justice. There were reports of general truculence and contempt, such as judges being sworn at and mobile phones ringing during cases. Judges were supposed to remove robes and wigs when dealing with defendants under eighteen, in case they intimidated them. Such defendants, often hulking six-footers facing charges of serious violence, were frequently allowed to sit outside the dock next to parents and social workers, supposedly because of their tender years. The old joke, 'Q: "What do you call a Liverpudlian in a suit?" A: "The defendant"', is now obsolete. Most defendants wear street clothes, as do juries. Tattoos, nose-rings and pony-tails were common among jurors, but jackets and ties were unheard-of. Jurors often lounged in relaxed attitudes. The old tongue-twisting jury oath, referring to the 'several issues joined before our Sovereign Lady the Queen', has been simplified so the illiterate or incoherent are no longer found out by it. The huge courthouse containing twenty-two criminal courtrooms is equipped with pictorial direction signs to help the growing number of illiterates find their way about.

Experienced court-watchers, speaking on condition of anonymity, believe that there is widespread but unacknowledged intimidation of juries and witnesses. Witnesses are followed into the lavatories or when they leave the building. Some estimate that as many as 20 per cent of contested cases collapse because witnesses either fail to appear or 'forget' critical evidence when in the witness box. Judges sometimes order the public to move their seats out of line of sight of the jury because of complaints that jury members are being subjected to intimidating stares. There are no police officers on duty in the building apart from those waiting to give evidence. Security, such as it is, is provided by shirtsleeved private guards, many of them women and few of them physically impressive. If there is serious trouble, as there sometimes is, the police must be called from their nearby headquarters.

There is no one obvious reason for the failure rate and demoralization of this place. Some believe that the split between the police and the Crown Prosecution Service leads inevitably to bureaucratic slip-ups and the postponement of cases. Some suspect the CPS is too worried about failing and drops charges too easily. Some blame the youth, inexperience and anti-authority attitudes of modern juries.

Others blame unscrupulous defence lawyers for exploiting the pettifogging provisions of the Police and Criminal Evidence Act 1984 and the current disclosure rules. All of these charges are partly justified. However, they add up to more than the sum of their parts. The system has no force or self-confidence and criminals know it.

The abolition of the property qualification, in the still-settled and restrained society of 1974, may have had little effect. However, it could equally have been a slow-burning fuse within the jury system which has finally detonated its bomb. At the present time, in which respectability and middle-class values are widely questioned, especially among the young, it may be starting to have a significant effect on attitudes towards the police and prosecution. It would certainly seem to be so on Merseyside.

Since research into individual jury decisions is sensibly and rightly forbidden by law we can only guess at the truth, although the figures for Liverpool, one of the least middle-class cities in the kingdom by any measure, seem to suggest that something of the kind may be involved. Another influence is almost certainly the age of jurors. The unintended result of the Morris committee's inquiry was that eighteen-year-olds, far younger in years and experience than the twenty-one-year-olds Morris envisaged, now serve on juries. Harold Wilson's decision to lower the age of majority to eighteen was not then in the manifesto of any organization except the Monster Raving Loony Party. Anecdotal evidence suggests that juries have been growing significantly younger in recent years, perhaps because of the over-sixty-fives' right to be excused, perhaps because older, employed people have taken advantage of the ease with which they, too, can avoid jury service.

It may even be that the new system is unintentionally discriminating in favour of juries containing high proportions of younger, unemployed men and women. With its long, time-wasting trials and seedy courtrooms, it repels the respectable, steadily employed and better-off, who have other things to do with their time and have the skill to avoid having to serve on juries. Research on this would be possible without invading the secrecy of the jury room and needs urgently to be undertaken if a serious campaign for jury reform – as opposed to jury restriction or abolition – is to get under way. Acquittals at the current rate will only increase political demands for the end of jury trial, when it is quite likely that it is the political reforms of the 1960s and 1970s that have brought juries to their present state. The acceptance of majority verdicts may also be having its effect – the exact opposite of the effect it was intended to have. In an anti-establishment culture it is those who want to convict who are likely to be in the besieged minority.

The bravely won independence established in the seventeenth and eighteenth centuries is now in doubt. In October 2001 the new establishment revealed its true feelings about the jury system in Lord Justice Auld's *Review of the Criminal Courts*. The Auld report followed three failed attempts by governments of both parties to abolish the right to jury trial. It was sidelined by the government in early 2002 when it became clear that a powerful coalition against it was still in being and that its proposals would be alarmingly expensive. Even so, its naked hostility towards defendants having any right to jury trial, and its desire to create a new tier of jury-free courts, provided a warning of what the elite state wants to do and will certainly do later if it can gain full control of the House of Lords. It was lack of parliamentary time, not a sudden rebirth of libertarian principle, that led to the temporary shelving of Auld. In July 2002 the government proposed judge-only trials in complex fraud cases and violated two ancient principles by suggesting the retrospective abolition of the rule against double jeopardy.

In the late autumn of 2002 a highly significant development signalled the determination of the Blair government to use crime as a pretext to limit liberty. This was made much easier by a major but little-noted constitutional reform in October, under which the Commons abandoned its main remaining power to obstruct the executive. Until that date, a bill which ran out of parliamentary time was completely lost at the end of the session. This gave opponents in the Commons and the Lords a powerful weapon with which they could force compromise on Downing Street. But under reforms sponsored by Robin Cook, leader of the Commons, this power was abolished.

Within two weeks the Prime Minister and the Home Secretary made it plain that jury trial should be even more restricted than the July 2002 White Paper suggested, and that the rule against double jeopardy would be dropped. They argued that this was part of a 'modernizing' and 'rebalancing' of the criminal justice system. In fact it was a recognition of the failure of all their anti-crime initiatives of the previous five years. It was also a clear sign that they had chosen the authoritarian route, rather than libertarianism, and that crime was to be the excuse for it. The basis of their proposals was plainly the Auld report.

Auld urged radical changes to the right to jury trial, effectively abolishing it as a right (a right that he did not believe had ever existed). He also suggested a law making it clear that 'juries have no right to acquit defendants in defiance of the law or in disregard of the evidence'. He argued:

> I regard the ability of jurors to acquit, and it also follows,
> convict, in defiance of the law and in disregard of their
> oaths, as more than illogicality. It is a blatant affront to the
> legal process and the main purpose of the criminal justice
> system – the control of crime – of which they are so
> important a part...
>
> They are not there to substitute their view of
> the propriety of the law for that of Parliament or its
> enforcement for that of its appointed Executive [Auld's
> capitalization], still less on what may be irrational, secret
> and unchallengeable grounds.

Auld urged that the law should be amended to allow the trial judge or the Court of Appeal to inquire into 'alleged impropriety by a jury, whether in the course of its deliberations or otherwise'. This power would have to be tested in use, but it is hard to see how it could exist without putting greater pressure on jurors to convict. Auld also noticed, as others eventually will, that Article Six of the European Convention on Human Rights, requiring reasoned judgements and verdicts, could be interpreted to mean that jury trial was contrary to the Human Rights Act. This unsettling discovery illustrates very clearly just how violently the Convention conflicts with English traditions of liberty and how the two cannot indefinitely coexist.

While he urged the creation of a law to rob juries of the right of defiance, Auld also mentioned an alternative which he seems to have found unthinkable but that actually exists in two American states, Maryland and Indiana. Their constitutions, he said, 'come close to conferring upon the jury the right to determine the law and the facts'. If adopted in England, stated Auld, a law of this kind would require judges to tell juries that they need not convict if they disagreed with the law or with the decision to prosecute. In truth, English juries believe that they have this right anyway and do not need to be informed of it by a judge. Only a judge would think that he needed to tell them about it. Auld, however, described such a clarification of the law as an 'enormity'.

Others might use the same word to describe his plan to extinguish jury independence. Such a statute, in the wrong hands and interpreted by the wrong judges, could cancel the liberties achieved in Bushell's case and the Fox Act, and might take England back to the days when Star Chamber tore up verdicts that did not suit the state. Perhaps because resistance in the House of Lords had recently defeated three government attacks on the right to jury trial, Auld's oppressive scheme did not attract very much attention on its publication in October 2001. Its burial, according to an unattributable government leak to the newspapers in January 2002, was not irrevocable and it has swiftly heaved itself out of the grave. With both Commons and Lords now severely weakened, the jury is in more danger than it has been for two hundred years.

Auld's view of juries contrasted with Lord Morris's attitude thirty-six years earlier. Gone was the reverence and awe for lamps of liberty and twofold protections. Gone was the awkward independence of the judiciary. In its place was a brusque, hard, official practicality and a seeming desire to serve the executive which, if typical of the modern judge, is quite alarming. Like much modern illiberal thinking, it was camouflaged with the cloak of the vaunted fight against crime. Yet there are many other ways in which the courts could be changed to shift the balance in favour of the prosecution of criminals. What Sir Robin Auld and a succession of Home Secretaries of both parties have not explained is why they are so determined to reduce the rights and powers of the jury rather than to take any other possible route. Yet that determination is blatant and unashamed.

Auld swept aside the idea that a right to jury trial existed in England at all. 'In England and Wales,' he declared, 'there is no constitutional or indeed any form of general right to trial by judge and jury, only a general obligation to submit to it in indictable cases.' He rejected Lord Morris's version of history: 'It is often claimed that Magna Carta, traditionally regarded as the foundation of our liberties, established such a right. The claim is incorrect.' This would-be reformer proclaimed:

> Quite independently of Magna Carta there is no legal
> basis for regarding the claimed 'right' to jury trial as a
> constitutional entitlement, that is as an entrenched right
> overriding all other legal instruments, as in the United
> States for offences carrying more than six months'
> imprisonment or under the Canadian Charter of Rights
> and Freedoms for offences punishable by five years'
> imprisonment or more, or as a right at all.

He was technically correct, but only because no such entrenched rights exist in English law. They are entrenched only in the minds of the people, but plainly not in his. It was interesting that Auld's brief history of the jury system did not mention Star Chamber, Bushell or Fox.

Irrelevantly, however, he said that juries had failed to prevent miscarriages of justice in the late 1980s and early 1990s. This is hardly surprising, as Auld himself pointed out that these miscarriages resulted mainly from falsification or concealment of evidence. Juries could have known nothing and done nothing about them. They could only decide on the basis of what was put before them by police and prosecution and what the judge allowed them to hear. Auld's interest was in showing that since 1855 the law has let accused citizens choose between jury and summary trial for a growing number of offences. This choice, actually granted so that defendants could avoid the length, expense and unpredictability of a jury trial, did not seem to Auld to be an argument for keeping a right to insist on a jury trial. He had a point, but not a very good one. His interest was in the workings of the jury system after it had already secured liberty of thought and speech. He failed to see that removal of the defendant's right to choose would give the state a dangerous power that it would be better off without.

As it happens (and as Auld noted), subtle methods of encouraging defendants to plead guilty, by rewarding them with lighter sentences, have already hugely reduced the numbers of jury trials. This has been achieved without forcing defendants to forgo jury trial, and was introduced in the recognition that many had simply been trying to spend more time in the better conditions given to remand prisoners. Auld, however, was not put off, even though his own evidence showed that criminals playing the system could be outmanoeuvred without the need to dilute the jury system. He revealed why in these telling words: 'I regard it as a matter of principle that the decision [about] where a defendant should be tried is one for a court, not for the defendant.' Why was that?

'This is a decision in which the public as well as the accused have an interest, and the decision should be an objective one, bearing both in mind, not a subjective choice of the defendant based solely on his own self-interest.' In this statement we hear again the cold voice of the elite state, so convinced of its own rightness and goodness that it requires no restraint.

Auld recommended that magistrates, not defendants, should decide whether the accused in so-called 'either-way' cases would go before a jury or a summary court. This would presently affect only a minority of trials. However, combined with his plan for a new bottom tier of courts without juries, his proposals were startlingly radical. If implemented, they would have removed a de facto right to jury trial for many offences and opened the way for its removal for many more. They would almost certainly have been the first stage in a restriction of jury trial that would eventually lead to its effective abolition.

Some hint of the reasoning behind this hostility to jury trial is to be found in Lord Hardie's words during a House of Lords debate in January 2000 on one of the present Labour government's anti-jury bills. Lord Hardie, approvingly quoted by Auld, said: 'What is essential in any system is that the various interests are balanced; that society's interests, as represented by victims and witnesses, are balanced against the interests of the accused. What must be ensured is that the accused is protected from the effect of arbitrary decisions. Who better to perform such a task than an independent judiciary?' These are curious words. Society's interests are not 'represented by victims and witnesses'. Society has an interest in justice and liberty, which is owed to itself as a whole. Sometimes that interest may lead to witnesses being disbelieved and victims seeing the defendant go free. In extreme circumstances (for example, burglars injured in the course of a burglary), it may even lead to truthful witnesses being discounted. The victim, which may be the state itself, may even have to see the defendant go free because the jury thinks he has committed no crime.

The idea that the courts act on behalf of victims is false. They act to enforce the Queen's peace, the property of us all, and the law of the land, also the property of us all. They also act to enforce the constitution and the liberties it guards, and, as long as they contain juries and are presided over by freedom-minded judges, they can even help to make the constitution. Without them, it is hard to see how judges can long remain independent, since all the forces acting on them will be the state's. The pity is that, when juries need as many friends as they can get, they have been so badly weakened by majority verdicts and the abolition of any kind of qualification based upon maturity, education or responsibility. The lower age limit of eighteen is also absurd. Who, remembering his own teens, would wish his future liberty to be in the hands of a teenager? If the politicians were serious about jury reform, they would re-examine these hasty and ill-thought-out changes rather than threatening the principle of jury trial. However, the elite state fears and mistrusts the independence of juries on principle, and sees an opportunity to get rid of them while appearing to pursue the objective of justice and order.

The worse crime becomes, the noisier and cruder the courts will become. When the Metropolitan Police Commissioner, Sir John Stevens, attacked the inadequacies of the criminal justice system in a ferocious speech in March 2001, he called for the implementation of the Auld report, while making little of the other factors that have paralysed the courts. His speech was instantly welcomed by the government and by its semi-official newspaper, the *Sun*. Had he attacked the Police and Criminal Evidence Act 1984, which has subjected the police to absurd codes of practice and rendered convictions far more difficult to achieve, he might not have received such kind treatment from the politicians or their press supporters. Had he urged the re-establishment of some sort of qualification for jury service, he would have been denounced as a snobbish elitist. It was an alarming moment for supporters of jury trial who also believe that crime should be punished and deterred. One notable supporter of juries, the conservative commentator and author, Simon Heffer, declared on the BBC's *Any Questions* programme that he might in future support the Continental inquisitorial system. Much of the attack on the present mess was directed at lawyers, who undoubtedly profit greatly from the adversarial jury system. The fact that lawyers profit from it does not, however, blot out the vital advantages of the jury for a free society, or the need for independent defence lawyers.

The increasing use of trials as crude propaganda is, however, a forewarning of the likely direction of the debate unless the defenders of freedom and the enemies of crime can combine. A combination of noisy 'tough on crime' populism and repression seems likely to be the elite state's response to increasing disorder. From the statements of the Home Secretary, David Blunkett, it is evident that he is politically unable to understand why crime is out of control. Mr Blunkett said in March 2002 that he knew the streets were not safe. He plainly did not understand why this was so, and could offer only the usual New Labour remedies of initiatives, targets and street crime summits at Downing Street. There was also talk of putting more police on the streets, without any understanding of why they are not there already, or why they can do so little when they are there.

With such people in charge of criminal justice, it is likely that the government will shortly resort to more populist measures designed to give the impression of resolution and action. The limiting of liberty can always be made to seem attractive in such times. Such crude crowd-pleasing will undoubtedly be used to undermine the principle of jury trial. This process, of using the courts as government anti-crime propaganda, has already begun. A worrying development of recent years has been this confusion of justice with propaganda, with policemen giving celebratory press conferences after convictions and prosecutors wasting the court's time with emotional descriptions of the victim's plight and wounds, often to disguise the fact that they have no proper evidence against the accused.

The idea that victim and court are in some way on the same side is a worrying and totalitarian one, reminiscent of the sort of state where the public prosecutor demands a heavy sentence. Such states do not have independent judiciaries. They have government servants who cannot be trusted to look after defendants' rights because it is not what they are paid to do or what will please their political masters. However bad the victim's injuries and loss, the court still has the same duty to find out the truth, and to acquit those against whom there is not enough evidence to secure a conviction. In this way, the interests of a truly just court have always been different from those of the victim, and always ought to be. So the answer to the question, 'who better to protect the defendant against arbitrary decisions than an independent judiciary?', is 'an independent jury'.

The attempt to remove the right to jury trial is a serious menace to liberty. Attacking juries will do nothing to aid the fight for the re-establishment of justice. However, it will greatly strengthen the elite state. In the end, if a time comes when it is in the interests of authority to suppress its opponents, restrictions on jury trial will threaten liberty of speech and thought. There is no clearer illustration of the way in which the failure to punish wrongdoing will lead in the end to the punishment of us all.

VIII

Institutional defeatism

'A racist incident is any incident which is
perceived to be racist by the victim or any
other person'
Macpherson report

The British establishment is now in favour of racial discrimination
by the police. Officers of the law are supposed to assume that
people of a different colour should be treated as if they were automatically people of a different culture. It is there, in bold print, on
page 316 of the much-praised and almost universally accepted
Macpherson report into the murder of Stephen Lawrence.
Paragraph 45.24 states: '"Colour-blind" policing must be outlawed.
The police must deliver a service which recognises the different
experiences, perceptions and needs of a diverse society.' These
words ended forty years of efforts to abolish racial discrimination in
this country. Until they were published, opponents of racialism (this
book's preferred term, as explained below) could still believe that
they should act as if colour did not matter, in the hope that eventually it would not matter.

From Macpherson onwards, rather than seeking to absorb new
citizens into British society through a policy of tolerance, this
country embarked on an official programme of adapting itself to the
supposed cultures of those new citizens. It assumed that a different-
coloured skin was the outward sign of a different cast of mind and a
reason to apply different rules of citizenship. For the previous forty
years enlightened people had been striving against any such belief,

insisting that colour was a meaningless distinction and that all could and should be absolutely equal in the eyes of the law. Any adaptation was expected to be by the new citizen to his adopted home.

Now the adopted home must adjust itself to its new citizens, treating them differently and with special consideration along more or less racial lines. The idea of a 'White Police Association' would have been repellent in the old era and also in the new. However, the idea of a Black Police Association is so acceptable to the new order that such a body actually exists, with official approval, and gave evidence to the Macpherson inquiry. Yet the new process of adaptation has been a highly selective one. Only some parts of some cultures are to be accorded this treatment. Open, official discrimination of this kind has not existed since the 1960s, when London police stations still displayed unashamedly racialist official notices advising different and special treatment for what were then called 'men of colour'.* To those who came to maturity in the years when racial discrimination was considered to be absolutely wrong and wicked in itself, the change has been disturbing.

The Macpherson report (*The Stephen Lawrence Inquiry: Report of an Inquiry by Sir William Macpherson of Cluny*, CM 4262-1, published by the Stationery Office in 1999) is one of the most extraordinary documents ever to be published by any British government. Its language, tone and style are quite unlike anything else ever printed by the austere presses of the state. Its accusation of 'institutional racism' against the police is by definition impossible to prove and therefore impossible to refute. Yet it has highly disreputable origins. The inventor of this idea and expression was the American black radical Stokely Carmichael, an anti-Semite who was at one time banned from this country and who proclaimed that Hitler was a

* The author clearly recalls seeing and being shocked by such notices when under arrest in two London police stations, West End Central and Cannon Row, in August 1969.

genius. Carmichael, originally a Black Panther, changed his name
before he died to Kwame Touré in honour of two of black Africa's
most disastrous despots, Kwame Nkrumah and Sékou Touré. He
once suggested that the people of Brixton should be armed with
hand grenades. Despite this tainted source, it has been difficult for
anyone to combat the new ideology presumably for fear of being
damned as institutionally racist themselves.

A full and devastating examination of this peculiar report's
assumptions and attitudes was made in *Racist Murder and Pressure
Group Politics* by Norman Dennis, George Erdos and Ahmed Al-
Shahi, published by the Institute for the Study of Civil Society.
This chapter cannot range so widely. It seeks only to examine the
effects that the Lawrence affair, and the official interpretation of it,
have had on the police. It also examines the similar but different
impact of the 1981 Brixton and other riots and the Scarman report on
them.

The strange nature of Sir William Macpherson's report suggests
that it was aimed not only at the organization and discipline of the
police but at their whole reason for existing. The report argued for a
revolutionary change in the official attitude towards solving the
country's racial problems, which has now affected every corner of
the public sector. The words calling for an end to 'colour-blind
policing' quoted above are wrapped in an apparently reassuring
blanket of tolerant worthiness. The paragraph in full reads:

> The message is uncompromising. A new atmosphere
> of mutual confidence and trust must be created. The
> onus to begin the process which will create that new
> atmosphere lies firmly and clearly with the police.
> The Police Services must examine every aspect of their
> policies and practices to assess whether the outcome
> of their actions creates or sustains patterns of
> discrimination. The provision of policing services to
> a diverse public must be appropriate and professional

in every case. Every individual must be treated with
respect. 'Colour-blind' policing must be outlawed.
The police must deliver a service which recognises
the different experiences, perceptions and needs of
a diverse society.

This declaration has to be read together with one of the report's
other revolutionary statements, namely the one appearing almost
immediately before it on page 314 (paragraph 45.17). This declares:
'A racist incident is any incident which is perceived to be racist by
the victim *or any other person*' (author's italics).

Before returning to these words, it is worth recording the main
objections to the Macpherson report voiced by Dennis, Erdos and
Al-Shahi. These criticisms, although published by a conservative
organization, did not come from the classical right. Dennis is a distinguished scholar of the left and active Labour Party member,
Erdos is a Hungarian-born ethical socialist. Al-Shahi, a British
citizen of Kurdish origin, is an anthropologist who is an expert on
tolerance and integration. After examining the Lawrence inquiry
and its report in great detail, they came to the unexpected conclusion that 'no evidence of racism on the part of the police was ever
produced.' They went on:

> There was no attempt to show that the Metropolitan
> Police Service was racist in the sense of being formally
> structured to put members of ethnic minorities at a
> disadvantage. Nor was any evidence produced that
> individual officers dealing with the murder of Stephen
> Lawrence had displayed racism, unless one includes the
> use of words like 'coloured', which are currently out of
> favour with professional race relations lobbyists. No
> evidence was produced to indicate that the police
> would have handled the investigation differently had
> the victim been white.

They added that: 'To question whether the murder of Stephen Lawrence was a purely racist crime was, in itself, adduced as evidence of racism. This was despite the fact that the suspects had been accused of violent offences against white people and were heard, in tape recordings made of their private conversations, to express violent hatred against white people.'

There is much to regret about the Lawrence case, most of all the murder itself, which, like all such crimes, is an immense and irreplaceable loss, made worse by the failure to bring the culprits to justice, and a woeful illustration of the lawlessness now infecting England. However, it is open to question whether it was so special as to justify the enormous controversy and campaign that grew up around it. Doubts have been cast on the competence of the police inquiries, which cannot be judged a success. But such police failure is all too common. The real issue is whether their behaviour in this case was in any way untypical of police work in modern Britain and whether, if so, it was untypical because of racial prejudice within the police.

The Lawrence family is one of many, black and white, who have yet to see justice done to the killers of close relatives. There is as yet no strong evidence that it was untypical, let alone that its failings were the result of racial prejudice. The Lawrence case is by no means the only unsolved murder on the books of the police forces of England. More to the point, it is not the only racial killing to have taken place in that part of London. As Macpherson says (paragraph 7.18 and others, pages 38–9):

> It should be recorded that racist crime and violence were not new to the district. Both Eltham and Thamesmead had bitter experience of such crime by 1993 [Stephen Lawrence was killed on 22 April 1993]. In May 1991 a black youth called Orville Blair was killed by a white man called Snell. Eventually Snell was convicted of manslaughter on the grounds of provocation. There is

some doubt whether this was in fact a racist crime, but it was so regarded by the community.

In February 1991 a white man named Thornburrow murdered a young 15 year old black youth named Rolan Adams, in a gross racist attack made at a bus stop after some altercation between rival gangs of white and black youths... Thornburrow was sentenced to life imprisonment...

On 11 July 1992 an Asian boy called Rohit Duggal was stabbed to death by a white youth named Peter Thompson outside the kebab shop in Tudor Parade. Thompson was found guilty of the murder in February 1993...

Macpherson mentions these cases to show possible connections to the suspects in the Lawrence killing and to complain about the 'lack of co-ordinated information about them', but also to 'highlight the regularity of such offences'.

They also show that, whatever their faults, the police were capable of catching such killers and of providing evidence on the basis of which they could be convicted. If there was a racial bias among the police in the area, then it was not so powerful that the families of Orville Blair, Rolan Adams and Rohit Duggal were deprived of justice. If all these cases had ended without convictions, then a serious case might have been made that there was something *institutionally* wrong with the area's police. Given that these other killings were all cleared up, Macpherson's evidence for a racial or general explanation for the Lawrence failure is remarkably weak.

But perhaps it had no need to be any stronger. It is worth remembering that the Macpherson report (1997–9) was not a response to the murder itself (1993), or to the initial failure to bring suspects to trial or to the failure of the private prosecution against three men (1996). It was not until July 1997 that Macpherson was asked to set up his inquiry, after Kent Police had already investigated the matter. The Macpherson inquiry was a response to the campaign that followed Stephen Lawrence's death. That campaign had a wider purpose than justice for Stephen Lawrence's family and punishment for his murderers. It had political objectives. The decision to set up the Macpherson investigation was also one of the earliest acts of a Labour government determined to extend Britain's cultural revolution into those institutions that had until then been only partly affected by it.

So in that light, let us return to those extraordinary words in the closing pages of the Macpherson report, that '"Colour-blind" policing must be outlawed', and that 'A racist incident is any incident which is perceived to be racist by the victim or any other person.' There is a third extract, too, which is also quite astonishing. It forms part of a lengthy quotation from a speech given in 1992 by Sir John Woodcock to the International Conference on Policing. At the time, Sir John was Her Majesty's Chief Inspector of Constabulary, a man with immense influence over the conduct of the police throughout England and Wales. His words give a startling clue to the real thinking of many senior police officers today.

Macpherson quotes him (paragraph 6.61, pages 34 and 35), alongside witnesses who called for a radical cultural transformation of the police. If the report had been solely about the Lawrence affair, the Woodcock speech really had no place in it at all. Its presence in the report is a clear sign that Macpherson was inquiring into the socially and culturally conservative culture of police officers and not just into one failed murder investigation. Admitting that the context was different, he specifically said that, even so, he believed Woodcock's words were apt. Since they have absolutely no direct bearing on the case, one has to wonder why. The central passage from Woodcock runs as follows:

The workplace values of the modern police service have
not yet fully cut free of the past and the police service

faces a massive task if it is to hold, as the community now
demands, integrity and respect for human rights, above
all other considerations…

What is happening to the police is that a 19th-century
institution is being dragged into the 21st century. *Despite
all the later mythology of Dixon, the police never really were the
police of the whole people but a mechanism set up to protect the
affluent from what the Victorians described as the dangerous
classes* [italics added]. I believe that the events of the last
few years have not only presented British policing with a
challenge so formidable that it has come close to disaster:
they have also now given the opportunity to the British
Police to reinvent themselves. It is now possible to see
that, through a fundamental shift of culture, the British
police service will remain at the worldwide forefront of
policing, with a style which draws its legitimacy from an
understanding of current public needs and of the nature
of the contract between police and a new generation of
the public.

Where did Her Majesty's Chief Inspector of Police get such ideas?
Dennis, Erdos and Al-Shahi comment: 'To ordinary non-affluent
people – the "labouring nation" who suffer from the crimes and
insecurity imposed on them by their neighbours, the idea pronounced by HM Inspector of Police, that the police service is
needed by nobody but the affluent, is incredible. Yet this is
included in the Macpherson report as particularly "apt in the
context of this Inquiry".'

Macpherson stated (paragraphs 6.62 and 6.63): 'Our conclusions
and recommendations are designed to guide all police officers
towards a transformation of their culture in partnership with others,
in the context of policing this present multi-cultural and multi-
ethnic Britain… We are confident that the Home Secretary and the
Government will perceive the pressures for change which this

THE ABOLITION OF LIBERTY

inquiry has uncovered, so that the necessary transformation will start to take place. The Inquiry itself cannot mould the future, but Government and society can together go forward.'

These three passages are the moral core of Macpherson. The first states clearly that it is the police who must change, rather than the society whose laws they seek to enforce. How must they change? No real suggestions are made about ways in which they might become more efficient and effective in their struggle against crime and disorder. Yet the need to increase their effectiveness is surely the main lesson of Stephen Lawrence's revolting murder and the failure of criminal justice that followed. However, almost all of Macpherson's recommendations concern elaborate and often bureaucratic steps to be taken against 'racism'.

Two of these – a new power to prosecute people for using 'racist' language in private and the suggestion, now adopted, that an accused person might be tried twice for the same offence – are frontal assaults on liberty which would be hard to justify in the midst of a war for national survival. Such ideas are typical of the 'liberal' response to disorder – an increase in the power, even over thought and speech, of the benevolent elite state. As such, they are a warning of what lies ahead for England under its new ruling class.

The police, meanwhile, are to be judged mainly on whether the 'outcome of their actions creates or sustains patterns of discrimination'. Taken to its limit, and put together with the statement that something is racist if anybody thinks it is, this leads to an astonishing conclusion. It means that any action the outcome of which is condemned as racist, even (perhaps especially) by a person of extreme and revolutionary views, is unquestionably wrong. In practice, the operational effect on the police will be unlimited. No officer, however junior, can take any action without fear for how it might one day be presented before some politically-correct inquisition in which his presumed attitude of mind, rather than his actions, will be on trial.

Add to this mix Sir John Woodcock's belief that the English police have until today been a shield guarding the rich from the poor and must now reinvent themselves, and you have a prescription for a cultural revolution in the police force. On another occasion, in his annual report quoted in *The Times* in June 1992, Sir John spoke of the need for cultural change which had to involve viewing the public as customers and meeting their demands. He went on: 'The abusing husband, the foul drunk, the lager lout and the belligerent squatter are customers, different but equally as much customers as the victims of crime, the frightened child, the tourist asking the time.' He said that the police had to be much more answerable and open because society had changed and was no longer acquiescent: 'Police can no longer say "These are the rules, this is what you must do." They must persuade, and answer, the public.' He said that changing the culture would take time but that younger officers had little difficulty in dealing with a discerning public.

In fact, changing the culture of the police has not been easy. Police officers, with a few interesting exceptions, have generally been conservative people. They are bound to be. The nature of the job does not attract individuals who reject the existing social order. Nor, until recently, were they educated much beyond grammar-school level. This did not mean that they were ignorant or stupid. On the contrary, a pre-1960s grammar-school education probably provided more knowledge and understanding than most modern university degrees. It did, however, mean that they were not sympathetic to idealist or theoretical views of life. Their own store of experience as constables would in any case have contradicted most such views. But, as I have shown elsewhere, this type of officer is rapidly disappearing. There are now many thousands of university graduates in the police and a far greater number of women, who could not apply the old-fashioned rough rules of policing even if they wanted to. These university-educated officers have been removed from conservative parental influences at an impressionable age and exposed to the egalitarian and socialistic theories that pervade most British university courses and are accepted as normal and obligatory among college students.

By the end of the twentieth century, the police force was balanced between the new graduate wing and the old common-sense and hard-knocks wing. Among senior officers, the academic, theoretical, business-school style had become dominant with the mergers of the late 1960s and the increasing influence of Bramshill and the Association of Chief Police Officers. However, the lower and middle ranks still contained many socially conservative people, imbued with older beliefs about what the law was and how it should be enforced. The distinction is best summed up in the difference between the old expression 'police force' and the new one, 'police service'. The older style of officer was often highly effective, although rarely promoted to high levels. Anyone seeking to transform the police as Sir John Woodcock wished to do would meet opposition from this large conservative body of men. And their continued existence and culture would affect and embrace many young recruits.

A forgotten aspect of the Labour Party's lurch into open extremism in the early 1980s is the widespread demand for political control over the police – 'police committees' in the language of the time. The left regarded the police much as Sir John Woodcock did, as the rich's army against the poor. They also viewed them as racialist and hostile to the sexual liberation and relaxed attitudes towards drugs that are common in leftist politics. However, that was in the days when Labour still clung to the old methods of openly seeking to change the nature of society by attacking or taking over established institutions. The left's great discovery in the later 1980s and early 1990s was that there was another method, less direct but equally effective: to leave the institution standing and apparently the same, but revolutionize its culture by more subtle means. Such an approach allows the left to win elections while appearing to be conservative, and to pursue radical policies once safely in office. It is at least possible that the left's desire to change the police has found a new and irresistible weapon in the form of political correctness.

That weapon can be wielded in the unending hunt for traces of 'institutional racism', the presence of which needs no objective evidence and can therefore be alleged whenever necessary.

There is no doubt at all that many individual policemen of the old sort are racially prejudiced in their private minds. It would be difficult for them not to be, given the backgrounds from which they come and the sort of people they are. There is also no doubt that the vast majority of them rightly keep these feelings to themselves and in many cases are actually ashamed of them. Yet it is also true that most of the operational successes of the police are still achieved by these old-fashioned, conservative, male officers. As a result, they still have the upper hand in the 'canteen culture' which determines how the mass of officers act, what they think and which idea of the law they cling to.

The cultural attack on them has been long and sustained. They were the main target of allegations of corruption and evidence-planting pursued by radical lawyers and activists from the 1960s onwards. The famous *Prime Suspect* series of television dramas about a female, culturally liberal officer challenging the sclerotic male dinosaurs of the force had an important impact on police and public attitudes. It has been much imitated. The effect of such programmes is enormous. Now, hardly a month goes by without a tribunal case or a complaint that exposes older male officers as boorish and out of step with the 'modern' world. Such officers and their 'canteen culture' were also the main target of the Police and Criminal Evidence Act 1984 and of the Police Complaints Authority, which acts on the assumption that the police cannot be trusted and that every action they take must therefore be recorded, regulated and subject to disciplinary inquiry.

The effect of Macpherson has been greater even than the impact of these exercises in cultural propaganda. For the first time, it has linked police blunders with racial prejudice in the public mind. Since racial prejudice affects only the old type of officer, it has dealt a wounding blow to their morale and prestige. It has also greatly strengthened the new wave of social-worker policemen and women. As a result, it is likely to lead to the final triumph of the new view of the law as mediator between offender and victim in an egalitarian and multicultural society – that is to say, in a society in which traditional deference, religion and morality have been dethroned. If the police force at all levels is dominated by those who believe in the new type of law beloved of Sir John Woodcock, then that will be the law that is universally enforced. The old type of policing, meanwhile, can be dismissed as wrong and false – as it was by Sir John, who believes that the police never really were the police of the whole people.

This result was not inevitable. It is particularly wretched that Britain's black people and their undoubted problems have been used for this purpose. Many black Britons were and are supporters of the traditional order. In fact, they suffer more than most from the crime and disorder of our society. Much of it is inflicted on them by other black people with whom they have nothing in common but their colour. In a strange inversion of racial prejudice, their plight and their decency alike have both been forgotten. They are black, therefore they must desire the changes recommended by Macpherson.

This liberal, racialist desire to confuse colour with culture is very difficult to oppose. If colour and culture are the same, then those who try to criticize a culture linked with a particular racial group can be attacked as 'racist' and be driven from the stage as personally odious. Yet such an attitude is profoundly racialist in itself because it classifies people by their race rather than by their actions. This book continues to use the term 'racialist' which the author remembers as being in common use in the days when he used to go on demonstrations against Enoch Powell in the 1960s. This is because it preserves the original straightforward meaning of the time: a racialist is one who judges a man by the colour of his skin rather than the content of his character, as Martin Luther King himself put it in his great speech at the Lincoln Memorial, Washington, DC on 28 August 1963.

The word 'racist' did not enter the language of England till much later and it seems to the author that it has an entirely different purpose. It is a slogan word which sucks meaning from a sentence, rather than an honourable word that aids understanding. It is easier to shout or paint on walls than 'racialist'. It sounds and looks like that other great vague abuse-word 'fascist' (so that it is sometimes written 'rascist'). Most significantly, it is often used against people who have no racial prejudice but who honourably object to cultural and moral change. Thanks to this verbal trickery, changes in culture and morals, and the growth of multiculturalism, have frequently been successful because opposition to them is deemed to be 'racist'.

A caricature of this problem is to be found in the attempted prosecution of the elderly retired seaman George Staunton in Liverpool in 1999 for 'racially aggravated criminal damage'. His offence was to paint on the wall of a derelict building the slogans 'Free Speech for England' and 'Remember the 1939 War', neither of which contains any racial sentiment whatever. The charges were eventually dropped, but only after newspaper criticism. The interesting thing is that he was charged at all. Mr Staunton's experience was an extreme example of what is happening to many other well-intentioned people. At some point, principled opposition to racial hatred ceased to be enough to guarantee political respectability. Active support for radical changes in English society became necessary to avoid the thought police and their irrational condemnations.

A significant moment in this process was the Scarman report into the Brixton riots of April 1981 (*The Brixton Disorders 10–12 April 1981, Report of an Inquiry by the Rt Hon the Lord Scarman OBE November 1981*, Cmnd 8427). What took place in Brixton was mass disorder by black and white youths, quite possibly organized, accompanied by a great deal of looting. During its two fiery and bloody days and nights 320 people were arrested and 587 injured, more than four hundred of them police officers. The country was deeply unsettled by such sights, unknown for many decades in mainland Britain.

Policing and criminal justice, although few were aware of it at the time, had already been greatly undermined by the reforms of the 1960s and 1970s, dealt with earlier in this book. Contact between the police and the people they served had diminished because of the abolition of beat patrols. Self-discipline, school discipline and family authority had also been weakened by liberal reforms of the schools and by the general demoralizing effect of the permissive society. An ambiguous official attitude towards narcotics had encouraged the widespread misuse of illegal drugs, only occasionally and unpredictably attacked by the law.

Mass immigration from the New Commonwealth had been badly mishandled, with pathetically little done to ensure that the new arrivals settled well and quickly. The housing policies of urban local authorities had led to the creation of disastrous pockets of social and moral deprivation and misery. Criminal gangs were seeking to take advantage of racial tension and social disorder to create areas where they could work undisturbed. All of these facts contributed to what happened on those two spring days in south London.

Much was wrong with that England. In 1981 much of it would have been a good deal easier to put right than it is now. However, the Scarman report made the disorders an occasion for an attack on police methods and attitudes. And, in anticipation of Macpherson, it sought to make England adapt itself to what it thought was the culture of Afro-Caribbean citizens. The strange and rather insulting implication of this was that the rioters were in some way representative of all such citizens, which, of course, they were not. For the report managed to admit quietly that the Brixton 'community' was divided on the issue of crime and law enforcement and that the majority was on the side of the law.

Scarman opened his report by offering only two significant reasons for the riots: one, that they were an anti-police protest caused by oppressive policing and the harassment of young blacks; and two, that they were a protest against society by 'deeply frustrated and deprived' people who saw 'in a violent attack upon the forces of law and order their one opportunity of compelling public attention to their grievances'. Scarman dismissed neither explanation out of hand, although he rightly said that both were oversimplifications and that neither, even if true, was the whole truth.

A third explanation – that lawless people, angered by a brief return of proper policing to what had become almost an outlaw zone, seized an opportunity to drive the police from the streets and to loot the local shops, and that political opportunists later sought to use the riots as a pretext for restraints on the police in future – seems not to have occurred to him. Why not?

His own report can be read in an entirely different way from the official interpretation. Take, for instance, the early hours of the rioting. Scarman wrote (paragraph 3.25): 'The crowd of black youths felt, with some reason, that they were being pursued. They turned and fought. Their action was criminal and is not to be condoned. It was not, however, planned. It was a spontaneous act of defiant aggression by young men who felt themselves hunted by a hostile police force.' This scene followed what many would think was entirely justifiable behaviour by the police in intercepting a suspicious vehicle, finding a wounded man in it and trying to get him to hospital because they feared he was seriously injured. It is quite extraordinary that one of Her Majesty's most distinguished judges should say that the fighting by black youths was criminal and not to be condoned and then go on to describe it as a 'spontaneous act of defiant aggression' by people who 'felt themselves hunted by a hostile police force'. If that is not exactly condoning the fighting, it goes a long way towards excusing it.

Dealing with Operation Swamp, the police attempt to contain and control street crime which preceded the riot, the guardian of the law is once again ambiguous about enforcing the law: 'I understand why it was decided to continue with the operation: street crime was a grave matter in Brixton, upon which the *silent law-abiding majority of residents* [my emphasis] felt very strongly. But I am bound to say that the wise course would have been to have discontinued the operation.' So protecting the interests of the law-abiding was understandable, but failing to protect them was wise. Which was *right*? The learned judge did not say.

And anyone searching for an actual cause for the outbreak of the riot will be disappointed. There was none. What is interesting about the account is that there is no major incident – only the searching of a minicab driver for drugs and the subsequent arrest of an allegedly abusive youth, not major incidents by the standards of the area at the time. Quite suddenly, there was a fully-formed riot, as if out of nowhere. Chief Superintendent Boyling 'noticed that the crowd in Atlantic Road was covering the full width of the road. Suddenly there was a cry of "Look out!" Looking through the air the Chief Superintendent saw bricks and stones coming through the air towards him.' Earlier, a Mr Tony Morgan (a young black man) had warned Mr Boyling (paragraph 3.37) that 'if he did not get his officers out of the area there would be a riot'. People with cameras had been seen at 4.40 p.m. on a nearby roof taking photographs. How did they know that there would be anything worth photographing at that place and time?

Mr Boyling had responded by toning down the police presence, walking round the crowd talking to as many people as possible. Scarman says: 'The general criticism was of the number of police officers present' (paragraph 3.38). He states that there were then about fifty or sixty in the area – hardly an army of occupation. By 5.45 p.m. the first petrol bombs were thrown. At 5.55 a number 2 bus was 'commandeered' (Scarman's curious term for a criminal hijack) by people in the crowd. The conductor was 'assaulted and *robbed of his takings* [my emphasis]', suggesting that this was not a wholly political act if indeed it was political at all. Meanwhile, the existence of demolition sites in Railton Road provided almost unlimited supplies of ammunition for stone-throwers. At 7.00 p.m. (paragraph 3.57) 'community leaders', including an Anglican vicar and two councillors, explained to the police commander 'that in their view the only way for the police to reduce tension was for the police to withdraw from the area and allow the crowd to disperse'.

The commander, Brian Fairbairn, said he would not withdraw and refused to go with the quartet to speak to the crowd, but lent them a loudhailer so that they could do so. The mediators were 'seized by some of the crowd' (paragraph 3.58) 'who told them their terms for dispersing. They wanted the police to withdraw, they wanted an end to police harassment and they wanted those arrested to be released.' Soon afterwards, there was an outbreak of wide-spread looting by *both whites and blacks* (paragraph 3.61, author's emphasis), again suggesting that the incidents were not exclusively racial or political. Scarman (paragraph 3.76), however, concluded:

> The inference is irresistible that many young people,
> and especially many young black people, were spoiling
> for a row as a result of their frustrations, fancied or real,
> and of their beliefs as to what happened on Friday. The
> young people who crowded the streets believed Friday's
> events to be yet another typical instance of police
> harassment of young blacks. And many of them were
> deceived by rumour into thinking that police callousness
> on the Friday had actually led to the death of the
> wounded man. The tinder for a major conflagration
> was there: the arrest outside the S & M car hire office
> was the spark which set it ablaze.

Another way of putting this is that false rumour, presumably spread by malicious people, led to a wholly unjustified confrontation between the police and a small, inflamed section of the Brixton public. The false rumour about the dead man was actually based on the decision by officers to call for an ambulance when they found a wounded man in a car they had stopped. He was not in fact seri-ously wounded and certainly did not die. Their action was humane and justified. Scarman has no thoughts about how the police are supposed to prevent the spreading of false rumours about humane actions.

He then (paragraph 3.77), astonishingly, adds:

> There is no need to probe deeper for the immediate cause of the Saturday riot. I have heard no evidence to suggest that there was any prior organisation or conspiracy. There was no 'D-Day' or 'H-Hour'. But many young people were itching to have a go. The spirit of defiance and aggression was in them. Many observers noted their elation as events developed to the disadvantage of the police. *They were enjoying themselves* [my emphasis]. Deeper causes undoubtedly existed and must be probed: but the immediate cause of Saturday's events was a spontaneous combustion set off by the spark of one single incident.

Yet, despite this insistence that there was no prior organization or conspiracy, Scarman earlier records (paragraph 3.53): 'A white man and a black youth appeared to one officer present to be directing operations' at the time of a concerted attack on the police line in Railton Road. He also notes that the fact that terms were offered by rioters to the police 'indicates plainly enough not only that there was a degree of direction but also that, after the disorders had begun, some strangers participated in the attacks upon the police, some leaders emerged and some used the disorders for the deliberate commission of criminal offences'.

Both these statements cannot simultaneously be correct. Spontaneous riots, if such things exist, do not need leaders either before they begin or after they have started. Scarman also refers (paragraph 3.104) to other events that suggest that the outbreak was not entirely spontaneous:

> The evidence does suggest that a sinister contribution
> was made by strangers in making and distributing petrol
> bombs. Indeed, it is possible, though the evidence is not
> sufficient to warrant a finding, that without the guidance
> and help of certain white people, the young blacks, who
> were the great majority of the rioting crowds, would not
> have used the bomb. Be that as it may – and I have to
> leave it as an open question – clear and credible evidence
> was given to me in private session by two witnesses who
> reside in streets adjacent to Railton Road, that they saw
> white men making, stacking and distributing petrol
> bombs in the Railton Road/Leeson Road area on Saturday.

What a question to leave open.

Yet it is easy to see why it was left open. The whole theory of spontaneous popular revolt by an oppressed and harassed racial and cultural minority is deeply undermined by a series of observations:

a) the possibility that petrol bombs were being made in an organized fashion;

b) the riot had enough of a directing intelligence to offer negotiating terms to the police;

c) the rioters lost no chance to loot and steal;

d) poisonous and lying rumours were spread in the hours before the riot;

e) there was not even a definable incident that can be said to have triggered the first violence;

f) white people were involved in both rioting and looting.

There is also the point, clearly made by Scarman himself, that the rioters were enjoying themselves. This is hard to square with the idea that the smashing, looting and violence were the expression of a rooted resentment.

Scarman argues (paragraph 3.105) that it is unlikely that the use of petrol bombs was premeditated. He says forward planning would not have been necessary because of the existence of materials readily to hand. These materials were looted bottles and petrol stolen from what the judge once again calls 'commandeered' vehicles – a strange use of a military term to describe an illegal act, especially from a judge. This is odd logic, since the making of petrol bombs requires not only materials but the wish to make and use them and the knowledge of how to do so, which has then to be shared among several people. They, in turn, must gather the bottles and petrol, find material for fuses, pick a site for bomb-making and organize the distribution of bombs to the crowd. Perhaps recognizing that he is contradicting himself, he adds: 'The bombs indicate the existence of a degree of organisation among the rioters *once the disorders began* [my italics]. There is convincing evidence of the existence of at least one makeshift "factory" in which petrol bombs were made for use by the rioters in Brixton on the Saturday.'

But if there was organization once the disorders began, does it not suggest that there might have been organization beforehand? At a distance of more than twenty years it would be quite impossible to establish this. At the time of Lord Scarman's report, when memories were still fresh, an investigation might have yielded some interesting results. And even if an organization only developed once the troubles were under way, what was its purpose and whom did it serve?

Repeatedly, Scarman reassures his readers (and himself) that (paragraph 3.109) 'The violence erupted from the spontaneous reaction of the crowds to what they believed to be police harassment', and (paragraph 3.110) that 'The riots were essentially an outburst of anger and resentment by young black people against the police'. Perhaps this is the right explanation. What is important is that Scarman's own report gives plenty of reasons to think that there might be another explanation altogether. Yet, as in the case of

Macpherson, one senses that Scarman's conclusions were designed to deal with the political aftermath of the riots rather than with the riots themselves.

There are many fascinating facts in the report that support the idea that the real issue was crime rather than discontent. One is the information (paragraph 4.40) that during the period of Operation Swamp (the allegedly tactless name of which was not publicly known at the time of the disorders) the number of robberies and burglaries in the area halved. Another is that a 'home beat' officer, expert on the neighbourhood, thought that the youths outside the car hire office where the disorders began were not local and were seeking a confrontation.

A vital section (paragraph 4.45) illustrates the police's dilemma and the existence of opposing views within a community that is usually portrayed as being united behind the rioters. The police had to do something about rising levels of street crime, but if they did so they would be criticized: 'There was an underlying feeling that no matter how hard they tried to meet the apparently conflict-ing expectations of the community and no matter what measures were adopted, their efforts would continue to be the target for unreasonable criticism.' Many police officers must have thought that much of the Scarman report, with its extensive use of hindsight about their behaviour, was yet more of that unreasonable criticism. We also learn (paragraph 4.44) that local 'community leaders' had withdrawn from a liaison committee with the police in February 1979, but nowhere does the report either question the right of these leaders to speak for the entire community, or subject them to the sort of criticism heaped on the police.

At the time, many police officers were baffled as to what they were now supposed to do about crime in Brixton or any other area where race might become an issue. Not yet worn down by two decades of political correctness, some officers were prepared to express doubts. James Jardine, the chairman of the Police Federation at the time, said: 'In my view Lord Scarman has not been able to provide a satisfactory answer to the most important question that he asked "How do the police in the inner city deal with a very high level of street crime, while at the same time retaining the support of all?"' He spoke of an 'upside down world' in which Scarman was persuaded to believe that action against mugging was a probable cause of the riots. Commander Brian Fairbairn, head of Lambeth district police and involved at the very centre of events, responded thus to the criticism of Operation Swamp as a serious mistake:

> I think perhaps in hindsight I should have got round the
> problem we had in a different manner... one wants to
> work with the community. It clearly pays the police to
> relate to and to have the full support of the community.
> At the same time if you are going to try to curb what in
> this instance is a very high crime rate, you may
> sometimes have, paradoxically, to do things which seem
> to work against this. It is difficult to please everyone all
> the time. In fact, it is impossible.

But others were already beginning to recognize that they were going to have to adapt to the new order. The division between old and new emerged during the hearings. Stephen Sedley, a former communist and future high court judge, was counsel for the Commission for Racial Equality at the inquiry. He contrasted the evidence given by Assistant Commissioner Wilfred Gibson with that of Geoffrey Dear, Deputy Assistant Commissioner in charge of training. He said: 'Through them the Metropolitan Police has spoken with two voices. Mr Gibson was basically defensive, un-self-critical and unseeing, while Mr Dear looked forward and was far-seeing.' It is not difficult to work out what Stephen Sedley's idea of a far-seeing policeman would have been. Probably it was not that different from Sir John Woodcock's.

The issue here is not one of whether police are able to stop and search black people more often or less often, or even of whether most muggers are black. So what if they are? The real point for most people is that mugging should be prevented, whoever does it. Most burglars are white. The answer is the same. The police record on race is not faultless. It would be absurd to pretend that it was. Stupidity and inexperience, and the chasm that car-borne patrolling has opened up between police and public, play their part in fraying relations between the police and *all* the public, not just black citizens. What is more, the methods of modern policing, with its inconsistency, unpredictability and temporary 'targeting' of certain areas, almost seem designed to cause trouble between police and young men. Years of laxity on drug possession have made the re-establishment of order in some districts a near-impossible task. Part of the magic of the old police uniform was based on its familiarity and its instant recognizability as a symbol of order and safety. Many younger people have never had a chance to develop the instinctive respect for the police that their elders feel. Stop and search, and actions such as Operation Swamp, are a poor replacement for the proper beat patrolling that might well have brought about a real relationship between the police and the law-abiding public in Brixton and many other areas. It might also have prevented the murder of Stephen Lawrence. He was casually knifed to death on a busy suburban road by people who obviously, and correctly, reckoned that they had a good chance of getting away with murder.

The question is whether the issue of race should be used to impose a new code of law on the police and thus on the people of this country. Should black Englishmen be insultingly stereotyped as prone to riot when subjected to the law? Should black Englishmen be assumed to be incapable of co-operating with the justice system, even in their own interests, unless treated with special consideration? Surely such ideas, in their naked simplicity, are grossly prejudiced and likely to create and fix racial divisions within our society? And who benefits from them? Certainly the black people of England do not, since these theories are used as excuses to withdraw what police protection there is from the areas where black people are concentrated.

There have been many racial riots since Brixton, some of them involving Muslim Asians who would once have been thought the least likely citizens in the country to take to the streets. There will, inevitably, be future murders similar to that of Stephen Lawrence. The Scarman and Macpherson inquiries, for all the talk of 'this must never be allowed to happen again', have failed in their supposed main purpose. However, they have succeeded in their less obvious purpose, which was to impose on the police of England a new kind of law, the law of the elite state rather than of the common people. That new kind of law originated with the wealthy liberal stratum whose religion is a guilty egalitarianism. It spread into the legal profession and the world of politics. However, it could not be finally effective until the old spirit of English policing, so despised by Sir John Woodcock, could be eliminated. The grievances and difficulties of black Englishmen have been used as the pretext for a reform that will leave them just as unprotected from crime as the rest of us, and which will in the end threaten the freedom of all Englishmen of every colour, race and creed.

IX

Justice denied

> And judgment is turned away backward, and
> justice standeth afar off: for truth is fallen in the
> street and equity cannot enter.
> *Isaiah 59:14*

There is usually a short interval between the crisis and the catastrophe. The barbarian raiders did not descend on the defenceless coasts of England the minute the Roman legions departed. It took some time for them to realize that the lush, comfortable land was defenceless. There is a long, slowly fading afterglow in the sky for some time after the sun has gone down below the horizon, during which the light survives though its source has gone.

We are now living in such an interval, gradually becoming aware of the grave change that has overtaken this country, but still living for the most part as if the legions had not departed and the sun had not yet set. Habits of mind, among those who are inclined to crime and those who are not, have still not adjusted to the real nature of things. For most of us, the moment when we become aware that we are no longer safe will be a personal shock: the grab at the handbag, the robbery on a corner we have passed in safety for years, the sound of broken glass and footsteps where there ought not to be footsteps in our homes at night.

Those who scoff at the law are also discovering their new freedom inch by inch. The young men and women who today beg aggressively for 'change' on the streets of many cities would once have been milder and more cautious. Not many years hence they will be more aggressive still, and probably violent. The burglars who hesitate to enter a house when its owner is at home have yet to digest the news from the courts – that they can most likely break in without fear that they will face a serious defence from the occupants. The thief faced by an inconvenient witness is not yet armed with a lethal weapon and is only slowly learning that it is a rational calculation to close that witness's mouth for ever.

They have not yet understood, and neither have their victims, that the police have permanently withdrawn from the streets and are unable to detect or prosecute most crimes. They are only just beginning to grasp that there is no reliable right of self-defence and that their victims are restrained by a fear of the law that does not trouble them. Only among sub-teenage children in the abandoned, marriage-free zones of the great housing estates is there already perfect knowledge of the feebleness of the police, the array of 'human rights' that prevent them from being prosecuted and the unwillingness of the authorities to punish them if by any chance they should ever be convicted. These people already behave with complete lawlessness, as those who live within range of them know painfully well. When they grow to manhood, we will all have much to fear.

The catastrophe will be gradual. If it were to happen overnight there would be a national revolt. Citizens have slowly grown used to the likelihood that they will return to car or home and find that thieves have broken in and stolen. Neighbourhood by neighbourhood, the puddles of broken glass left by the car thieves begin to appear, at first alarming, then commonplace. Word spreads quietly that it is not wise to use such and such a cash machine late at night. The yellow 'murder-boards' appear, at first a novelty, then a tedious and dispiriting nuisance. It is now generally thought unwise to intervene in violent or angry incidents in public places, and many who would once have gone to the rescue think twice before doing so, mainly for fear of knives.

It is foolish to expect help of any kind to come in incidents on the street or on public transport. Shopkeepers in many areas accept that their goods will be pilfered by violent youths who will return and attack them and their shops if they are challenged. They know that it is futile to call the police, and probably worse than futile since it will only bring about some sort of vengeance. It is a new and crude form of protection racket, instinctive rather than organized. In large parts of the big cities residents are accustoming themselves to the sound of gunfire by night, to the blood-encrusted needles of the drug-takers and the whispered commerce of the drug-dealers. Dangerous and demoralizing narcotics which ought to be discouraged are effectively legal and ignored by the police even when they see them being sold in the open. Once-normal roads and highways are consciously or semi-consciously avoided, especially by women and at certain times, because they are considered to be unsafe. Homes and vehicles must be protected with all the resources of technology, although the main effect of this has been to displace rather than to suppress crime. CCTV cameras in town centres send thieves to the unwatched suburbs. A burglar alarm system says 'rob the house next door, not mine'. Car alarms and immobilizers persuade thieves to hijack cars with their owners, and keys, still in them. The lock and bolt industry has never flourished as it is flourishing now, along with the alarm manufacturers. The only sort of alarm that the public cannot obtain is the sort that would alert the political classes to the true state of affairs.

If all these things had happened at once there would have been outrage and political anger. Because they are gradual and happen to each of us as individuals, we adapt to them and, while we complain, we are not angry enough to act or to try to make sense of what is happening to us. The realization that, if we are in serious trouble or danger, there is nobody out there to help has come to many thousands of people in recent times. However, it has happened to each one of them in isolation. The fear and even shame at their humiliation and defeat that now infect their lives are experienced alone or inside the family. Many probably blame themselves. They ought to be blaming the rulers of the country who have utterly betrayed them while pretending to guard them.

As for those rulers, whose failure in their most basic duty is one of the true scandals of modern England, they have so far escaped most of the consequences of their own folly. Since most crime is about geography and convenience, the political classes have not yet experienced it very much. They drive rather than walk, they live in areas of the capital where there is still some sort of police presence and where trouble is still some distance away. If they are politicians, they are surrounded by uniformed policemen. In fact, the Houses of Parliament are probably the last remaining place in the country where a uniformed constable is a frequent and regular sight. If the police guards of MPs and ministers were to be withdrawn, as ours have been, they would quickly realize how serious matters have become. This will not happen. The deployment of the police as bodyguards for the governing class is part of their new function. Because the new type of policeman serves power rather than the law, the seclusion of the elite from normal life has become one of his main activities.

Our rulers throw us sops and concessions. Schemes for community policing come and, more usually, go. Neighbourhood Watch, supposedly an advance in crime-fighting, is in fact an insulting invitation by the police to the public – to do for themselves the job that the hired constabulary ought to be doing. Packages of noisy 'tough' legislation are rammed through Parliament, frequently damaging civil liberties. They make no difference because the problem does not arise from there being too few laws, or laws that are too weak, but from the fact that laws must be enforced to be effective, and the police refuse to enforce them or are prevented by other legislation from doing so.

That is why so much of the current public argument about crime and punishment is futile. Why quibble about the length of a prison term when professional criminals do not fear prison and are most unlikely to end up there? When the main objective of the Home Office is to keep the prisons from overflowing, or from exploding into riot, and when it openly and specifically states that it does not want to punish convicts, it is hardly surprising that prison has no deterrent effect. Indeed, most criminals have to be exceptionally unlucky and incompetent to get sent to prison at all, or to be made to stay there for more than a few months before being tagged, paroled or otherwise returned to the 'community'. It may well be true that some of the people in our prisons ought not to be there. It is certainly true that thousands who ought to be in them are not, either out on bail, tagged, or left at liberty by the anti-establishment juries created by government folly.

The refusal of the English system to take human life more seriously than property means that levels of violence and the use of weapons increase unchecked. Carrying a gun or a knife is now most definitely worth the risk for the professional criminal, making victims more likely to give up their goods and aiding escape. The slow and unco-ordinated arming of the police, and the rapid and draconian disarming of the lawful population, do nothing to check this trend and make mistaken state killing more likely than ever.

The police themselves are the victims of the mistrust of the liberal elite. No doubt many of the methods used by the police in former times were not ideal. It was an open secret that the police might use violence and other types of rough justice against what they regarded as the criminal classes. The use of informers, still the most effective way of detecting crime, was always bound to be close to corruption and sometimes was corrupt. No system devised by humans can be perfect. But generally fair and just courts usually ensured that the police could not go too far in this direction. The public, it has to be said, were also satisfied with the way in which the old system worked. While it operated criminals feared the law, and both property and lives were far safer than they are now. It was prejudiced in favour of the public, and especially in favour of those who 'worked hard and played by the rules' – to use an expression so much liked by the present government that they stole it from President Clinton.

The growing influence of socially liberal thought on the legal and political elite in the 1960s and 1970s destroyed the informal independence of action against the criminal classes that the police once enjoyed. When cases of police wrongdoing were exposed, punishment of the individuals involved was not enough. Each event became the pretext for a general cause – that of restraining the police with rules and forcing them to do all their business on the record. The various commissions and campaigns whose work led to the Police and Criminal Evidence Act of 1984 and the establishment of the Police Complaints Authority were not set up because of public discontent with the performance of the police. There was little or no such discontent at the time, outside left-wing circles.

Nor were they intended to have the effects they did have. Legal liberals do not like crime any more than the rest of the population and usually try to live as far away from it as possible. They were set up because this country was passing through a revolution – a revolution that needed to change the nature of the law, the police and the courts. The Police and Criminal Evidence Act, with its pages of codes of practice governing every minute action by an arresting officer, is often blamed for the current state of affairs. However, it merely finished the work already done by the abolition of the beat system. The constable was already a radio-controlled automaton sent to crime scenes after the event, robbed of his initiative and of his main function, the enforcement of the public will. Now, bound by the Act and threatened with the career-ruining procedures of the Police Complaints Authority, the police officer is almost powerless to act even when an arrest could be made. Officially, he is not trusted to do the job for which he is paid. The removal of the police prosecution function and its transfer to the Crown Prosecution Service, a body governed by central bureaucracy and fearful of risking defeat in court, completed the transformation of effective police force into ineffectual police service. There are now proposals to remove even the right of the police to charge suspects and hand that over to the CPS as well.

At the same time, the state has obtained powers for itself and for the police force that make it theoretically possible to use immense pressure against those of whom the state does, from time to time, disapprove. On the excuse of fighting against terrorism, suspects can be held for lengthy periods without charge, yet actual terrorists are released early from prison and their political spokesmen serve as ministers. Under the pretext of the fight against crime a suspect's exercise of his right to silence can now be taken by the courts as a sign of guilt, yet actual criminals are rarely brought to court, and the sacrifice of this ancient principle (in the Criminal Justice and Public Order Act of 1994) has brought few obvious benefits. Strong public order powers to restrain demonstrations are also a new feature of English law. A police force reluctant to take to the streets singly in pursuit of crime is curiously ready to appear in hundreds to confront demonstrators or protestors. Any excuse serves to denigrate the ancient principle of jury trial. The courts, the police and the prisons now serve the new benevolent elite state rather than the law of the land.

In February 2002, an extraordinary event revealed just how far this process has gone. One of the most senior officers in the Metropolitan Police, Commander Brian Paddick, revealed his innermost thoughts to a website, rashly believing that they would stay private. Commander Paddick, a highly intelligent Oxford graduate plainly marked for rapid promotion, was already known for his open and frequently declared homosexuality. Something that would once have endangered his entire career had become, in effect, an asset and an advantage, and there were those who whispered that Mr Paddick was promoted by the Metropolitan Police because they wished to show that they had fully adopted the new moral and social agenda. Such claims cannot be proved or disproved. He was also well known for his decision to abandon the prosecution of those possessing supposedly 'soft' drugs such as cannabis in the Lambeth district of London where he was in operational charge. This policy had been keenly endorsed by the Home Office and was extended to other parts of the country.

In his Internet conversation, Mr Paddick revealed a worldview that owed a good deal more to Rousseau and other revolutionaries than it did to the stolid reassurance of George Dixon. 'The concept of anarchism has always appealed to me,' he wrote, 'the idea of the innate goodness of the individual corrupted by society or the system. I believe many people are forced into causing harm to others by the way society operates. They would not behave in this way if the current system did not exist or was radically different.' Other samples of his thought included: 'What to do about crack and smack, especially in Brixton? Bottom line – screw the dealers, help the addicts', and 'Do not treat all police officers as lapdogs of a corrupt capitalist system. Dogs sometimes turn on their owners.'

Mr Paddick is plainly a taker of risks. Perhaps comparable to the London mayor Ken Livingstone, he is open about matters that others do not yet have the nerve to discuss. His rash pioneering will make it easier for his successors to say such things as if they were normal, even if he becomes a marginal figure as a result. But there is not all that much of a gap between him and the thoughts of Her Majesty's Chief Inspector, Sir John Woodcock, quoted approvingly in the Macpherson report.

In fact, in many ways Mr Paddick is the ideal post-Macpherson senior officer, a committed member of the liberal elite, equipped with correct ideas on sexuality, gender and 'racism', seeing drug-takers as victims, viewing the police as the defenders of wealth rather than of law. And in the same week that his words were published, the Metropolitan Police took another step away from their traditional duties. It was revealed, in the *Daily Mail* in February 2002, that they are considering 'downgrading' some supposedly minor crimes by no longer automatically sending officers to investigate them. These include burglary, shoplifting and the epidemic crime of driving away from petrol stations without paying. This, if implemented, would not make much difference in practice since arriving after the event is in any case fairly futile. However, it does demonstrate the complete defeat of Sir Robert Peel's original, conservative concept of a police force ranged on the side of the public, sharing its morals and culture.

In the same week a group of traders who sought to sell their goods in the ancient and picturesque imperial measures, known to generations of Englishmen and women, lost an appeal against convictions for breaking the law. But what law had they broken? An Act devised to protect the public from short measure and cheating was used instead to attack entirely honest men for defying an aspect of the cultural revolution. This was an entirely novel use of the criminal law in this country, a fact lost in the justified and equally important legal arguments about its constitutional implications. The 'metric martyrs' were convicted and fined for something that is not an offence against any form of natural law. They were not dishonest, violent or destructive. They were, however, not modern men like Commander Brian Paddick. Both cases are extreme. But, since one was carried to the Court of Appeal and the other involved one of the highest-ranking police officers in the capital, they cannot be dismissed as marginal.

I have sought to explain in this book what appears to be the driving force of the new law. It is based, like the other changes that have overturned English life since 1960, on the new secular religion of the educated elite. Socialist and collectivist in origin, it worships the welfare state. It believes neither in absolute truth nor in absolute right and wrong. It demands special protection for cultures and lifestyles that consciously and deliberately undermine the morality and beliefs of the older generation. It uses the grievances of activists within racial and sexual minorities as the pretext for general change. It rejects the whole idea of punishment and affects to believe in rehabilitation while failing to pursue this objective with any real consistency. It is careless of the ancient liberties of the English constitution, which it often has not heard of, preferring arbitrary group rights granted to favoured lobbies over binding restraints on the power of the state. Having taken possession of the state, it believes that government is essentially benevolent and does not need to be restrained. It is hostile to individual self-improvement by the masses, although members of the elite are permitted to improve their own lives and even to become extremely rich. It is suspicious of individual wealth and most types of property. It sympathizes with the drug-abuser and can see the burglar's point of view. It sees respectability and restraint as repression. It regards what remains of the police force as the army of the rich against the poor, of the morally conservative against the liberated.

However, the elite state hardly ever declares its purpose openly. Often it is too inarticulate or incoherent to do so and merely gropes towards its objectives, seizing opportunities as they come. Since the repeated electoral defeats of radical leftism from 1979 to 1992, it has been justifiably cautious about disclosing its aims in public. Because of this its purpose can only be divined from the results of its actions, which have now had thirty years to reveal their true effects: demoralization; lawlessness; licence; unchecked public debauchery and violence; disrespect for the old; contempt for private or public property; indulgence of hedonism at almost any cost; scorn for the lawful and neglect for the robbed, the injured, the bereaved; furious prosecution of those who defend themselves and feeble pursuit of those who attacked them in the first place; courts that are not respected and prisons that are not feared; an utter complacency about the great misery that all this has caused to the gentle and the good. These are the consequences of the elite state's great project to 'modernize' England into something and somewhere else. In that, at least, it has had great success.

If that were the end of it, things would be bad enough. It is not. Having overthrown a successful and functioning system of law enforcement and justice in the pursuit of an unattainable ideal, the elite state finds that the resulting disorder is unpopular with its own supporters, who are the first to feel the pain of lawlessness. Year by year, the fear and hatred of crime and chaos grows among all classes, as do the demands that something must be done.

There are simple and obvious measures that would begin to deal with this: the return of preventive patrolling; the disciplining of the prisons; the removal of the ludicrous codes of practice which hamper prosecution; the scrapping of the Crown Prosecution Service and the Police Complaints Authority; the breaking up of the merged police forces into smaller units linked to the places they serve; the introduction of educational and other qualifications for jury service. These would hold the line while a remoralization of society was begun in homes and schools, and broadcasters were held to account for their encouragement of violence and licence.

None of these ideas, however, is even contemplated. Instead, the elite state reaches increasingly for instruments of repression long abolished in this country. Some of them it thinks of itself, like the Auld report's assault on juries, the centralization of the police sought in the Police Reform Bill, Mr Blunkett's 'anti-terror' measures, identity cards, the abolition of the rule against being tried twice and the end of the right to silence. Others it welcomes from the European Union, like the abolition of habeas corpus implicit in the European arrest warrant, and the construction of an unaccountable and all-powerful European prosecution service and police force, based upon a European constitution, court and 'charter of rights', which simply ignore the practical success of centuries of English experience and ask us to rely instead on purely theoretical protections.

Arrayed as a 'fight against crime', or against drugs, or against terror, or whatever happens to be the suitable bogeyman of the moment, these measures are in fact the gravest threat to English liberty since the seventeenth century – not least because they are highly popular with a badly-educated public which increasingly believes what it is told and would tolerate much in return for a real attack on crime. In truth, such measures are unlikely to have much effect on crime unless they are taken to the point where the country actually becomes a police state.

There may be people on the left, and on the right for that matter, who genuinely and sincerely believe that this country would be happier if it were less free. There must surely be many more, from both traditions, who believe that freedom is our most precious possession and that no arguments of necessity should be allowed to weaken or destroy it.

Postscript

Shortly after I finished writing this book, a series of disturbing events took place which suggest that there is now a direct, as well as an indirect threat to liberty. This danger comes mainly from attitudes within the reformed police forces and the increasingly politicised Crown Prosecution Service. I believe it originates from the same source as the wider attack on liberty, namely the elite state's certainty that its benevolence and goodness are beyond dispute. This means, by implication, that opposition to its ideas and beliefs are actively offensive, dangerous and subject to legal sanction. We may be witnessing the early stages of the gradual transformation of a free country into a closed society in which some ideas can no longer be publicly expressed. If this is so then the message of this book is even more urgent than it otherwise would be.

The most important of these events was the prosecution of the late Mr Harry Hammond, an elderly eccentric living in Bournemouth. I visited Mr Hammond shortly before his death, and – with colleagues from the *Mail on Sunday* – investigated the background to his arrest and prosecution in great detail. The case is extraordinary in almost every way, and reveals the depth of the conflict between the two traditions of policing now striving for mastery.

Mr Hammond, a passionate evangelical Christian in his late

sixties, liked to preach the Gospel in the open air of Bournemouth, whether anyone was listening to him or not. In April 2002 he was prosecuted under the Public Order Act of 1986, which makes it an offence to display any writing, sign or other visible representation that is threatening, abusive or insulting, within the hearing or sight of a person likely to be caused harassment, alarm and distress thereby. Mr Hammond's crime was to display a placard – now destroyed by order of the bench – on which was written: 'Stop immorality. Stop homosexuality. Stop lesbianism.'

As Mr Hammond hoisted his six-word manifesto in the centre of town on a busy Saturday in October 2001, a small crowd gathered round him, partly hecklers but mostly curious onlookers. The hecklers were rough with him. A young woman tried to tug the placard from his hands. During this tussle, Mr Hammond fell flat on his back and had to be helped to his feet by security guards from a nearby shop. Soon afterwards, Mr Hammond's enlightened liberal critics flung clods of earth at him, one striking him on the chest and one on the head. Another of these campaigners for tolerance crept up behind Mr Hammond and emptied a bottle of water over his bald cranium.

Yet when the police were called, it was Mr Hammond who was arrested. Mr Hammond's case may well be the most bizarre arrest in the history of English policing, since the two officers involved disagreed over what to do and did not resolve their disagreement. A more experienced male constable, Wayne Elliott, thought that Mr Hammond should be protected. His younger female colleague, Nicola Gandy, thought that he should be taken in. They argued for 20 minutes before her view prevailed. At the trial the two officers gave evidence on opposite sides, PC Elliott appearing for the defence, while PC Gandy spoke for the prosecution. The Crown Prosecutor laid into Mr Hammond as if he were a serious malefactor. He said the offending placard was 'insulting to people and people's intelligence. It was insulting to gay people and gay people's friends and he knew that'. A magistrate ruled that the sign 'clearly insulted members of the crowd who had gathered round him'. She pronounced him guilty and fined him £300 plus £300 in costs. She also ordered that his placard be destroyed. Afterwards, PC Elliott said: 'I did not want to arrest him. He was entitled to his viewpoint. My attitude was to protect him from members of the crowd rather than protect other people from what he had to say.'

PC Gandy stood by her decision to arrest Mr Hammond. She said: 'He was provoking and inciting violence with highly inappropriate behaviour.' Asked about her motives for taking a strong stance, she explained: 'My agenda was to try to maintain the peace. I was not very impressed with Mr Hammond's conduct, I don't think he is a very good representative of the Christian faith.' It is interesting that police officers now feel able to comment in public on the religious opinions of citizens.

Mr Hammond planned to appeal, but died in the summer of 2002, before the case could be heard. He would have been disappointed, but not surprised by the failure of his posthumous appeal in early 2004. It is worth noting that there is a 1999 precedent in his favour, and that it was set by none other than Lord Justice Sedley, who features more than once elsewhere in this book as a champion of the new liberalism. However, in this case, he stood up nobly for an older principle, which is encouraging news for those, like me, who hope that the civilized left may yet rally to the support of liberty. He allowed an appeal by a fundamentalist preacher, Alison Redmond-Bate, convicted of obstructing the police on the steps of Wakefield Cathedral, saying that freedom of speech covered the 'the irritating, the contentious, the eccentric, the heretical, the unwelcome and the provocative.' It seems that the times have changed so much even since 1999 that Lord Justice Sedley's view no longer prevails. It certainly had no influence over the policewoman who arrested Mr Hammond, the prosecutors who took him to court or the bench that convicted him, and many in his position might have been in no position to mount an appeal.

Such prosecutions are based on an assumption which is dangerous to proper free speech. They suggest that condemnation of an action is deemed to be insulting to anyone who does that action. If this is so, then the public declaration of almost all absolute morality is outlawed, since in law it is both disturbing and offensive to those whose actions are condemned by it.

A different sort of unease arises from the prosecution of Alistair Scott, of Exeter, sentenced in October 2002 to 200 hours of community service, and ordered to pay £100 compensation, for having rude and emotional arguments with his Muslim neighbours. It is very difficult to find out exactly what Mr Scott said to these neighbours, since his account differs from theirs – one of many objections to prosecuting people for what they say. Mr Scott denied saying several of the things he is accused to have uttered, but admitted to having been rude, which is why he pleaded guilty. It is not clear whether he really said he hated Muslims, as was alleged against him. 'I deny being a racist although I would say I'm a faithist,' Mr Scott said after his trial. 'I accept that the way I went about it was wrong and unacceptable.' Mr Scott certainly did not behave well. But his opponent Mohammed Hudaib, who was not prosecuted, was also far from saintly. In an argument about the destruction of the Twin Towers Mr Hudaib said that 11 September 2001 was a 'glorious day' and that Osama Bin Laden was a great man. He also called Mr Scott a Zionist pigf*****.

The police charged Mr Scott with harassment, though in a free society they would not have charged either man with anything, as nobody was hurt and both had used pungent language. Since the Macpherson report, all British police forces are nervous that they will be accused of institutional racism and so would probably charge a brick wall with harassment if a member of a racial or religious minority drove into it. But the Crown Prosecution Service then altered the charge to 'religiously aggravated threatening behaviour'. This offence – to which Mr Scott pleaded guilty – was invented in the unbalanced few weeks immediately after the Twin Towers outrage, which Mr Hudaib believed was a glorious day. During this period most politicians simply took leave of their senses, which is presumably why the enemies of free speech in the Home Office chose this opportunity to slip such legislation past them. But they succeeded and in the way of such things, it is now the law and the authorities were presumably anxious to apply it at the first available opportunity. Having done so once – and Mr Scott's guilty plea rules out any chance of an appeal – there is every reason to think that they will do it again.

The third unsettling event was the arrest in November 2002 of Robin Page, a former presenter of the TV show *One Man and his Dog*. Mr Page was arrested and locked in a filthy police cell, more than two months after he had spoken to a countryside rally in Gloucestershire. He began by saying: 'In case any of you are of a fragile disposition and easily offended, please go for a walk round the lake and come back when I have finished. If there is a black, vegetarian, Muslim, asylum-seeking, one-legged, lesbian lorry driver present then you may be offended at what I am going to say, as I want the same rights that you have got already.'

Some time later, he was approached by Gloucestershire Police, who said they had received complaints about his speech. Then he learned that the following advertisement had been placed in at least one Gloucestershire local newspaper, the *Stroud News and Journal*: 'Propaganda Claims Investigated: Claims that Frampton Country Fair was hijacked by the pro-hunting lobby are being investigated by Stonehouse police. Countryside campaigner Robin Page was accused of bombarding visitors with pro-hunting propaganda during his commentary at the fair in September. Sgt Geoff Clark would like to hear from anyone who was upset by the commentary.'

Mr Page says that, when Sergeant Clark arrived at his home, he told him he was there to interview him under caution, with a view to possible prosecution. Mr Page had no lawyer present and declined to be interviewed. Mr Page says the officer then formally arrested him and took him to the nearest police station, where he says he was locked in a squalid cell, his shoelaces, belt and tie removed. He says he was told that if he wanted to wait for his own chosen lawyer he would have to spend the night in the cell.

He says: 'I had no choice but to agree to be interviewed there and then.' He was then told that it was alleged he had begun his speech with racist comments. According to Mr Page's account, the officer then asked him what it was he had said. Mr Page says the two then had a bizarre conversation in which he alleges the police officer asked him if he were a racist. Mr Page also says the sergeant appeared to indicate a dislike of traditional country people, called him an eccentric and remarked that people like him caused a lot of trouble because they offended moderates. In late January 2003 the Crown Prosecution Service decided that there was insufficient evidence to take the case further.

Plenty of people might dislike Mr Page and his views or see him as an eccentric. They would be entitled to their opinions, as he is to his. Our society contains many different sorts of human being and some of them are destined not to get on with each other. What is important about this astonishing account is that the power of the law and the resources of the police are being deployed to investigate speeches and personal, private opinions. If the police are allowed to form judgements on whether we are eccentric or not, how long before they are forming judgements on whether we are institutionally racist, xenophobic or homophobic? Mr Page, who is well-known and articulate, is able to resist. But how many others are not? In an era when few local newspapers report the courts as thoroughly as they once did, how many individuals have been pursued in this way without anyone ever hearing about it? How many now fear that, if they speak their minds, they risk such treatment? It is impossible to know. But it is disturbing that English police officers think that such interrogations are part of their duties.

One other incident needs to be recorded here. It involves Anne Robinson, the TV presenter, who was rude about the Welsh people on a BBC TV programme *Room 101*. There were many complaints about her rudeness and following these accusations, North Wales Police took it upon themselves to suggest to the BBC that they should not repeat the programme. This is interesting in itself. I asked the North Wales Police under what law they had the power to take such action and they have yet to reply. When the programme was repeated, they sent officers hundreds of miles to interview Greg Dyke, then Director General of the BBC, but eventually wrote to him to say that they would not be seeking a prosecution. However, this was not because the very idea was preposterous but because there was said to be insufficient evidence.

A very short time ago, anyone in England would have thought all these cases were comical, silly bungles by heavy-handed, inexperienced and humourless juniors, without any greater significance. This kind of thing does not happen here, we would have thought; therefore we may safely laugh at it. And yet this kind of thing does happen here, not by mistake but through the conscious and deliberate actions of powerful public officials. A pattern is perceptible in these incidents which is not reassuring. It seems likely that similar prosecutions and investigations will happen with increasing frequency and seriousness. Such speech codes have been rigorously enforced on many university campuses for some years (the author, for example, has had his microphone switched off in mid-speech by student officials following baseless allegations of racism. Such officials frequently find their way into national politics, and the expansion of the universities means that many police officers, lawyers and court officials will have been exposed to – and possibly infected by – such attitudes during their education.) They are now spreading into the country as a whole as the intolerant campus consensus infects the police and the prosecuting authorities. New European Union provisions, under the Racism and Xenophobia directive, threaten to provide a legal basis for more official widespread persecution of certain opinions. One major purpose of this book is to warn that there is now a real threat to liberty of thought and speech in this country, a threat which cannot be lightly dismissed by any observant or alert citizen. I hope the warning will, for once, be heeded.